Desert Wisdom

Desert Wisdom

SACRED MIDDLE EASTERN
WRITINGS FROM THE
GODDESS THROUGH
THE SUFIS

Translations, Commentaries,
and Body Prayers by

Neil Douglas-Klotz

HarperSanFrancisco
A Division of HarperCollins*Publishers*

Harper San Francisco and the author, in association with The Basic Foundation, a not-for-profit organization whose primary mission is reforestation, will facilitate the planting of two trees for every one tree used in the manufacture of this book.
A TREE CLAUSE BOOK®

FIRST EDITION
Book design by Ralph Fowler
Set in Granjon by TBH Typecast, Inc.

Library of Congress Cataloging-in-Publication Data
Douglas-Klotz, Neil.
Desert wisdom : sacred Middle Eastern writings from the Goddess through the Sufis / Neil Douglas-Klotz. —1st ed.
p.   cm.
ISBN 0–06–061996–1 (cloth: alk. paper)
ISBN 0–06–061997–X (pbk.: alk. paper)
1. Middle East—Religion.   1. Mysticism—Middle East.   I. Title
BL1060.D68   1995
291.8'0939'4—dc20   94–31792
                                                                 CIP

95 96 97 98 99   RRD(H)   10 9 8 7 6 5 4 3 2 1

This edition is printed on acid-free paper that meets the American National Standards Institute Z39.48 Standard.

For my father,
Verner H. Klotz,
who taught me that
love is stronger
than death.

Contents

Table of Source Threads

ARAMAIC GOSPEL THREADS

DEAD SEA AND NAG HAMMADI THREADS

Preface

Every part of the earth has evolved crucial insights and wisdom that can offer solutions to the unfolding story of the human species on the earth today. This wisdom comes through the mystics, prophets, poets, and artists who, by their own willingness to experience a sense of deep communion with the universe, give voice to enduring meaning and beauty. We need all of this wisdom to meet the ecological, economic, political, and spiritual challenges we face today—no one voice has all the answers.

This book aims to convey both wisdom and spiritual practice from the Native Middle Eastern tradition that will help us to regain a healthy relationship to the earth and to fulfill our purpose in being here. For similar wisdom, many people have begun to listen seriously to voices of the native traditions of the Americas, Europe, Africa, Asia, and Oceania. Likewise a voice of desert wisdom from the Native Middle Eastern tradition is waiting to be heard.

The term *Native Middle Eastern* may seem unusual. By this I mean a spirituality that arises from a bioregion that ranges from northeastern Africa around the Mediterranean Sea to the Anatolian peninsula (present-day Turkey) and extends southeast through the Arabian peninsula and northeast through present-day Iran into the Caucasus Mountains. Human beings in this area of the earth evolved unique forms of cosmology, spirituality, and psychology over the past eight to ten thousand years that helped to connect them with the natural world and make sense of their lives. This wisdom can be heard as separate voices and as a harmonious chorus. Just as Native American spirituality presents many varieties of ritual, spiritual practice, and tribal organization, yet can also be heard as a unified voice, so also can the heart of Native Middle Eastern spirituality offer a perfume that transcends its apparent differences. The fact that this perfume is hard to catch has much to do with the history of relations between the European West and the Middle East.

For the past two thousand years, the West has extracted, refined, and harnessed the spiritual resources of the Middle East to create and fuel its version of modern culture and religion. Foremost among these products were the European versions of Christianity and Judaism, whose prophets were born in the Middle East and spoke Semitic languages. Conflicts between and among the Western versions of these "classical" religions and their various sects, heresies, and competing orthodoxies have dominated political and cultural life in the common era.

Even the roots of modern science and mathematics arose in the Islamic Middle East and were carried to Europe during its "dark ages." Scientists then fought with religious hierarchies over who would dominate the spiritual and imaginative life of the West. When the politician and the industrialist both entered this battle about three hundred years ago, they irreparably tipped the scales away from a shared worldview of spirit and nature. Without any common vision of purpose, which is the gift of cosmology and spirituality, human life became an ever more divisive fight for resources and wealth.

Over the past century, the West has returned to the Middle East to extract, refine, and harness its earth energy resources—oil—as it previously did the Middle East's spiritual resources. In elaborate political chess games, Western nations carved out countries and engaged in a belated spasm of empire building to protect their "strategic" interests. Most recently, in various attempts to further peace in the region, the West has not only confronted its own previous interference but has also found itself embroiled in conflicts that are deeply rooted in the indigenous spirituality of this region. After a few hundred years of ignorance, fear, and manipulation, how can anyone in the West make sense of the deeper story embedded in the spirituality that has evolved there and that controls events?

Like a person awakening from amnesia, the West now turns to the Middle East with vague inklings of the childhood of Judaism and Christianity, with fear and mistrust of the little it really knows of Islam, and with virtual ignorance of the varied indigenous spiritualities that were never labeled "classical religions" by the West. As drilling for oil continues, another type of digging continues to unearth ancient manuscripts like the Dead Sea Scrolls and the Nag Hammadi Library, which call into question the previously accepted stories of the origins of Western Christianity and, to a lesser extent, Judaism.

While the desire to secure sources of oil leads the West into increasingly dangerous conflicts in the Middle East, our culture also confronts the overall question of human survival into a postmodern age. How much oil is enough? How much of the earth's resources do we need to feed an addictive lifestyle that is maiming the earth for the next generation of human beings?

On the deepest level, what are we trying to get from the Middle East? What does this region mean for us in the West and for all of humanity at this time? What answers can it contribute to the overall question of human survival on the earth?

To begin to answer these questions, I maintain that Western culture needs to return to the Middle East as a student and partner, not as a teacher and dominator. As the West found in its relations with the former Soviet Union, when cultural stereotypes begin to break down, fear and superstition do also. The "enemy" begins to look more like us. But mere cross-cultural understanding, which seldom extends beyond mental concepts, is not enough. We must begin to experience a part of our collective psyche that was left behind when the mythic oil was extracted from the earth and used to fuel so-called Western religion.

As we recover this psychic territory, we may be able to release the ways we seek, as a culture, to fill an inner void by taking more and more from the earth around us. Put another way, the extent to which Western culture has been unwilling to look at its own religious roots in terms of indigenous, earth-based spirituality may reflect the extent of its denial of the body and the earth.

This collection offers to begin a process of recovery by sharing the words of Native Middle Eastern mystics linked to the indigenous spiritual practices that make their wisdom an embodied experience. Ultimately, myth arises from a profound, direct experience of the natural world and intimations of its connection with the entire cosmos. Spiritual practice opens the door to such direct experience. Trying to take the myth without the embodied practice is at best a form of voyeurism. At worst it is a form of spiritual strip-mining: It raises psychic and mental energy without really grounding it—that is, giving it back to the earth through our own bodies.

For the past twenty years, I have studied the spiritual practice of the Native Middle Eastern tradition with Sufis, dervishes, rabbis, Kabbalists, monks, mystics, and shamans. I have researched their sacred writings in Hebrew, Aramaic, Arabic, Persian, and other languages. I am aware of the religious and theological differences that divide creed from creed and sect from sect. I leave these to those for whom they have interest. I am also aware of a greater common ground of spirituality that unites not only the "great" religions but all religious experience in this area. What I have experienced and understood I offer here in translations, commentary, and body prayers that evoke the wisdom of the Native Middle Eastern tradition.

We need all the wisdom practices we can get. In her book *States of Grace* (1991), the ecofeminist author Charlene Spretnak calls such worldwide spiritual wisdom, disentangled from its fundamentalistic religious aspects, our "saving grace" for dealing with the ecological, economic, and political problems we face.

Further, scientist Brian Swimme and historian Thomas Berry, in their landmark book *The Universe Story* (1992), maintain that the wisdom that developed in each of the earth's bioregions must be viewed as part of the evolution of the entire cosmos, not just of the human species. All the findings of the new physics show that the universe itself is not an inert room we inhabit, not a collection of unchanging, mathematical laws, but an unfolding event, an ongoing story in which every event affects what happens next. After centuries of accelerated degradation by the human species, the earth has reached a crisis point just as the possibility arises for human beings to realize their true role in the story. This role is not to exploit other species but to act as a partner with them and to be the awakening consciousness of the universe becoming conscious of itself.

The approach to the wisdom we need now cannot be made as though from the outside, in a pseudoscientific, reductionist way. As the findings of the new physics show, there is ultimately no "outside." Observing something changes it, and we are all "inside" whether we like it or not. Most theologians, biblical scholars, linguists, and anthropologists have not even begun to confront this phenomenological aspect of their work: "insider" means "unscholarly" and "subjective" in most academic circles enchanted with the presuppositions of postmodern deconstructionism.

I have made common cause with Swimme and Berry by applying their model of the "universe as story" and their search for bioregional wisdom to the area that historically has held the most fear, energy, and attraction for modern culture: the Middle East.

Acknowledgments

My special thanks go to Kamae A Miller, my partner and best editorial eye, for her support in ways too numerous to mention. This work was undertaken and completed in a nomadic fashion in northern California, Germany, Austria, Jordan, Israel, Syria, England, and back to northern California. My thanks go to all my friends and hosts who provided hospitality and a place to spread innumerable papers and a laptop computer. For helping draw out and support the wisdom necessary for this time, my thanks also go to the many friends of the Abwoon Study Circle, the students and faculty at the Institute in Culture and Creation Spirituality in Oakland, California, and the worldwide circles of the International Center for the Dances of Universal Peace.

For introducing me to and helping me maintain a living practice that touches the depths of self, my special thanks to Murshid Moineddin Jablonski and the late Frida Waterhouse. For their deeply ecumenical wisdom and example over the years, my thanks go to Matthew Fox, Joseph Kilikevice, O.P., Marlene DeNardo, S.N.D., and Archbishop Dionysius Behnam Jajjawi of Jerusalem; Murshid Wali Ali Meyer, Murshida Vera Corda, Pir Vilayat Inayat Khan, Ali Kianfar, and Nahid Angha; Rabbi Zalman Schachter-Shalomi, Joanna Macy, and Brian Swimme. Finally, special thanks to my editor at Harper San Francisco, Tom Grady, for his patience and help in bringing this caravan of a project to its appropriate destination.

Introduction

In September 1993 I was in Jerusalem with a group of citizen diplomats and students of spirituality as peace accords were due to be signed between representatives of the Israeli government and the Palestine Liberation Organization. Euphoria and dread, hope and fear ruled the reactions of people whom we met in Israel, the Occupied Territories, and Jordan. The general consensus seemed to be: things could get much better, or they could get much worse. What would make the difference?

One answer came in the middle of the Christian quarter of Old Jerusalem. There we met with the Syrian Orthodox archbishop, Dionysius Behnam Jajjawi, who, according to his tradition, is the direct successor to Saint James, the first bishop of Jerusalem. His monastery occupies the original house of Saint Luke, where it is said Mary, Jesus' mother, also lived for a while. Currently the monastery is virtually empty. A native Aramaic speaker now in his sixties, Archbishop Jajjawi has lost most of his congregation to war, dislocation, and emigration. He told us of his arrival in Jerusalem from Iraq, the country of his birth, many years before and said that he had truly been in awe while walking on the earth where so many sacred events had occurred. But as he looked around him, he saw everyone going about their business, each religion (or religious denomination) carving out a little piece of the Holy Land for itself and holding on for dear life.

"My friends," he said, "the Middle East has too much religion, not enough spirituality."

In taking a new look at some familiar sacred scriptures, I also wish to shift the focus from religion to spirituality. I would define spirituality as experiences of the sacred, and religion as orthodox concepts (often rigidly enforced) about the sacred. While the word *religion* originally meant that which "binds together," in the last half of the twentieth century many have questioned the value of bonds that have served to divide human beings from one another and from the natural world. Old communities of meaning fall apart as new ones form in a search for "postmodern" forms of spiritual community.

To shift one's point of view from religion to spirituality means unraveling the very language of and the approach to translation of ancient texts that has dominated Western religion and scholarship.

Here I wish to discuss how I organized this book, what it contains, how I did the translations, and why I feel that radically new translations of well-known sacred texts are needed for a healthy spirituality to develop in the West. Appendix A relates how I became connected to an ancient Middle Eastern tradition of mystical translation.

THE ORGANIZATION OF THIS BOOK

As a collection of wisdom and practice, this book is a personal selection. I have chosen from among many alternatives and have had to leave much for another time. When translating from the Hebrew Scriptures, the Gospels, and the Quran, I attempted to include key sacred texts that are familiar and important for understanding the essence of the tradition. Rather than segregate the voices according to their particular tradition, I have interwoven them, along with appropriate body prayer practices, to correspond with certain themes and key sacred words. I feel that these themes contribute to a dialogue of wisdom among all sacred traditions concerning our purpose as human beings on the earth at this time.

Not all the voices within a particular chapter agree. My purpose is not to show that everyone is saying the same thing. They aren't. Each strand of the Native Middle Eastern tradition, as represented here, has its own unique voice to offer, as does the entire tradition when heard as a multivoiced chorus. I hope that this approach will offer a way to understand both the unique depth of each tradition represented as well as the literal common ground from which they all spring.

I intended this book, like my previous one, to be "porous"—able to be opened at any point by readers seeking inspiration. Because of the much larger amount of material involved, this desire led me to place many of the textual notes and explanations at the end of each chapter rather than interspersed throughout. I have included some textual notes in the body prayer sections where readers will need them to understand the practices involved. There are many ways to read a book like this. Some readers may wish to focus on meaning and practice; others may wish to investigate in depth each selection and the derivation of the translation. Some may wish to do both at various times. In arranging the textual notes, I have tried to keep a door open to all these paths to understanding.

Parts and Chapters

The book is divided into three parts. Each corresponds to one of the three foundational principles of how the universe and life on this planet have evolved based on the research of modern physics, paleontology, and biology. These three principles have been articulated by scientist Brian Swimme and historian Thomas Berry in *The Universe Story* (1992). They are diversity, inner presence, and communion.

Because the universe as we know it developed through the principle of *diversity,* no two individuals are ever exactly alike, whether they are galaxies, planets, living beings, atoms, or elements. Because the universe developed through the principle of *interiority,* each individual organizes a "self" that seems to move toward its own unique goals and purpose. Because the universe developed through the principle of *communion,* every individual self maintains or tries to maintain a relationship with other selves around it.

About these three principles, Swimme and Berry comment: "Were there no differentiation, the universe would collapse into a homogenous smudge; were there no subjectivity, the universe would collapse into inert, dead extension; were there no communion, the universe would collapse into isolated singularities of being" (p. 73).

To the extent that modern culture has lost touch with nature, it faces collapse in all three areas. The Native Middle Eastern tradition, in the form of orthodox religion, has been used to justify this collapse. But its voices of wisdom, prophecy, and mysticism speak strongly to all three of these universe—and universal—principles. And they may help us recover parts of our psychic life that have been suffering from collective amnesia.

Within each part, the chapters offer wisdom clustered around particular themes that I feel are unique gifts from this tradition.

To contribute to our experience of diversity, the Native Middle Eastern tradition offers rich understandings of the sacred realities of vibration and form, creativity, light and dark, time, and spaciousness. To contribute to our experience of inner presence, this tradition offers practical and subtle insights about inner sensation and emotional feeling, the subconscious soul-self, its relation to the universal "I Am," the self's journey of discovery, and how it relates to an "other." To contribute to our experience of communion, this tradition offers a clear, rich expression of the interplay between sexual passion, desire, love, death, healing, devotion, and thankfulness. A short synopsis of each theme precedes each chapter.

The Body Prayers

I have based the body prayers that relate to various selections on spiritual practices from the Middle Eastern region. Some derive from Jewish or Sufi mystical practices that are actively used today. Others have been re-created based on my understanding of the texts and revised in order to provide a balanced experience for readers—that is, one that can be integrated into their everyday lives. Some of these practices have never been put into print before. This is not because they are dangerous but because what makes them work is the spiritual relationship in which they are usually given. This relationship is like a current that flows from one pole to another in a battery. When the poles are not connected, no current flows.

I encourage readers (1) to use the body prayers individually to find their way into the world of experience they offer and (2) to use them with another person or in small, cooperative study groups where experiences can be shared. I feel that the need of the planet at this time calls all of us to the integration of feeling and wisdom that previously was the province of the "mystic." I also encourage readers to carefully seek out experienced teachers from these traditions who can serve as touchstones for one's growth in wisdom about the purpose of being human today. For me, such growth is worth a life's dedication, and nothing else—not appeals to fear, not the promise of power, not grandiosity or compulsion, not ritual, robes, or ceremony—can induce my devotion.

Many of the body prayers rely on intoning, chanting, or breathing with the words of power used in the texts. My rendering of Hebrew, Aramaic, and Arabic into English characters does not use formal transliteration script and, like my previous work, is not intended to teach a person these languages, which can be a long study. This book is intended for general readers, most of whom cannot read formal transliteration scripts (which look, for example, like this: yirᵊ'at yᵊhwɔh re'šiyt dɔ'at ḥɔkᵊmɔh). My transliterations intend only to approximate the sounds involved so that the general reader can understand how the translations arose and can participate in the body prayers. A simple key precedes the text.*

*Readers may also want to use a pronunciation tape I have prepared of the major words involved, along with melodies that can be used for their own meditative and creative expressions of prayer. Please see the reference list at the end of this book.

The body prayers themselves follow their own themes and work with different aspects of one's being. They also develop progressively, building gradually on the ability to sense, feel, concentrate, and articulate one's inner awareness. Some body prayers may work for you immediately, some only over time or after practice, some not at all. Please take what is of value in your own unfolding, and do not concern yourself with the rest. The body prayer themes are Sound and Embodiment, Simple Presence, Heart Awareness, Depths of the Self, Celebration, and Thankfulness.

The Threads: Texts Used

The image I carried while completing this book was that of a nomadically hand-loomed Middle Eastern carpet, created from various interwoven strands in which certain patterns emerge depending upon one's distance and angle of viewing. In the second part of the table of contents I have also grouped all the threads of a common background together, so that readers can follow a search for wisdom in one voice rather than several.

Below I have listed the major threads and the reasons why I chose them.

1. *Genesis Threads.* These include the original seven "days" of creation according to the Hebrew text. This text has had an unparalleled impact on Western culture, especially in its literalistic translations, which render deep divisions between "heaven" and "earth" as well as between "man" and the rest of "nature."

The block-script "Hebrew" letters we know today are actually Chaldean characters appropriated by the Jews during the seventy-year captivity of the southern kingdom of Judah in Babylon in the sixth century B.C.E. According to Hebrew scholar Fabre D'Olivet (1815), Genesis and the original "books of Moses" were composed much earlier in a more ancient form of Hebrew. Archaeologists in this century have rediscovered various forms of this proto-Hebrew in inscriptions that date to the era in question. After the Babylonians were conquered by the Persians, the Zoroastrian king Cyrus allowed the Jews in Babylon to return to Jerusalem to rebuild the city. It seems to have been at this time that the scribe Ezra and his party converted the original books of Moses to the Chaldean script, combined them with other literature popular at the time, and made various editorial additions to form a first rendition of the Hebrew scriptural canon.

My expanded translation from the Hebrew could be called a mysti-cal commentary on the scripture, or *midrash*. In these renditions, I have taken full advantage of the vocabulary that the new physics has evolved to describe the origins of the universe. At the same time I have been as faithful as possible to the sense of the Hebrew words. Details of this are explained in the textual notes. I do not think Genesis explains or predicts all of the new scientific cosmology, but I do believe that the presence of new vocabulary in English offers us the possibility to get beyond overly literal and mechanistic renditions like that of the King James Version. The account of the first seven days in Genesis in fact goes far beyond current scientific and psychological insights in its subtle teaching about how the interiority of a self actually organizes itself. The Genesis thread runs throughout this book and in many ways helped organize the loca-tion of the themes I have chosen.

2. *Other Hebrew Threads.* These include translations from the Hebrew of sections of Proverbs (the voice of Holy Wisdom), the Song of Songs (the passage about love and death), Deuteronomy 6:4 (the Shema), and Isaiah 6 (the vision of the divine "throne"). The Isaiah passage has historically been connected with one of the earliest recorded Jewish mys-tical practices, which involved the experience of the *merkabah* (the divine chariot or throne). According to Jewish scholar Gershom Scholem (1954, p. 47), references to this experience involved paradoxical descriptions of both "descent" and "ascent" in order to attain to the vision. In retranslat-ing the Isaiah passages and adding body prayers to them, I have tried to show one way in which this experience might have occurred.

For comparison with my translations of all these Hebrew scripture texts, I have also given the most common (and popularly influential) pre-vious English translation—that of the King James Bible.

I have also included a later "Hebrew thread" from the thirteenth-century Aramaic mystical treatise called the *Zohar,* which illustrates the three faces of the soul or self. According to various points of view, the *Zohar* is either a compilation of much older texts that reach back to the early Palestinian Jewish experience or the work of a single author (per-haps the Spanish Kabbalist Moses De Leon) who created the text to appear older.

3. *Ancient Middle Eastern Threads.* These are versions from sacred scriptures, liturgies, and poetry from Sumer, Babylonia, Assyria, and Egypt. The voices of these texts sometimes contrast, sometimes harmo-nize with others around them. I hope that my renderings expand and

illuminate this older heritage of native mysticism, which has influenced all of our classical religions.

In this category I have also included brief texts from the Mandaean and Zoroastrian traditions, both of which were once as pervasive in power and influence as the "classical" religions and both of which still survive today in vitality if not in great numbers.

These old voices reveal wild, stark, intense passion and awe at the processes and mysteries of the universe. The poets and ritual voices grope for explanations that can express both the terror and wonder of being alive in their time. As human beings, we need to recover these qualities today as we face different terrors and wonders, with far too many unquestioned explanations.

For comparison with my translations and versions of these texts, I have given the first few lines of some previous literal translations. Since most people are unaware of these texts, or don't regard them as anything more than a curiosity, none of these previous translations have really affected the popular mind in the West. My translations seek to place them clearly within the overall wisdom tradition of the other selections rather than to obscure them with awkward syntax.

4. *Aramaic Gospel Threads.* These are further expanded translations of the words of Jesus (*Isho'a* in Aramaic) from the Gospels. My source text is the Peshitta version of the Christian scriptures in Syriac Aramaic commonly used by Aramaic-speaking Christian churches in the Middle East up to the present day. Without going into an extensive explanation, which is contained in my previous book (1990), these translations and versions illuminate an aspect of Jesus' native language, idiom, and culture almost completely removed from the Greek versions. Imagine, for example, trying to render the *Tao Te Ching* exclusively from a Latin version, then suddenly discovering it was composed (or at least originally spoken) in Chinese.

Facing the Aramaic Jesus means confronting Christianity's "lost childhood," which is a project few Christian scripture scholars have been willing to undertake. Readers who wish more background on the Aramaic roots of the words of Jesus may consult the works of George Lamsa, Rocco Errico, and Matthew Black, which are cited in the bibliography.

In these selections I have attempted to retranslate sayings that have proved problematic to many readers because of Greek-based translations and later theological interpretations. I have also attempted a further version of one Beatitude as well as a condensed translation of the Lord's

Prayer based on my earlier work. Again, for comparison with my translations of these texts, I have also given the King James Version.

5. *Dead Sea and Nag Hammadi Threads.* My primary selections here are a new translation of a blessing from the Dead Sea Scrolls (itself a version of the blessing in Numbers 6) and a new version of the Coptic text usually called *Thunder, Perfect Mind* from the library of scrolls found buried near Nag Hammadi, Egypt, in 1945.

There is yet much controversy about the communities that buried each set of scrolls. Up until most recently, the Dead Sea Scrolls were dated and analyzed as sufficiently far removed from the early "Jesus movement" to have no influence on it. The community of ascetics living at Qumran, on a bluff overlooking the Dead Sea, had no direct connection to the origins of Christianity or to Jesus himself, stated the group of scholars who monopolized the scrolls' translation (and often nontranslation) for almost fifty years. In 1992, due to public pressure instigated in large part by the Biblical Archaeology Society, the Dead Sea Scrolls were released for the perusal of other scholars. Some scholars now seriously question the previous assumptions about the date, purpose, and nature of the Qumran community as well as the scrolls themselves. Previously untranslated scrolls reveal versions of a set of "beatitudes" as well as references to phrases like "son of God" and apparent texts cited by Saint Paul. There are a number of excellent, and often conflicting, scholarly texts on the subject of the scrolls' discovery and interpretation, some of which I have cited in my bibliography.

The Nag Hammadi texts have been in translation much longer, even though they were discovered about the same time as the Dead Sea Scrolls. Usually scholars refer to these books as "gnostic" texts from a period before the Jesus movement became an orthodox religion. However, the varieties of belief that the texts represent make it difficult to attribute them to any one group. The Coptic language text that I have re-rendered seems to me clearly in the tradition of *hokhmah*, or "holy wisdom," as mentioned in Proverbs, even though most scholars are at pains to give it a Greek parentage. In addition, the text illustrates a very Middle Eastern view of the subconscious soul-self and its unfoldment, an aspect that previous works have not explored.

No doubt both sets of scrolls deserve more representation than I have given them here, and I hope to return to them in the future. For comparison to my versions of the Nag Hammadi text and translation of the Qumran text, I have again given the first lines of previous literal translations.

6. *Quran and Hadith Threads.* No Middle Eastern tradition has been stereotyped as badly as has Islam, especially by the Western popular media. As discussed at length in Appendix A (which relates my personal experiences with a mystical teacher-translator of the Quran), from the Muslim point of view there can never be an adequate translation of this text. The Quran is viewed by Muslims as a material symbol pointing to the divine presence in every atom of being. It not only relates meaning; its Arabic words *are* Sacred Meaning. For this reason, I hope that my "meditations" on the Arabic of the Quran will inspire readers to look further for wisdom from this source. The essence of the Quran has much to offer toward reenvisioning the entire natural world and cosmos as a sacred sanctuary, a point of view much needed today.

According to Western Quranic scholar Kenneth Cragg (1988), "The Quran requires us to interpret our human status as that of guests within a hospitality where theology might be likened to the art of courtesy. . . . 'Letting God be God,' in all its implications, is a comprehending and comprehensive summary of the Quran" (pp. 73–74).

The suras (chapters) and portions of suras I have rendered include those that are used as part of the ritual prayers of Islam, which were initiated after the example of Muhammad. In addition, I have included one of the *hadith* (traditional sayings) of Muhammad. The distinction made by Muslims is that in the Quran the voice of the One is said to speak directly; in the *hadith,* Muhammad speaks.

Since there is no common, popularly influential English translation of the Quran, I have cited for comparison a number of versions that are considered standards in the field.

7. *Sufi Threads.* While the roots of Sufism seem to be very ancient, as a Middle Eastern mystical movement and path it attained an outward brilliance during the ninth to twelfth centuries as expressed in writers and poets such as Mevlana Jelaluddin Rumi, Sa'adi of Shiraz, Hafiz of Shiraz, and Mahmud Shabistari.

The origins of Sufism are shrouded in mystery. By some accounts, a circle of mystics formed around Muhammad while he and his community were in exile in Medina (about 623 C.E.). According to some scholars, certain of these mystics were already members of or influenced by preexisting circles of Christian mystical ascetics living in Arabia and Syria. According to other scholars, there was no prior influence, a position frankly difficult to maintain considering that Muhammad himself acknowledged and honored the previous influence of Jesus and other Semitic mystics.

The term *sufi* was based on a word meaning "wise, pure, and woolly" (from the robes of wool that were traditional clothing in these early pre-Islamic desert groups). As we shall see, the word also has its origins in early Semitic sacred phrases, particularly in the words of Jesus. According to most accounts of early Sufism, the term was not formally adopted until almost 150 years after the time of Muhammad by the Syrian mystic Abu Hashim. An early European translator of Sufi texts, H. Wilberforce Clarke (1891), comments:

> *Some say that the seed of sufism*
> *was sown in the time of Adam,*
> *germed in the time of Nûh [Noah],*
> *budded in the time of Ibrâhim [Abraham],*
> *began to develop in the time of Mûsâ [Moses],*
> *reached maturity in the time of Christ,*
> *produced pure wine in the time of Muhammed.*
> *Those who loved this wine have so drunk of it as to become*
> *selfless. They exclaim:*
> *"Praise be mine! Greater than I, is any?*
> *The truth (God), am I: there is no other God than I." (p. 2)*

Such attitudes, however, have traditionally landed Sufis in hot water, and not a few of them have been persecuted, tortured, and executed by Muslim authorities over the centuries.

While the works of Jelaluddin Rumi are relatively well known through the fine work of my friend Coleman Barks, the other Sufi poets whose work I offer here have not had as good a hearing due to the absence of any contemporary English versions. By employing Coleman's method of "informants" (that is, comparing previous antiquated English language translations) and keeping in mind the underlying Sufi terminology and psychology used, I have attempted to add my own versions to the growing body of poetry already available. I have not given any comparison to my versions from previous literal translations here, since most of the latter suffer mainly from outdated syntax and word choice. In some cases, the nineteenth-century British translators were also clearly unaware of certain key sacred terms in Sufism. However, like many others, I remain in the debt of these early translators for their pioneering work of opening the Western mind to the classical Sufi poets.

Wisdom, Translation, and the Problem of Language

Translators traditionally make apologies—both in the sense of remorse for and defense of what they have done. This book is no exception.

The need for new solutions and new wisdom to meet the challenges facing human beings on the earth today also demands new language and new translations of sacred texts. The Christian theologian Matthew Fox notes: "A paradigm shift requires a new pair of glasses by which to look anew at our inherited treasures. Just as all translations of our mystics are affected by the ideology or worldview of the translator, so the same is true of our Scriptures. Those who have lost a cosmology and the mysticism that accompanies it hardly recognize that fact when they translate the Bible for us" (1990, ix).

A parallel revolution in Western science currently challenges the way scientists use language to discuss "reality." In considering the new findings of physics about the origin and development of the universe, Brian Swimme and Thomas Berry (1992) doubt whether we even have the language to properly convey "the Universe Story": "To articulate anew our orientation in the universe requires the use of language which does not yet exist, for each extant language harbors its own attitudes, its own assumptions, its own cosmology. . . . Any cosmology whose language can be completely understood by using one of the standard dictionaries belongs to a former era" (1992, p. 24).

Swimme and Berry go on to point out that, while science formerly repudiated any "anthropomorphic" language in speaking about the universe—that is, any description of the cosmos acting like a human being—it made an equally grievous error in seeking to describe the universe in terms of a machine. During the rise of Newtonian science, they explain, "the Western mind had become completely fascinated with the physical dimensions of the universe. . . . A univocal language was needed, one whose words were in direct, one-to-one relationship with the particular physical aspects under consideration. In this way, anthropomorphic language was abandoned in favor of mechanomorphic language" (p. 36).

This machine model for language has also infected the translations and study of sacred scriptures in the West for the past several hundred years. It led first to an overemphasis on "literalism"—the study of what was supposedly present in the original with nothing added or deleted—and second to the extreme relativism of literary criticism, which ended up dividing and analyzing virtually all meaning and wisdom out of sacred texts.

As new scientific insights of the present and mystical insights of the past come closer together, each looks for a language that will have the vitality to galvanize and actually change human behavior as did earlier sacred revelations. Swimme and Berry note:

> *Among the greatest challenges linguistically is the change from our present efforts at an exclusively univocal, literal, scientific, objective language to a multivalent language much richer in its symbolic and poetic qualities. This is required because of the multivalent aspects of each reality. Scientific language, however useful in scientific investigation, can be harmful to the total human process once it is accepted as the only way to speak about the true reality of things. (p. 258)*

One place where rich, symbolic, multivalent language is found is in the ancient expressions of native mystics. Historically these words have carried the psychic energy to motivate large numbers of people. This is also why they have produced so much sectarian conflict. In essence, human beings were not ready to absorb the same amount of life energy that the mystics themselves experienced. So this energy had to be channeled into making divisions and creating conflict over the acquisition of resources.

Today, as the earth presents us with a bill for the last several centuries of overconsumption and sectarian conflict, we may be ready for another look at mystics who have, up until now, been used as projection screens for various religious, economic, and political power grabs. However, to translate the words of Native Middle Eastern mystics in a literal, univocal way collapses their wisdom into a lifeless corpse.

In most translation, one can focus on form (rhythm, sentence structure, stress, meter, rhyme, and sound) or meaning or both. As I pointed out in my earlier work, *Prayers of the Cosmos* (1990), to focus on meaning in Middle Eastern sacred languages and scriptures leads to the question, Which level of meaning? Hebrew, Aramaic, and Arabic all lend themselves, by virtue of their root-and-pattern construction of meaning, to multileveled interpretations.

Further, there is a long, clear tradition (which survives today in both Jewish and Islamic mysticism) that stipulates that all scriptures, sacred texts, and mystical or prophetic expressions have several levels of meaning incapable of being rendered by a single translation. All must be constantly translated to our experience of life today. Jesus put it more simply, "Those who have ears to hear, let them hear."

In Christianity this tradition of multilevel meaning was explicitly suppressed when the words of a native mystic in a Middle Eastern language were strained out through a European language, Greek, which then became the orthodox standard for translation and interpretation. However, the tradition of multileveled, mystical translation still exists in both the Jewish and Sufi traditions (see Appendix A).

The English Christian mystic C. S. Lewis confronted the basic absurdity of a narrow form of literalism in relation to the Bible when he considered the problem of "miracles":

> What we now call the "literal and metaphorical" meanings [of the Bible] have both been disengaged by analysis from an ancient unity of meaning which was neither or both. . . . As long as we are trying to read back into that ancient unity either the one or the other of the two opposites which have since been analyzed out of it, we shall misread all early literature and ignore many states of consciousness which we ourselves still from time to time experience. (1969, p. 276)

For these reasons, I have chosen, as in *Prayers of the Cosmos,* to use an "expanded" translation style when dealing with sacred texts in Hebrew, Aramaic, and Arabic in this collection. By "translation" I mean a rendering directly from the original language. By "expanded" I mean an interweaving of the multiple levels of meaning possible without the necessity of limiting the expression to one "literal translation." For my purposes, these translations are all literal, and in the original sense of the word "translate"—to carry across—they bring more of the wisdom of this tradition across the cultural gulf than a single translation does.

There is, of course, always the danger that I have read in meaning where none exists; however, given the well-established Middle Eastern tradition of multiple levels of meaning in sacred texts, there is more evidence that previous translations have, for reasons of theological purity, "read out" the additional meanings. To ask whether persons living at the time of Jesus would have understood the Lord's Prayer or the Beatitudes to mean all the things I rendered in my previous translations is to misunderstand the nature of language. Those Aramaic-speaking persons of the first century had no need for English approximations—they had the Aramaic itself. And if they had ears, they heard.

Because of this, I also do not believe that any translation of these scriptures is a substitute for their Hebrew, Aramaic, or Arabic originals. Much of the sound and rhythmic expression of the texts, their value as words of power, is lost in translation. For this reason also I have included body prayers based on Middle Eastern spiritual practices that focus on key sacred words using sound, awareness of breathing, and other methods. My translations and versions, I hope, open a window to wisdom and a full experience of life. The body prayers invite one to walk through a particular door to enter that experience.

In working with texts from the "nonclassical" Middle Eastern spiritual voices—those that were not included in any orthodox religious tradition—I discovered that less "unraveling" was necessary. These voices may have been considered heretical at various times or banned outright, but by not being included in a religious orthodoxy their modern translations were not restricted by any sort of test of purity. In this category are ancient writings of the Sumerians and Babylonians discovered in the last hundred years, texts such as the Dead Sea Scrolls and the Nag Hammadi Library, which were buried under the threat of destruction and discovered only in the last fifty years, and the mystical poetry of the Sufis of the eleventh through fourteenth centuries, all of which already have several literal renderings but relatively few in contemporary English. In these cases, I have done "versions" based on several previous literal translations and with an understanding of the key sacred words involved.

The closely related languages—Hebrew, Aramaic, and Arabic—contain many words that either have no English equivalents or need not only a new coinage but a whole new psychology. For instance, all three languages describe in one word root, SHM, a state of reality that embraces personal and impersonal sound, light, name, vibration, and atmosphere and that extends infinitely. This one root forms the basis for the word usually translated as "heaven" in European languages—something distinctly separate from "earth." By contrast, in Middle Eastern languages this word is much closer in meaning to the concept of "wave," as used by physicists to describe the behavior of light, which can also behave simultaneously as a "particle."

In fact, the language evolving to describe the new story of the universe, its origins and unfolding, will significantly add to our understanding of sacred texts, which have often been denuded of their value as wisdom. This does not mean that we are reading new science concepts into sacred texts. It does means that a mystic like Jesus or the writer of

Genesis 1 grasped an essential reality of the cosmos that not only is still relevant today but that we are in a position to understand in a deeper way in translation for the first time.

Swimme and Berry again challenge those in all disciplines of science, education, and religion to reconsider their purpose in light of the new scientific story of the universe:

> *The important thing to appreciate is that the story as told here is not the story of a mechanistic, essentially meaningless universe but the story of a universe that has from the beginning had its mysterious self-organizing power. . . . Nor is it the case that this story suppresses the other stories that have over the millennia guided and energized the human venture. It is rather a case of providing a more comprehensive context in which all these earlier stories discover in themselves a new validity and a more expansive role.*
> *(1992, p. 238)*

Two final points need to be made about the touchy subject of gender.

First, I have avoided in most cases the translation of any divine name as "God" or "Goddess" largely because I have found no Middle Eastern sacred name that is linguistically equivalent to these Western generic terms, both of which stem from a Germanic root meaning "good" (that is, not "evil"). I believe that the use of this inherently dualistic term has had a cumulative schizophrenic effect on the Western religious psyche. By contrast, names like *Elat* (Old Canaanite), *Elohim* (Hebrew), *Alaha* (Aramaic), and *Allah* (Arabic) center around roots that mean more closely Oneness, the All, Divine Unity, or the Being of the Universe. I have therefore employed these as well as similar variations. In other cases, such as the Babylonian sacred names *Nintu, Mami,* and *Ninhursag,* I have retained a transliteration of the names and rendered their various meanings.

Second, I have been extremely circumspect in the gendering of divine names. First, some names seem to have changed gender back and forth over the centuries. For example, while the Babylonian sun deity Shamash is usually referred to by scholars as male, there is equally good evidence that Babylonians saw Shamash as female (see McCrickland, 1990). No doubt the Sumerian-Babylonian pair Inanna and Dumuzi were female and male, as were the Egyptian Ast (Isis in Greek) and Usari (Osiris), but they were not split along sky-god and earth-goddess lines, as has been assumed by some contemporary psychological writers.

With regard to the classical religions—Judaism, Christianity, and Islam—devotees of all faiths affirm that the most exalted names (like Elohim, Alaha, and Allah) can never really be seen as male or female. Nevertheless they have been consistently rendered male in most translations. Considering that these names were taken over wholesale from earlier traditions where they were gendered oppositely (that is, as the female Elat), the exclusive use of the male pronoun has again served only to fragment and polarize the Western spiritual psyche. My use of gender (or lack of it) in these translations is in the spirit of achieving a balance after centuries of relentless use of the male pronoun in combination with divine names.

Additionally, as my translation of Genesis 1:27–28 shows, the early "archetypes" of male and female in this tradition are much simpler and less stereotypical than we might imagine. For instance, from what I have experienced working with all of these traditions, the sun and sky (with all their implications) are not "naturally" male any more than the moon and earth are "naturally" female. There are many moon or earth gods in Native Middle Eastern mythology as well as sun and/or sky goddesses.

I would like to declare a moratorium on easy gender stereotyping by everyone interested in hearing the wisdom of native traditions. Let us allow the space for our own evolving story today to tell us how we can balance the relations between the male and female sides of ourselves. As some of my selections show, the Native Middle Eastern tradition carries much erotic energy and tension, some of which made it into biblical literature like the Song of Songs. While previous translations have toned this energy down considerably, my goal has been to reclaim the sacredness of sexual passion so that we can make use of it in transforming our relationships and lives.

As with all handwoven carpets, I beg the reader's indulgence for any stray threads that have been left unknotted or hanging out. This lack of machine-fabricated perfection is said to add to the value of the piece. As well, it provides some room for readers to fill in their own pattern of experience; this personal empowerment increases the magic of any carpet. If I have succeeded, I hope that this piece of weaving transports readers through the power and beauty of the Native Middle Eastern tradition to take a closer look at their own place in the cosmos.

A Key to Special Characters in the Transliterations

â = a in father
a = a in hat
ê = e in bear or pear
e = often indistinct or like the *a* in bad
î = as in pique or *ee* in bee
i = i as in sit
ô = o in whole
û = o in move or *oo* in pool
ch = ch in Scottish *loch* (no English equivalent)
kh = usually like ch in German *ich* or Bach
th = th in thing
' = no precise English equivalent, gutteral like an emphasized *e* in they but without the *y* sound

PART ONE

Voices of Diversity

Diversity reflects the way in which the universe tends to create what is new, unique, and complex. No two cells, blades of grass, fingerprints, bodies, or events are ever exactly alike. On a personal level, this wisdom helps us find our purpose in life as well as the work that expresses this purpose rather than deadens our soul. On the deepest spiritual level, these voices deal with hearing our own unique place in the story of the universe.

Chapter One

Vibration
and Form

The instant of beginning contains the seed of
what follows, according to Native Middle
Eastern spirituality. Focusing attention at the
beginning reveals two intertwined realities—
vibration and form—that create life anew
each instant. These two realities help us
understand the communal and individual
dimensions of our existence.

PARTICLE AND WAVE

An expanded translation of Genesis 1:1

Berêshîth bârâ Elohîm êth-ha-shâmaîm w'êth-hâ-âretz.

KJV: In the beginning God created the heaven and the earth.

In the beginning . . .
which means:
in archetypal form—
with the power to be something in principle—
like a point that unfolds itself
in wings, in flame,
in all directions,
conceiving the idea of a universe
for better and for worse . . .

In that time before time and space,
the Being of beings,
the I-They-Who-Are,
the One that is Many,
the Ultimate Pronoun . . .

Drew upon unknowable Otherness,
to convert into knowable Essence
two tendencies of our universe-to-be:

the cosmic tendency toward the Limitless:
the ocean of light, sound,
name and vibration—
all that shines in glorious space,
that rises in sublime time

as well as

the cosmic tendency toward the Limited:
a formed and fixed energy that moves
straight toward goals and solutions:

*the sense of purpose that we see in
earth, water, fire, and air.*

*In Principle,
In Beginning-ness,
Oneness envisioned the wave and the particle.*

BODY PRAYER: WAVE AND PARTICLE

This version of Genesis 1:1 combines several literal translations of the key words in Hebrew to give one possible expanded and multileveled sense of the mystical meanings behind the verse. For a much more extensive discussion of this approach to Genesis, please see the work of Hebrew scholar and mystic Fabre D'Olivet (1815).

The initial word, *berêshîth,* combines the primary roots R with ASH to denote something happening in principle or archetypal form—that is, involving the *power to be* but not actual manifestation. In Middle Eastern mystical cosmology, this power to envision a new reality precedes the reality itself, whether that reality is seen or unseen. *Berêshîth* can also mean before anything else or in the beginning-ness. The roots themselves show a central point or dot, which unfolds itself into a circle. As it unfolds, this circle either has wings or is surrounded by flames.

The "actor" in this unfolding process is *Elohîm,* which translated literally means the "Being of Beings," the Ultimate Pronoun. While singular in meaning, the word has a plural ending that leads to the difficult translation "It-They-Who-Are." *Elohîm* is the answer that the composer of Genesis gives to the question physicists now ask: "What existed before the Big Bang?" It could also be translated "the inherent intelligence of the divine That-ness," which includes both the One and the Many.

In Hebrew, the roots of the verb *bârâ* mean not only "to create," but also to draw from an unknown element or to render "same" what was "other." The centuries-old argument by some scholars as to whether the verb means "to create something from nothing" or "to create something from something" misses the point from a Middle Eastern mystical view. "Some-thing" and "no-thing" do not apply at this level. The process described concerns a change of state from unknown to known, from nonbeing to being. D'Olivet proposes that to translate *bârâ,* one must coin a new, and not very elegant, verb: "to thing."

In principle, what the Being of Beings (Elohîm) created before anything else was *shâmaîm* and *hâ-âretz*. As I have pointed out elsewhere (1990), the difficulty of translating *shâmaîm* as "heaven" is that, to the Western mind, the latter word has historically connoted something separate from and specifically above "earth." Shâmaîm could unequivocally be translated as the "world of vibration," or life seen as the farthest extent of light, sound, name, atmosphere, time, and space—all of which are vibration or wave phenomena. To the Middle Eastern mystic, even the sound of our own name can link us to the source of all names, the sound of the universe heard as one sound. The "sky," from this viewpoint, is a graphic example of shâmaîm, but this greater vibratory reality is in no way limited to what is "above" us.

The strict division of matter from spirit, cause from effect, inner from outer is a habit of the Western mind inherited from Greek and Latin abstract philosophy. The exaggeration of this type of dualistic thinking has brought the modern world to the brink of destruction by turning nonhuman reality into objects for our use. Similar to other ancient cosmologies, the Native Middle Eastern tradition (as expressed through the mystical writings in Hebrew, Aramaic, Arabic, Ugaritic, and other languages) rejects dualistic, pseudo-objective categories in favor of mutually coexisting paradoxes (like wave and particle, shâmaîm and hâ-âretz).

Hâ-âretz can certainly be translated "earth," but in principle it includes all ideas of a power that is stable, defined by relative limits or boundaries, and yet continues to move. From the Middle Eastern mystical view, this defines life seen as discrete entities or particles. It is not exclusively female any more than shâmaîm is exclusively male. According to D'Olivet, hâ-âretz also indicates the primary divisions of matter into earth, water, fire, air, ether (the combination of the first four), and light (in its individual or particle form). As expressed by the roots of hâ-âretz, particles and individuals move toward limits, solutions, ends, and goals. By comparison, the wave reality shows no such movement toward boundaries and purposes. It is ultimate communion.

Translations influenced by a mechanistic, dualistic worldview artificially widen the gulf between "heaven" and "earth." In the mystical sense of the Hebrew words, both realities exist simultaneously: one as vibration, one as form. Most people in modern culture have heard that scientists now view light as both wave and particle, that energy and matter are convertible. If we were to substitute these close equivalents for the Middle Eastern mystical rendition of "heaven" and "earth," we might begin to recover the cosmology of the writer of Genesis 1:1, which existed "in the beginning."

To balance our sense of individuality and communion, of particle and wave, one may need a lifetime of experience. Middle Eastern mystical writings return to this paradox repeatedly. Body prayers that work with hâ-âretz (individual form) and shâmaîm (communal connection) follow.

Sound and Embodiment

1. When feeling out of contact with your body and with the earth, due to mental distraction, exhaustion, or just plain busyness: Sit comfortably on the earth directly, or on a chair. Then sit briefly on your hands, feeling a distinct connection between the solid part in you, the bones of your pelvis, and what is solid underneath you and supporting you, the body of the earth. While feeling this connection (either with hands underneath or removed), intone the Hebrew word *âretz* for four counts (for instance, "a-ah-re-etz"). Try to feel the bones vibrating with the sound. After a few times, breathe with the sound and feeling.

2. When feeling introverted, locked up in yourself, or overly bound: Place hands lightly over the heart and begin to sense all the movement and pulsing underneath, the blood radiating out to all parts of the body. You might also feel your own heart's pulsation as a continuation of the mysterious pulse that began the universe. While doing so, intone the sound "shâm-a-îm" for four counts (for instance, "shahm-ay-ee-eem"). As much as possible, feel the sound radiating outward from the center of the heart. Once you feel this, try opening your hands and arms to allow the sound and feeling to radiate outward. To emphasize your own creative fire in unison with the cosmos, you might imagine the heart as the center of a fireball. To emphasize the freedom of the cosmos in you, you might imagine your own arms opening like wings, allowing the heart to fly. After some moments of intoning, simply breathe with the sound and feeling.

3. To balance the two sensations, intone one sound after the other. Feel both the particle and wave realities of your being balance each other and work in harmony together. Then breathe with both sensations while sitting or walking: try inhaling, feeling the sound "a-ah-re-etz," and exhaling, feeling the sound "shahm-ay-ee-eem." Then reverse these and notice the difference in feeling.

CHARACTER DEVELOPMENT   Sumerian

A portion of a hymn on the creation, approximately second millennium B.C.E.

First lines of C. J. Gadd version: When in heaven and earth the steadfast
twain had been completed, and the goddess-mother Inanna, she [too]
had been created, when the earth had been laid down in the place made
[for it], when the designs of heaven and earth had been decided . . .

> *After the beginning,*
> *Vibration and Form, the two elementary principles,*
> *became more of themselves and divided.*
> *(Yet they are always found entwined.)*
>
> *After this Inanna, the divine Mother of life, took form:*
> *It is she who begins the countless generations of relationship,*
> *the primordial lineages, clans, and families who*
> *travel together throughout created time*
> *as new emanations linked to prior waves and forms.*
>
> *Then earth began to fix its place in space and time.*
> *The heights and depths were fastened*
> *like a jewel in the cosmic bezel of the prior void.*
> *And wave-atmospheres-sky—earth's partner—*
> *responded in harmonious embrace.*
>
> *From this embrace of partnership,*
> *the denser waves found form on earth*
> *and limited themselves to stream and sea.*
> *Tigris and Euphrates, our two glittering ones,*
> *remind us of this time when wave and form*
> *set bounds and banks,*
> *developing their characters more uniquely*
> *to further life's unfoldment.*

BINDING AND LETTING GO   Aramaic

A translation of Matthew 18:18–20 from the Peshitta version of the Gospels

Isho'a said

W'âmêyn âmar anâ l'khôn
d'khul mâ d'têsrûn b'ar'âh nihwih lâkh asîr bashmayâ
w'midiq d'tishrôn b'ar'ah nihwih shri' bashmayâ. (18)

KJV: Verily I say unto you, Whatsoever ye shall bind on earth shall be bound in heaven: and whatsoever ye shall loose on earth shall be loosed in heaven.

> *By the living ground on which we stand, I say:*
>
> *In whatever you deeply bind your individual self,*
> *whatever passion you harness in earthiness,*
> *whatever foundation you build*
> *on the particle reality,*
> *that same part of you will be tied up,*
> *the passion already occupied*
> *within the communal reality of the universe,*
> *the wave-penetrated cosmos.*
>
> *On the other hand:*
> *Whatever passion you liberate and release,*
> *whatever circles you open in order to give birth,*
> *letting go of the created and loved one*
> *in form, substance, and earthiness,*
> *that same part of you will be released,*
> *the opening already accomplished*
> *within the vibrating communion of the divine Name—*
> *the heavens, within and among you.* (18)

Tûbw âmar anâ l'khôn
din t'rêyn min'khôn nisht'wôn b'arâh 'al kul tz'bwû d'nishalûn
nihwih lhôn min l'mâth âbwy d'bashmayâ. (19)

KJV: Again I say unto you, That if two of you shall agree on earth as touching any thing that they shall ask, it shall be done for them of my Father which is in heaven.

> *Another way to say what I mean is this:*
> *If two of you, in your earthy, particular natures,*
> *are in balanced agreement with each other,*
> *exemplifying the harmony of the heavens*
> *(the communion of wave, sound, and name),*
> *then anything which you ask in that communal mind—*
> *tranquil, straightforward, without deception—*
> *will occur by the power that gave me birth,*
> *by the Breathing Life of All,*
> *the Mother-Father of the Cosmos.* (19)

Aykâ' gêyr dathrêyn âw t'lâthâ k̲'nîshîn b'shêmy tamân anâ' baynâthhôn. (20)

KJV: For where two or three are gathered together in my name, there am I in the midst of them.

> *This occurs because*
> *wherever two or three*
> *gather and wrap themselves*
> *b'shêmy—in my sound and name,*
> *in my atmosphere and light,*
> *in my experience of*
> *the wave reality of the cosmos—*
> *wherever this power becomes tangible*
> *and names itself through their devotion,*
> *then "I Am" is really there*
> *among, around, and inside them.*
> *My being is present in their own simple presence,*
> *ready for the next instant of reality.* (20)

Body Prayer: Simple Presence

This translation of Matthew 18:18–20 from the original language of
Jesus, Aramaic, is taken from the Bible used by Assyrian and Syrian
Orthodox Christians, the "Peshitta" version meaning pure, straight, and
unadulterated. For further background on this text and my approach in
rendering it, please see the introduction as well as my previous work,
Prayers of the Cosmos (1990).

As I mentioned there, the Greek translators of the words of Jesus
experienced considerable difficulty in translating Aramaic idioms, Middle Eastern cultural expressions, and Semitic language psychology and
cosmology into a more abstract, metaphysical language containing many
dualistic concepts. This resulted in the greater part of the mystical
expression of Jesus being strained out and left on the other side of a linguistic sieve. The resulting Greek-based texts were ripe for theological
formulations and political manipulation that tended to separate
"heaven" and "earth" as well as to create the impression of an exclusive
religious and priestly elite that had the sole power to "bind" and "loose."

When Christianity became institutionalized as the state religion of
the Roman Empire in the fourth century C.E., the link between theology
and politics became even stronger. The Greek scriptures were declared
the "original" versions of the words of Jesus. They remain so to this day
in most seminaries and universities, even though scholars find it difficult
or impossible to defend the position that Jesus taught in Greek (see also
Fitzmyer, 1992). For textual notes on words translated but not included
in this body prayer, please see the end of this chapter.

In the first passage (v. 18), the Aramaic words translated as "bind"
and "loose" are related in a very sublime wordplay. The first word,
d'têsrûn . . . asîr (based on the root ASR), can mean to bind, tie, engage,
or enmesh oneself in something; to harness one's energies, and symboli-
cally to enclose one's directed passion in a closed circle. The energy so
enclosed is the "straight-line" variety: It is meant to flow through conditions back to its Source and not ultimately to be held onto by any one
form. We shall see the appearance of this straight-line energy again later
as the Genesis story unfolds.

The second word, *d'tishrôn . . . shri'* (based on the root SHR, very
similar in sound to the one just cited), shows in symbolic form this same
closed circle opening up. This leads to the additional meanings of liberation, loosening, and solution. The root also suggests the image of the

severing of the umbilical cord after birth, a graphic image of the letting go that follows a harmonious act of creation in the cosmos.

In the final verse (v. 20), the Aramaic word *k'nîshîn* can mean to gather, hide, or wrap oneself in something. In this case, Jesus suggests wrapping oneself "with my *shem*" (*b'shêmy*), an expression that the Greek translation limited to the meaning "in my name." The Aramaic translation again shows the variety of meanings that the word *shem* holds. Like the creation described in Genesis 1:1, *shem* points to all wave- and vibration-related reality, the realm of communion that connects us through light, sound, vibration, and atmosphere. The Aramaic word *baynâthhôn,* usually translated as "in the midst of" or "among," can also mean "alongside of," "inside," and "available for" whatever comes next.

When feeling not present, unintegrated, or without safe boundaries: Feel your own breathing as the point at the center of a circle. Inhale from and exhale to this point, feeling the unique sense of "I-ness" you experience now. What is the particular essence or atmosphere of the divine expressing itself through you at this moment? From what place or places in your body do these feelings or sensations arise? After a short period, continue to inhale from the "point" and gradually begin to exhale to the circumference of the imagined circle, sensing your boundaries as whole and complete. After a time, you may also allow the body sensation of boundaries to become porous, yet complete, on all sides. Release the image of the circle and continue to breathe and feel for a few moments.

THE NEXT THING, PART 1 Arabic

A meditation on the Holy Quran, Sura 1: Fateha, "The Opening"

Bismillâh

A. Yusuf Ali translation: In the name of Allah . . .

> *We affirm that*
> *the next thing that happens occurs only*
>
> *Through the waves of the whole universe yearning toward a*
>   *goal,*
> *By means of the entire unfolding cosmos,*
> *In the light of one single unity of purpose—*
>   *which is the clear sign and name of the Only Being,*
>   *the Ultimate Force behind being and nothingness.*
>
> *We begin*
> *With the Divine Void calling our name before we rayed into*
>   *existence.*

BODY PRAYER: BEGINNINGS

Every sura, or chapter, of the Quran begins with the Arabic formula *bismillâhir-rahmânir-rahîm,* often translated "In the name of Allah, most Gracious, most Merciful." The whole of the Quran is said to be mystically contained in its first chapter. In even more powerful fashion, this essence condenses in its first phrase and most powerfully in its first word.

As a word of power, *bismillâh* came to be used by many of the Sufi mystics as a remembrance to begin everything with the SM—name, light, sound—of Cosmic Unity. Like its Hebrew and Aramaic equivalent SHM, the Arabic root SM also points to the entire sphere of a being, its connections and atmosphere, the sign by which it is known. The prefixed preposition *b-* indicates whatever comes next, what advances or opens, a mouth, an instrument or means, in addition to the usual meanings of "by," "with," or "in."

Bismillâh takes the same linguistic form as the statement Jesus makes in Matthew 18 about how to pray and come together in communion—b'shêmy, that is, "with my name, light, sound, experience, atmosphere." In the Quran the mystical formula for all beginnings affirms the same reality: "with the name, light, sound, experience, atmosphere of Unity." For more on the subtle difference between these, see the textual notes for this chapter.

The word *Allah* (whose form is shortened in the second half of Bismillâh) is not a proprietary name of the divinity invented by Muslims but a continuation of the same root/word of power that had existed for at least six thousand years in the Middle East, beginning with the Old Canaanite *Elat* and extending through the Hebrew *Elohîm* and the Aramaic *Alaha.* All of these words indicate a name pointing to the reality of Cosmic Unity and Oneness, the ultimate force behind being and nothingness, which includes the most mysterious concept: Holy Absence, the "No" (LA) that balances the "Yes" (AL).

Sacred use of the bismillâh phrase continues today as a practice throughout the many Sufi esoteric schools in the East and the West. Murshid Samuel L. Lewis (Sufi Ahmed Murad Chisti), the Western Sufi and spiritual teacher who began the Dances of Universal Peace, wrote that seemingly impossible and unimaginable things could, with devotion, be accomplished through the use of this practice. Ultimately the intention of this word of power calls us to remember our Source before we approach "the next thing."

By comparison Christian theologian Matthew Fox (1986) has named the seminal reality of the Judeo-Christian tradition "original blessing" (in contradistinction to the nonbiblical theology of "original sin" later developed by the institutional church). Using the sound of either the Aramaic phrase b'shêmy or the Arabic phrase bismillâh as a body prayer may remind us of our real origin and potential in a way that leads us beyond concepts into an actual experience of blessing.

Heart Awareness 1

When about to begin any project or relationship, or upon arising in the morning: With eyes closed, breathe easily and naturally, noticing the rise and fall of the breath and the way in which it forms its own rhythm in combination with the sensation of your heartbeat. To feel this, it may help to place one hand lightly on or near the heart. Then bring into this "swing" of the breath one of the two words of power—*Bismillâh* or *B'shêmy*. Allow a natural four-count rhythm of the phrase, inhaling and exhaling, to shape the breath (for instance, "Bis-mil-la-ah" or "Be-sheh-em-ee"). Sense heartbeat and breathing as forming the boundaries of a clear, conscious, creative space in the middle of the chest. Hold this sacred space free and expectant, ready for the next instant of being.

During the silence, you might contemplate the face of the universe before its origin. You might consider the intelligence, passion, creativity, and blessing that extended itself throughout the entire story of the universe and that continues with you, breathing, reconnecting to your place in it.

Gradually release the word-focus and follow the feeling that arises. If you try this body prayer at the beginning of the day, you might conclude by continuing to breathe in the heart while you focus on what lies ahead. If beginning a project, allow any images or intuitions to arise in the silence before going on to "the next thing."

Many beautiful melodies have been generated for the phrase *bismillâhir-rahmânir-rahîm* that enable the practice to be chanted, sounded, and experienced in a more extroverted way. You might start by chanting either *Bismillâh, B'shêmy, Allah,* or *Alaha* slowly on one note. Feel your way into the right note for you, one that resonates with the core of your body and being. Then notice where the chant leads you, deeper into the body or outward to a new melody, as expressed through your own creativity. Conclude the practice with a short period of breathing the phrase, as above.

Textual Notes

1. *Character Development.* This version is based on reading number 17 from a Sumerian account of creation included in a collection of transliterated Sumerian language texts compiled by Gadd (1924, pp. 133–37).

2. *Binding and Letting Go, Matthew 18:18–20.* In verse 19, the Aramaic word *nisht'wôn,* translated as "agree," may also mean to be worthy by being in harmony or equilibrium, to be fitting or qualified because of a balance of the forces between movement and stillness, or between any other two coextensive but paradoxical realities, such as individuality and communion. The root of the Aramaic word for "ask," *d'nishalûn,* is the same word as *pray* in Jesus' vocabulary. The word points to a direct, straightforward, passionate energy, like a line traced from one object to another, or like birds going to their watering place. We shall encounter this word again in chapter 10 in one of Jesus' sayings (see also *Prayers of the Cosmos,* pp. 86ff.).

As mentioned in my earlier work, the word translated as "father," *âbwy,* may also indicate the "breathing life of all" and ultimately the archetype of all parenting, which is the active emanation of *ruhî,* the sacred breath, or spirit, coming into form. The Aramaic version clearly shows that it is the quality of "wholeheartedness" in harmony with the intention of the universe that affects whether prayer is answered, rather than some inherent privilege of membership in a particular group.

3. *The Next Thing, Part 1—Sura Fateha, first word.* In the teaching of Jesus, one touches the *shem* of the One by attuning first to the atmosphere of another human being ("in my *shem* . . .") and then by following that atmosphere to the source. In other words, there is a bridge between the particle and wave realities through the atmosphere of a mystic who could be at the center of both. The Quran, instead of pointing to Muhammad, affirms a direct connection to the shem of the Only Being.

One could say that the message coming through Muhammad at the time recognized the danger of a "mediated" experience of the divine in the way that the institutional Christian church had developed. Relying on dualistic translations that could not catch the nuances of Aramaic words like *shemaya* and *ar'ah,* the church began to create creeds that made mystical experiences into concretized beliefs. It began to insist on the particular person of Jesus (not just his shem) as standing between humanity and Cosmos.

In a conscious critique of this, Muhammad insisted that no pictures or statues of himself should ever be made. Interestingly, none were made of Jesus either until after Christianity became the Roman imperial religion after the conversion of the Emperor Constantine in the fourth century and the various Western creeds began to be composed (thereby also creating "heresy"). Yet even in Islam, after the death of Muhammad, the prophet's personal way of life, prayer, and conversation took on increasing importance, and notes about it were collected as *hadith,* or traditions. By doing so, Muhammad's followers also built a human bridge to the direct experience of Oneness—Allah. Even though Muhammad had outlawed a separate priestly class, his recorded example became a sort of legal precedent that spurred discussion and argument (similar to Christian theology) between the legal "experts" of the various branches of Islam.

Chapter Two

THE BREATH
FROM THE WOMB

There is a breath of warmth, compassion, and creativity that comes from inside, from the darkness, from the womb of all beings. According to the Native Middle Eastern tradition, the womb reality was present at the beginning, preparing for the primeval fireball. In this process of birth, some part of individuality is sacrificed and cleansed with each new creation. This womb reality is available in our bodies and our collective psyche both as the fear of darkness and as a power of rejuvenation.

Before the Fireball Hebrew

An expanded translation of Genesis 1:2

W'ha-âretz haîthah thohoû wa-bohoû, (A)
w'hoshech hal-pheneî th'hôm, (B)
w'roûah Elohîm merahepheth hal-pheneî ha-maîm. (C)

KJV: And the earth was without form, and void; (A) and darkness was
upon the face of the deep. (B) And the Spirit of God moved upon the
face of the waters. (C)

The story continues:

> *Now particles—the Power of Limits—*
> *were still only things in principle.*
> *They were like the germ of a solution*
> *within the shell of a surrounding problem,*
> *the inkling of an answer*
> *to the question of "What next?"*
> *a kernel of purpose embedded in*
> *a dream of the Universe's heart.*
> *This "earthiness" of all the elements was yet*
> *unformed and waiting while* (A)

> *On the surface of the Primordial (yet unawakened) Womb,*
> *at the billowing edge of the abyss of existence where*
> *phenomena, time, and space were yet to appear,*
> *a struggle raged:*

> *A spark of cosmic desire wanted immediate return to Source*
> *from the realm of limits, contraction, and chaos.*
> *This self-involved fire forgot its purpose and set off*
> *the first violence of a being*
> *that wants to be where it is not.*
> *Its barren wanting strangled its own voice until* (B)

> *The breath of Universe Being touched the face of Beloved*
> *Possibility.*
> *Pure expansive power stirred the primordial soup.*
> *The Being of Beings*

inspired, animated, and reminded Flow,
that same edge of possible phenomena,
of the expansive growth awaiting it.
One could say that Cosmic Breath moved with pregnant
    possibility
into the deep and massive nether of Chaotic Dark—
awakening Womb for what?
An intimacy yet unknown. (c)

Body Prayer: Layers of the Deep

The Hebrew expression *thohoû wa-bohoû* (translated "without form and void" by the King James Version) refers to a potential germ of being contained within another such potential existence, revealing the layered idea of the abyss of being that is essential to Native Middle Eastern cosmology. Here the writer of Genesis describes the primordial state of the Universe as being a seed of possibility enclosed within the shell of another possibility. Shell and seed coexist like problem and solution, question and answer. Does the inside push its way through the outside, or does the outside call forth the latent potential of the inside? This question helped begin the Universe, says the writer of these passages.

The story continues when a disturbance happens on the "surface" of these potentials. The Hebrew word *hoshech* (which is translated as "darkness" by the KJV) actually refers to a violent, disordered movement caused by an inner ardor that seeks to extend itself out of harmony with its surroundings. Hoshech is simultaneously a compression and a contraction, a tightening as well as a force trying to liberate itself—perhaps a graphic image of unhealthy stress. This theme returns throughout the Middle Eastern wisdom as various forms of "unripeness" (usually translated as "evil")—that is, action that is not in the proper time and place relative to its surroundings. This type of action shows an imbalance of the individual (particle) and communal (wave) realities of life. Yet this imbalance itself helps further the unfoldment of the cosmos.

Roûah (usually translated "spirit") is the force here that reminds stressful self-involvement of its place in the universe's unfolding. Roûah is the animating power of breathing that can also be variously translated as "soul," "wind," "ethereal breath," or "the force of expansion." As this passage closes, the breath of the Source touches the *maîm*. Much more than just "the waters," the latter word refers to the primordial, unawakened womb of existence, a fluid reality associated with the female principle of generation, the intimate essence of which, according to this cosmology, remains forever unknown.

As the primordial womb (which combines the roots MH and IM) is awakened by the divine breath roûah, it becomes RHM or *rahm*—the activated womb, a raying forth of creativity, heat, compassion, and mercy. Although the word *rahm* is not mentioned here, it is implied by the burst of light and energy that follows in the next verse. As we shall see, in its various forms in the Hebrew, Aramaic, and Arabic scriptures, rahm is the principal archetype of what we call unconditional love. For textual notes on words translated but not included in this body prayer, please see the notes at end of this chapter.

Depths of the Self 1

When feeling tense, contracted, or overly stressed by life, follow the feeling of breathing down: Sense it actually going lower in the body. As much as possible, relax into the bottom of the breathing wave, where it is all out and begins to come back naturally.

Don't hold the breath. Allow yourself to enter the gentle darkness at the "bottom" of things. Use the awareness of breathing as a way to remain connected to the part of you that observes and witnesses all of the interactions within. Are there any voices, sensations, or feelings on the "surface" of your own depths that have been waiting to be heard and recognized? If so, you might begin by asking their names and needs. This process can begin a long, gradual journey to establish a relationship with the subconscious self, called *nephesh* in Hebrew (*naphsha* or *nafs* in Aramaic and Arabic respectively). It can be returned to layer by layer and is best done as a regular "check-in."

To conclude the journey, breathe toward the self (or selves) in your depths with as much love and thanks as you are capable of breathing in and out. Ask for help by aligning your breath to the breath that began the cosmos, the "Holy Breath," and feel your own potential for creation, which arises from "what waits in the darkness."

THE MOTHER WOMB CREATES THE HUMAN

Babylonian-Assyrian

Version from portions of incantation texts, approximately second millennium B.C.E.

First lines of E. A. Speiser translation: That which is slight he shall raise
to abundance; the word of god man shall bear! The goddess they called
to enquire, The midwife of the gods, the wise Mami . . .

> *"From what is small and fragile*
> *let abundance and power come:*
> *let humanity take on the consciousness*
> *of the whole creation*
> *and be absorbed by this task."*
>
> *So spoke the Great Ones,*
> *shining centers of awareness,*
> *the original archetypes of existence,*
> *in the primordial beginning.*
> *From the energizing dark waves*
> *they summoned the Great One in the form of*
> *the Mother, Wise Mami—*
> *she whose name means*
> *the one who responds to cries:*
>
> *"You are the Mother Womb,*
> *radiant source of warmth and life,*
> *the one from whose depths*
> *humanity may arise.*
>
> *"Create this unique form*
> *as a spiral of life into matter—*
> *one force of its being always leaving,*
> *the other always returning home,*
> *the tension balanced*
> *by the awareness of the void.*

"Create humanity as a thin veil
which shrouds the Universal Reality.
Let its purpose spread open and fertile
like a fresh field to be plowed.
Let it embrace the empty core of Being
covered in layers of activity
like an onion's skin."

Then the Great One in the form of Nintu—
    she who bears all new generations,
      preserver of the chain of being—
told the other shining archetypes:

"From my essence comes everything
which helps the cosmos unfold.
So let lullu—*this new spiral being—appear!*
Let the universe develop through its efforts!
Let this human being be
formed from the earth
and enlivened with blood!"

Then Enki,
    the "I Am" compressed into form,
      the archetype of being made manifest,
suggested to the others:

"In the month when the land is cleansed,
when it returns to healing emptiness,
when the earth's beings
see the fruits of their labor
and feel the mother's support underneath,

"Let them kill one of us holy ones,
    shining archetypes of awareness,
      mythic shells of psychic energy,
let all of us be cleansed thereby.

"With the flesh and blood of the divine
let the Great One, also called Ninhursag—
        she who expands the circle of illuminated being—
mix and mingle the clay of the earth.

"Let both the worlds—
shining-waved and particle-formed—
be forever changed by
this new mixture:
the human being.
And we shall hear its tale unfold
from ages to ages."

FROM THEIR INNER WOMBS   Aramaic

Expanded translations of Matthew 3:7 from the Peshitta version of the Gospels

Tubwayhun lamrahmane dalayhun nehwun rahme.

KJV: Blessed are the merciful; for they shall obtain mercy.

> *Ripe are those who from their inner wombs birth mercy;*
> *they shall sense the relief of all prayers answered.*

> *Ripe are those who from their inner wombs birth*
> *   compassion;*
> *they shall feel the delivery of unconditional love.*

> *Ripe are those who from their inner wombs birth radiance;*
> *upon them shall be the rays of divine warmth and heat.*

> *Ripe are those who from their inner wombs birth ardor;*
> *they shall feel a breath from the heart of the Universe.*

> *Ripe are those who from their inner wombs birth*
> *   illumination;*
> *upon, around, and within them will the Cosmic Body shine.*

BODY PRAYER: BLESSINGS OF THE WOMB OF LIFE

These translations of one of the Beatitudes in Aramaic center on the key words *lamrahmane* and *rahme,* which are usually translated as "mercy" or "compassion." Following the older roots back to their source gives the additional meanings associated with *rahm,* the archetype of the original Sacred Womb: a long, heartfelt breath, shining from deep within a body, the sensation of all prayers answered, radiance of warmth, heat, and ardor. For textual notes on words translated but not included in this body prayer, please see the end of this chapter.

Sound and Embodiment

When feeling in need of warmth, heat, or compassion for yourself or another person or in need of reconnection to the creativity that comes "from the darkness," try the following:

1. Lie or sit comfortably and place your hands lightly over the belly, sensing all the movement and fluidity there. Breathe into this center, gently feeling the sound "rah-hm" as the breath rises and falls. You might focus on the power of the creativity that can come from the unknown, on the layers of "dark matter" throughout the Universe from which new stars and galaxies are born in the same moment as your breath.

Then slowly begin to intone the sound "rah-hm" on one note, sensing the movement it evokes in your body. "Ra" is the raying forth energy; "hm" is the breath from the inside, Holy Wisdom (who returns later in our journey). To conclude, allow yourself time to breathe again with the sound and integrate this creative "going out" with its connection to a grounded, embodied, yet mysterious knowing within.

2. This contemplation can be aligned with the seasons around the time of the winter solstice and done in ritual fashion as a group chant. It can also be used to celebrate the fireball that began the universe fifteen billion years ago, a one-time event in the unfolding story of life.

THE WOMB IS A GREAT WORLD   Mandaean

Version of a gnostic text from Iran in Aramaic from about the first century C.E.

First lines of E. S. Drower translation: In the name of the Great Life. . . .
Each of them that existeth in the Body is a world; when separated (taken
separately) each of them is a world. . . . The head is one world; one
world the neck, one world the breast . . .

In the name and light of the most powerful Life!

Worlds combined to form the first Body.
Each head, neck, breast, leg, liver, spleen, stomach,
each male and female organ, skin, hair, nails,
was originally its own world.
They all carry on a friendly conversation.
When they don't—or one does not join in—
then the whole Body is in trouble.

Next came the Soul, a renewing, gracious self that
links us to the sphere of luminous vibration.

After Soul took shape,
the Body formed the Breath of its own radiant life.
This vital spirit animates and connects it to all other Bodies.
And after Body, Soul, and Breath took shape,
then the Womb was formed:
an enclosing darkness from which new life radiates.

The Womb is a great world,
there is none greater or more powerful.

The Blood within the womb radiates pure purpose.
The Blood within the heart radiates precious refinement.
The Blood within the liver radiates plentiful beauty.
The Blood within the veins radiates pure surrender.
These four radiant vibrations control the whole Body.
If there were only three, there would be no Body.

BODY PRAYER: THE BLOOD OF THE WOMB

The Mandaeans are a surviving offshoot of first-century C.E. Gnostics and heterodox Jewish sects, living today mostly in Iran. Their complex cosmology emphasizes knowledge (which is the meaning, in eastern Aramaic, of their name) as the solution to the usual states of "drunkenness," "oblivion," or "sleep" in which most people wander through life. Despite this ascetic-sounding philosophy, the Mandaeans take an interest in penetrating the mysterious depths of embodiment and somatic sensation. Isolated from the theological developments in mainstream Christianity and Judaism, they continue to celebrate the sacred power of body, soul (pictured as an individualized ray of divine light—*nishimta*), breath (*ruha*), and womb (*marba*—the emanation of birth from within).

Gratitude for the Body

To cultivate thankfulness and gratitude, lie comfortably, perhaps before going to sleep, and sense the blood renewing your creative womb with a sense of purpose. Similarly, you might feel this renewing power refining the many feelings the heart experiences each day. The blood circulates through the liver to distinguish between the beauty we can use and that which we can't. And it returns to the heart through the veins as the blood surrenders what we need to release with each breath. Each "world" is a vastness for which we can be thankful, pulse by pulse, heartbeat by heartbeat. They all provide doorways for the renewal and rebirth of our connection to the sacred cosmos of which we are a part.

A Conversation about Rebirth   Aramaic

An expanded translation of John 3:3–8 from the Peshitta version of the Gospels

He [Niqadimaw, a Pharisee] came to Isho'a at night and said to him: Teacher, we know that you are sent from Alaha, the Source, because no one can do what you are doing unless the Source is with him. Isho'a answered and said:

Amêyn Amêyn amar ana lakh

KJV: Verily, verily I say unto thee . . .

> *By the earth on which we stand*
> *what I am going to say is*
> *the ground of truth and*
> *the source from which my actions grow.*

Din anâsh la mithîlidh min d'rîsh
la mishkach d'nichzê malkutêh d'Alaha. (3)

KJV: Except a man be born again, he cannot see the kingdom of God.

> *Unless a human being is completely regenerated,*
> *propagated and reborn*
> *from the Center of existence,*
> *from the primal origin of light and fire,*
> *that person will not see the sudden vision,*
> *be illuminated by the flash*
> *of the "I can" of the Cosmos,*
> *the creative fire of the soul's Source.*

Niqadimaw then said to Isho'a:

Aykana mishkach d'nithîlidh gawra sawa.
D'alma mishkach tûbw l'karsa dimêh d'tarteyn zabwneen l'mi'al
wa nithîlidh. (4)

KJV: How can a man be born when he is old? Can he enter the second time into his mother's womb, and be born?

How can an old man be reborn? Can he physically pass
through his mother's vagina and enter the space inside a
second time? Can he be born again?

Isho'a answered:

Amêyn Amêyn amar ana laкh
dim nash la mithîlidh min maya wa ru'cha
la mishka'ch d'ni'al l'malkûtha d'Alaha. (5)

KJV: Verily, verily, I say unto thee, Except a man be born of water and
of the Spirit, he cannot enter into the kingdom of God.

> *As surely as I stand on this earth,*
> *unless a human being returns*
> *to that sameness with the cosmos*
> *which feels like death—*
> *the dark moist place of birthing,*
> *the place where only flow and animating spirit,*
> *only water and breathing,*
> *only giving way and stirring exist—*
> *that person cannot enter*
> *the reign of Unity,*
> *the "I can" of the cosmos,*
> *the queen- and kingdom of the One.*
> *That person cannot extend*
> *to touch and feel at home in*
> *the power and beauty of the Source.*

Midam dîlîdh min bisrâ bisrâhû
wa midam dîlîdh min rûcha rûchahû. (6)
Lâ tetdamar di'amreth lâкh d'wâlih
l'кhûn l'mithîlâdw min d'rîsh. (7)

KJV: That which is born of the flesh is flesh; and that which is born of
the Spirit is spirit. Marvel not that I said unto thee, Ye must be born
again.

That which is generated from a base sense of things,
crushed down and tread upon with heavy feet,
will show the impression of that density.
That which is generated from inspiration,
breathed from and with the spirit of the cosmos,
will show the force that
moves the universal winds.

Is this surprising that I have told you
you must be born from the first Becoming,
leaving everything else behind?

Rû'cha atar d's'awya nashbâ wa qalah sham'a anat
ala la yada'a anat aymika âthya wala yka âzala
hakana aîthawhy k'lnash dîlîdh min rû'cha. (8)

KJV: The wind bloweth where it listeth, and thou hearest the sound thereof, but canst not tell whence it cometh, and whither it goeth; so is every one that is born of the Spirit.

The breath, the wind, and the spirit
all move by becoming small and large,
by heating and cooling.
They obey their own impulses and
their own harmonious laws.
You are touched by their signature,
you know they exist without a doubt
when you hear their gentle, rapid voices.
But you do not notice or understand
how they attract each other and come together
or how they rise and fall as they
seek their own relationship to the earth.

Just as mysteriously moves every human being
who has returned to the Source
and been reborn from the Great Dark
through the power of breathing and spirit.

Body Prayer:
Celebration of the First Winds

In verse 2, the word *ameyn* can mean firmly, truly, and in faithfulness. It can also mean to stand in firmness or to assert by what is firm underneath. The word was regularly used as an affirmation either before or after an important statement. George Lamsa comments about the place of this word in his native Aramaic-Assyrian culture: "When a priest or prince makes a statement the people generally respond by saying 'Amen' to indicate their ready acceptance and belief. When oral laws are enacted and proclaimed, the people raise their hands and say 'Amen' as a mark of approval and loyalty" (1939, p. 214).

The older roots of the word combine AM, meaning "the mother" or "the matrix" of things, with IN, indicating manifested, individual existence. No doubt there is a relationship here to the Egyptian sacred word *ament*, which could be translated as "the ground of being" and was seen as the "underworld," which held the forms of those departed. As in many surviving Neolithic cosmologies, the "Lady of the Ament" in one of her forms presided over this land of death and rebirth.

The phrase *mithîlidh min d'rîsh*, usually translated "born again," literally says born from the source or from the primary origin of all life in light and fire. The word *rîsh* is related to the Hebrew root in *berêshith*, the first word of Genesis 1:1, which describes the beginning of the universe in its archetypal form.

The word *nihzê* in verse 3 points to an inner vision or contemplation (just as in Matthew 5:8, the Beatitude that mentions "seeing God"). The roots of the word point to being illuminated by a flash of lightning, an instantaneous sense of enlightenment. The phrase *malkutêh d'Alaha*, used in many forms by Jesus, could best be translated as the "I can" of the cosmos, a combined sense of creative fire and willingness to take responsibility for an idea or vision. It also points to all ruling visions that can dominate the collective mind of humanity. When queens, and later kings, became part of Middle Eastern polity, this same word root was used to name them, thereby leading to the translations "queen" or "king." Here the "I can" is that of *Alaha*, the One behind all beings. For more on this construction, please see my earlier work (1990).

In his response (3:4), Nicodemus clearly misunderstands Jesus' reference to returning to the source of existence, since he uses the construction *l'karsa dimêh . . . l'mia'hl*, an expression that means to enter in physical form the space created by womb or belly, or the opening of the vagina.

In verse 5, the words *maya* and *rucha* are the same primordial waters and breath we encountered in Genesis 1:2. Jesus uses the word *d'ni'al* to reflect the one used by Nicodemus, indicating that entering the "I can" of the cosmos can be experienced through one's embodied senses.

In verse 6, Jesus plays with *bisrâ,* the word for "density" and "earthiness," both to contrast it with *rûcha*—breath, wind, or inspiration—and to show Nicodemus his mistake in trying to apply particle-reality rules to wave-reality wisdom.

In verse 8, Jesus continues this theme by pointing to the mysteries involved in the breath and winds. There were then—and still are now—many things we do not understand about why air masses move and come together as they do. The weather is barely more predictable now than it was at the time of Jesus. And these mysterious movements—the coming together and bonding with which the entire universe embraces itself, the search for a harmonious relationship to the earth and embodiment—still drive most of our lives. The person who has returned to contemplate the Source moves in unison with the movements of the whole cosmos.

Sound and Embodiment

About 4.45 billion years ago, the earth began to develop an atmosphere of methane, ammonia, hydrogen, and carbon dioxide. This highly ionized, violent atmosphere seethed with gigantic lightning storms for about a half billion years, charging and changing the primeval earth and seas. From this one-time (as far as we know), spectacular manifestation of the universal winds, the first living cell arose.

As you feel the wind passing over your skin, open to its sound, texture, and resonance with the first life on this planet, which still lives as a memory within you. Feel your own being as breath and wind inside and outside, with only a thin layer of skin in between. The skin itself evolved from the same embryonic layer in you as your brain. It is the organized embodiment of our contact with the whole cosmos, our intelligence. Intone gently the word *rû-châh* on one note, uniting your voice to that of the wind. Follow the feeling of the wind back to its source, inside and outside you. Celebrate those earlier winds that began life here, and thank the intelligence behind them.

THE NEXT THING, PART 2   Arabic

A meditation on the Holy Quran, Sura 1: Fateha, "The Opening"

Bismillâhir-rahmânir-rahîm

A. Yusuf Ali version: In the name of Allah, Most Gracious,
Most Merciful.

> *We affirm that*
> *the next thing that happens occurs only*
>
> *With the Divine Void calling our name before we rayed into*
>   *existence.*
>
> *From this Original Womb comes both grace and mercy.*
> *The first, a supreme unconditioned love:*
>   *before any need arose, a vital power enveloped itself,*
>   *creating warmth, heat, radiation from a center*
>   *without regard to what was lost or gained,*
> *a natural gift of the Cosmic Self.*
> *This always continues.*
>
> *The second, a tender response to all cries,*
> *all unfulfilled potentials:*
>   *the primordial pull of cosmic kinship bears*
>   *acts of compassion, responding to all needs*
>   *as though heard for the first time—*
> *the breath of love in response to a sighing universe,*
> *the quality of mercy.*
>
> *We begin*
> *by means of the Entire Unfolding Cosmos*
> *from whose Womb is born the Sun and Moon of Love.*

Textual Notes

1. *Before the Fireball, Genesis 1:2.* The Hebrew says *hoshech hal-phenei th'hôm,* which the King James Version translates as "darkness was upon the face of the deep." *Phenei* can mean the surface or the edge of something, or what first appears as phenomena, the initial aspect or countenance of anything. It can also mean the manner in which anything becomes present or enters the world of phenomena, or the idea of presence itself.

Th'hom is similar to *thohoû,* the layered depths of existence. In addition, the collective sign *m* unites all this "depth" into the absolute abyss of existence, which also paradoxically contains its most vital power.

The King James Version talks about *roûah* "moving" on the face of the waters. The Hebrew *merahepheth* could also mean "to agitate," "to expand," "to dilate," or "to generate something actively."

2. *The Mother Womb Creates the Human.* Version based partially on the translation of E. A. Speiser from the Old Babylonian and Assyrian as contained in James B. Pritchard's collection (1955, pp. 99–100). In certain instances, I have retranslated some of the Old Babylonian for greater clarity, including the following:

Speiser renders the Old Babylonian word *suq* in my lines 3–5 as the "burden of creation," which he says is a "pure guess." From the later Semitic roots this word is similar to SHQ, which in Aramaic (latter Assyrian) means both a burden, something carried, as well as any inclination to possess or to be enveloped or absorbed by a task. This movement to envelop returns to itself as self-absorption or, in its more profound sense, reflexive consciousness, which is pictured as a layered state, like the skin of an onion.

The name for primal humanity, *lullu,* refers to a contradictory movement of two opposing forces—one drawing itself to a center and the other drawing away—linked by the vowel *u,* which in sound meaning is the link between being and nothingness, the universal connector, the archetypal *and/or.*

In the first name of the Great One in the text, *Mami,* can be seen the original mother-root AM, which indicates all sources of maternity, creative possibility, the matrix of life. Or as a compound root, MA plus MI shows a being that embraces both generative power and energized fluidity. Further, as a combination of the sign of water doubled, MM, enlivened by the creative principle (A) and energizing life (I), we find yet another image of one of humanity's first, and most enduring, names for the Mother.

The latter two names of the Great One in the text (*Nintu* and *Ninhursag*) are variations of the root NN. This root indicates the continuity of existence through the continuance of generations, families, and lineages: The new replaces, yet is linked to, the old. The word *Ninhursag* adds to the basic root the image of a circle gradually expanding from its center to embrace and augment new growth. In Babylonian mythology, Ninhursag was also associated with mountains, the breasts of the earth, similar to the original meaning of the Hebrew word *Shaddai*.

3. *From Their Inner Wombs, Matthew 3:7.* I have translated the initial word, *tubwayhun,* this time as "ripe" in distinction to the Aramaic word *bisha,* "unripeness." These two words are often contrasted in Jesus' teachings and are usually translated in all Greek-based versions as "good" and "evil." The earth image revealed by the Aramaic text opens up the meaning considerably. *Tubwayhun* may also be translated as "happy" or "blessed" (because in tune with the present), "aligned with the One," "healthy" or "healed," "integrated" or "resisting the effects of entropy and deterioration," and "tuned to the Source." For further translations that offer these nuances of the saying, see my earlier work.

4. *The Womb Is a Great World.* This version is based on a selection from Book I, Part 2 of Lady E. S. Drower's collection of Mandaean literature, *The Thousand and Twelve Questions* (1960, pp. 162–64). Additionally I have retranslated various qualities and concepts based on the Mandaean Aramaic transliteration she provides.

5. *The Next Thing, Part 2.* The Arabic words *rahman* and *rahim* are both derived from the primitive Semitic root RHM, or "womb" (*rahmat* in Arabic), previously discussed. Here the primordial Womb emanates the first two qualities from the One: the active and receptive sides of warmth, heat, compassion, mercy, and love. *Rahman* is the active, or solar, side, radiating regardless of its reception. It is, in Jesus' words, the sun that shines on the just and unjust. *Rahim* is the receptive, or lunar, side, responding without limit to needs expressed. Shakespeare expressed this energy of the universe well in *The Merchant of Venice* with: "The quality of mercy is not strained. It droppeth as the gentle rain from heaven."

This important sacred phrase affirms that whenever we remember our true origins, we can begin our lives anew with the same sacred energy that began the cosmos.

Chapter Three

THE GIFT OF
LIGHT AND DARK

Light and dark come as a package in one of
the original gifts of the Universe's diversity.
In developing the fullness of our humanity,
we develop an awareness of both; neither can
exist without the other, and both lead us back
to the Source of all Being.

LIGHT SHALL BE   Hebrew

An expanded translation of Genesis 1:3–4

Wa îâomer Elohîm îehî-âôr, wa-îehî-âôr. (3)

KJV: And God said, Let there be light: and there was light.

> *And then the Universe declared—*
> *that is, its own intelligence surfaced,*
> *infinitely straight, focused, and*
> *reflected from its own depth of being.*
> *It called wave and form to action:*
>
> *"Light Shall Be!"*
> *and because in its "beginningness"*
> *this massive radiance and*
> *flaring forth of light, heat,*
> *and all elements already was,*
> *so "Light Shall Be!" meant "Light It Was!"*
> *The call of the future ignited*
> *the reality of the present.*

Wa-îara Elohîm aeth-ha-aôr 'chi tôb,
wa-îabeddel Elohîm beîn ha-âôr w'beîn ha-hoshe'ch. (4)

KJV: And God saw the light, that it was good: and God divided the light
from the darkness.

> *Next, that Universe Being that brought*
> *elementary life into existence, from nonbeing to being,*
> *sent a pure, straight ray of its intelligence toward*
> *the flaring forth of pre-elementary wave and particle—*
> *   the Light.*
> *The Cosmos drenched itself in lucidity*
> *and recognized the Light as ripe, that is*
> *capable of advancing the cosmic story.*
> *It was an appropriate balance to the older Dark.*
> *This new character development led to the instant*
> *that would begin what we call time.*

Within the tendency of Universe Being
to foster peculiarity for the sake of abundance,
a natural differentiation then occurred:
the Being of Beings divided
Light,
the flaring forth, expanding energy—
straightforward, direct, intelligible,
the mystery of all illumination, teaching and knowing
from
Dark,
the gyrating, concentrated ardor—
self-involved, curved, unknowable, and dense,
the mystery of all chaotic and violent creation.

Body Prayer: The Pull of the Future

The key word here, *aor,* refers to all varieties of light, intelligence, and elemental energy, everything that is enlightening or that produces joy, happiness, and grace. It is a direct, straight-line energy, not whirling or spiraling like its counterpart *ash* (which appears later). The wonderful and mysterious phrase *îehî âôr wa îehî âôr* presents an essential feature of this (and perhaps all) native mysticism: That which is created initially in principle, archetype, or vision draws present reality into manifestation and embodied existence in accordance with the original vision. There is, so to speak, a pull of the future on the present that causes tendencies to unfold now that will be used to further a being's purpose later.

Some scientists now regard the action of the future on the present as a fundamental principle of the development of the universe. To bring us to where we are today, they say, required more than a random series of developmental changes. The tendency or texture of the universe was toward a type of complexity that predisposed its entire development to the unique conditions that brought life as we know it into being on this planet. According to Swimme and Berry (1992, pp. 70–79), the universe is predisposed toward creating forms that are characterized by differentiation, autopoiesis (or interiority), and communion:

> *The universe arises into being as spontaneities governed by the primordial orderings of diversity, self-manifestation, and mutuality. These orderings are real in that they are efficacious in shaping the occurrences of events and thereby establishing the overriding meaning of the universe. (pp. 72–73)*

Celebration of the Moving Toward the Light

For developing a sense of purpose, a forward direction to the unfoldment of life: At dawn, find a quiet place to observe the changing of darkness into light as the earth again rolls to face the sun. Instead of seeing the sun as rising, imagine that you (and the rest of the earth in your region) are moving forward to meet the sun. This is the actual condition. With the eyes slightly closed take the feeling and sensation of the sun into your inner being by breathing gently and "inhaling" it. You may also find it helpful to intone the word *a-or* gently on one note. Translate the outer sensation of returning to light into the inner sensation of clarity, lucidity, and purpose. It is the same light, and it is the same sensation, according to the Native Middle Eastern tradition.

If you are willing, ask the Universe to shape your life in accordance with its own best unfolding. This is what Jesus meant in the fourth line of his prayer (Matthew 6:10) when he asked in Aramaic *Nehwey tzevyanach aykana d'bwashmaya aph b'ar'ah:* "Let your desire be done through us equally in all the waves of vibration as in all the particles of form." Follow whatever light you feel, inner or outer, back to its own source and begin a relationship with a personal source of guidance, a Greater Self or Soul that calls us from the future.

YOUR RADIANCE SUCKLES EVERY
BLADE OF GRASS   Egyptian

*Version from a hymn to Aton as the Sun from the time of Akh-en-Aton, Pharaoh Amen-hotep IV,
1380–1362 B.C.E.*

First lines of John Wilson translation: Praise of Re Har-akhti, Rejoicing
on the Horizon, in His Name as Shu Who Is in the Aton-disc, living
forever and ever . . .

Praise to the Three-in-One of the Sun:
Praise to Re, the streak of light we see.
Praise to Har-akhti, who appears pregnant at dawn.
Praise to Shu, who maintains a balance of heat and power.
All live eternally in the disk of Aton—
the ultimate Thou-and-I in all beings,
our Mutual Soul.

You appear with beauty on heaven's horizon,
beginning life anew each day.
When we approach you in the east, glistening and gracious,
your rays encircle and embrace all you have made.
Though you are far away, we feel your radiance.
Though you touch our faces, no one knows your coming
        and going.

When we leave you in the west,
the whole earth lies in the darkness of death.
We sleep in our rooms, heads wrapped in night:
one eye does not see the other
and everything we think we own can disappear
without our knowing.
Lions roam around, things creep and sting.
Darkness covers us like a shroud.
The earth becomes still like a tomb,
for the one who made us rests
beyond our horizon.

At dawn we approach you again,
as you appear from beyond the border of being.

Harper San Francisco
ATTN: Jill Boeve
1160 Battery Street
San Francisco, CA 94111-1213

Harper San Francisco
is a leading publisher of books
that explore spiritual, philosophical,
and psychological questions.
If you would like to know more about our books,
please complete this card and mail it to us.
We will be pleased to send you a catalogue.

_____

Name (please print or type)

_____

Street

_____

City   *State*   *Zip*

Area(s) of interest —— *Religion* —— *Psychology*
—— *New Culture/Self-Help/Wellness/Spirituality*

_____

Title of the book in which you found this card

HarperSanFrancisco

The symbol of our Mutual Soul
you drive away all darkness and give
the Two Lands cause for a daily festival:
Awake, standing on our feet—
for you have raised us—
we wash and pull our clothes on over our heads,
our arms raising in praise as we see you.
The whole earth takes up your work again!

You create women's seed, men's semen.
You comfort and nurse the child in its mother's womb;
you soothe even its inner weeping.
When the time comes for it to descend,
to breathe and face the outer world,
you open the infant's mouth wide to
receive what it needs from you.
When the chick rouses and speaks within the egg,
you give it enough breath
and the fullness of time
to break the shell
and come forth into the day.

Your radiance suckles every blade of grass.
When you approach, each sprout lives and grows for you.
You created seasons to teach us maturity:
the winter cools us, the heat reminds us of your taste.

You appear, shining;
you approach and withdraw:
by this alone, millions of forms have come from you.

Every being that glances up sees you,
radiant one of the earth's day,
symbol of our Mutual Soul.

The "I Am" Illuminates   <small>Aramaic</small>

Translations of John 8:12 from the Peshitta version of the Gospels

Isho'a said:

Ina(i)na nûhrêh d'alma.

KJV: "I am the light of the world."

> The depth of Identity is the light of the worlds of form.
>
> The "I am" illuminates all primal existence.
>
> The self conscious of its Self enlightens all that grows and greens.
>
> The eye of the whirlwind of self-interest guides the infant of the world.
>
> The ego, fully aware of its ephemeral nature, instructs each leaf on the tree of life.
>
> The germ of the seed of individuality grows the shining joy of creation.
>
> Simple Presence is the radiant force behind nature's expansive power.

Body Prayer: "I Am" and Radiance

Many scholars believe that John's Gospel was written in Greek. However, if Jesus spoke these words, he spoke them in Aramaic. I will leave the reader to judge whether an Aramaic commentary on these words—and the other "I am" statements in John's Gospel—which are often interpreted to mean "Jesus is the only way," can be helpful in discerning the wisdom behind the later theological overlays.

In the Aramaic subtext of Jesus' "I am" statements, we have the Native Middle Eastern approach to the problem of individuality. If everything is linked in communion with the One, why do we have individuality, and how does it serve the universe's unfolding? In the Aramaic word Jesus uses here, *ina(i)na,* we have an intensification of the word for "I," literally the "I-I" or "the I of I." This is not an abstraction of the "I" but a distillation of its essence, as the alternative meanings of the roots show.

As mentioned in textual note 3 in chapter 1, the "wave reality" or atmosphere of the individual mystic is a bridge to her or his consciousness of the Only Individual. So in using "I am" as he does here, Jesus is both including and pointing beyond his personal awareness of cosmic Unity. He is the bridge for those who attune to him in this way.

Here Jesus points out that a deep, unfolding sense of "I" is what illuminates and guides all primal matter. This sense of unfolding is built into every atom of the cosmos, not only so-called organic life. For textual notes on words translated but not included in this body prayer, please see the notes at the end of this chapter.

Simple Presence 2

For developing further a sense of presence: Sit comfortably, eyes closed, and feel the rise and fall of the breath. With each breath, reach out to whatever feelings or sensations appear and feel the breath illuminating each with awareness. Each sensation is also an "I"—a momentary individual awareness. Where does it find its source? You might use the interior sound of the word *nuhr* to help build a bridge of awareness between the individual feelings and sensations and their source. Try opening the eyes very slowly and keeping the same awareness of presence for a few moments.

METAPHORS OF LIGHT   Arabic

A meditation on the Verse of Light, from the Holy Quran, Sura 24:35

Bismillâhir-rahmânir-rahîm (A)
'Allâhu Nûrus-samâwati wal-'arz. (B)
Masalu Nûrihî ka-Mishkâtin-fîhâ Misbâh: (C)
'Al-Misbâhu fî Zujâjah: (D)
'az-zujâjatu ka-'annabâ kawkabun durriyyuny (E)
yûqadu min Shajaratim-mubârakakin- (F)
Zaytûnatil-lâ Sharqiyyatinw-wa la Garbiyyatiny-yakâdu
Zaytuhâ yuzî-'u wa law lam tansas-hu nâr: (G)
Nûrun 'alâ Nûr. (H)
Yahdillâhu li-Nûrihî many-yashâ' (I)
wa yazribullâhul amsâla linnâs (J)
wallâhu bi-kulli shay-'im 'Alîm. (K)

A. J. Arberry translation: In the Name of God, the Merciful, the Compassionate (A). God is the Light of the heavens and the earth (B). The
likeness of His Light is as a niche wherein is a lamp (C), the lamp in a
glass (D), the glass as it were a glittering star (E), kindled from a Blessed
Tree (F), an olive that is neither of the East nor of the West whose oil
well nigh would shine, even if no fire touched it (G): Light upon Light
(H); God guides to His Light whom He will (I). And God strikes simili-
tudes for men (J), and God has knowledge of everything. (K)

> *We begin with the Light of Unity, the Sun and Moon of*
> *Love.* (A)
> *One Being illuminates all waves, all particles—*
> *both communal and individual existence.* (B)
> *Models and symbols surround us:*
> *Our consciousness sculpts space like a recess*
> *or a shade designed to hold and focus light.* (C)
> *Within the shade, glass surrounds the fire element,*
> *protecting, magnifying it, or—if dusty—*
> *obscuring the light.*
> *This glass is the way our embodied life develops—*
> *the contours of our personal history, its twists and*
> *turns.* (D)

Finally, within the glass is light itself—
      pure fire, heat, illumination, soul-force produced from
burning earth, burning matter.
This fire, this light, this illumination is
the same as the stars we see. (E)
All stars are lit from another growing force,
a tree of light and life we cannot find in space, (F)
neither of East nor of West.
But like the oil of our olive tree,
its essence—our soul—exudes light.
At moments we can see it
break the bounds of the material body
and shine, producing brilliance
even before fire touches it. (G)
Light upon light upon light—
      back and back we trace it to its Source. (H)
From this One comes the ultimate ray of
light and sound,
      a voice, an echo
guiding those who hear the desire behind
the unfolding Universe's story,
who come to its call
like a flock of thirsty birds to water. (I)

The Universal One is the matrix of meaning.
It creates models, signs, symbols, and parables
everywhere we look to remind human beings
of their Source. (J)
And the One behind all
comprehends and embraces all—
the past and future journey of primal matter,
all particles, from seed to star. (K)

Body Prayer: Light upon Light

Whole books have been written on the spiritual significance of this one verse of the Quran, and no translation can do it justice. My expanded version includes some of the alternative meanings of the Arabic text, but the mystery to which the verse points is still more a matter of experience than of mental understanding. For textual notes on words translated but not included in this body prayer, please see the notes at end of this chapter.

Sound and Embodiment

For developing the embodied sensation of light:

1. Breathe the sound *nûr* in and out, gently focusing on a sense of divine guidance for one's life. Then slowly intone the sound on one note several times, feeling the sounds in the body as much as possible. Return to breathing the sound and finally release it while you hold only the feeling for a few more breaths.

You may also modify the practice by breathing in *nur* and breathing out the sound *mû-nâw-wir.* This modification of the basic root points to embodied light—the light in the lamp or in the olive oil. Then intone both words alternately as above, invoking names of the divine chanted by the Sufis: *Ya Nur Ya Munawwir,* meaning "O all-pervading Light, O all-embodied Light."

2. To this body prayer you might also add a brief contemplation on the clear light present in a substance like olive oil, along the lines suggested by the sura itself. Place the oil in a clear glass before you and slowly breathe with its essence, allowing your eyes to be soft and your mind to take in the feeling of the oil more than its exact details. Then allow the eyes to close for a few moments and hold the feeling that presented itself. It's best to start with the eyes opened for about a minute, and closed for a minute. After holding the feeling of the image, allow it to lead you. Follow the feeling to its source. End by opening the eyes again slowly and breathing the phrase a few more moments, looking for its presence in everything around you.

UNITY'S DISGUISES   Arabic

Version from a recorded saying [hadith] *of the Prophet Muhammad*

Inna lillâhi la-sa'bîna alfa hijâbin min nûrin wa zulmatin.

A. Yusuf Ali version: God has Seventy Thousand Veils of Light and Darkness.

> *Cosmic Unity has seventy thousand ways to hide.*
>
> *The One Being wraps itself in countless disguises:*
> *It veils itself in light and darkness,*
> *in appearance and disappearance,*
> *in sage guidance,*
>   *a torch to understanding,*
> *and in foolish advice,*
>   *the extinction of wisdom.*
>
> *In the rising and setting of enlightenment.*
>
> *One moment we shield our eyes from the glare,*
> *the next we shudder in shadow.*
> *Eclipse and Brilliance both obscure from mind's view*
> *the Universe's single-minded purpose.*

From The Diwan of Shams-i-Tabriz *by the Sufi poet Mevlana Jelaluddin Rumi, thirteenth-century Anatolia*

David asked God: "We know you don't need
either this world or the one beyond,
so what was the wisdom in creating them?"
God replied: "Humanity is enmeshed in time,
how shall I answer so you can understand?

"I was a hidden treasure,
abundant, radiating love.
To reveal this treasure
I created a mirror:
its face the heart of being,
its back the worlds of phenomena.
The back seems better than the face—
if that's the only side you know."

When dust clouds the glass,
how can the mirror be clear?
When you remove the dust,
the rays return without a detour.
Grape juice does not ferment overnight:
wine ages a while in a bottle.
If you want your heart to brighten,
expect to exert yourself a bit.

Listen to this story:
When the soul left the body,
it was stopped by God
at heaven's gates:
"You have returned just as you left.
Life is a blessing of opportunity:
where are the bumps and scratches
left by the journey?"

Everyone knows the legend about
the alchemist who turns copper to gold.

A rarer alchemy has transmuted our copper,
my beloved Shams and I:
Shams, the sun, needs no hat or robe
to block the intense, uncompromising
rays of Grace.
His being alone covers a hundred bald heads
and clothes ten naked bodies.

My child-self!
For humility alone, Jesus rode an ass.
Why else should the wind mount a donkey?
My intuitive self!
In this search, direct your head
to mimic the behavior of stream water.
My logical self!
If you want a life worth living,
walk the path holding death's hand.

Remember Unity until you forget separation.
Then you may lose your way in the Named,
without the side-trip
of namer and name.

BODY PRAYER: THE MIRROR

The Sufi poet Mevlana Jelaluddin Rumi is renowned throughout the
Middle East as the greatest mystical poet of all time. He met his teacher
and beloved friend Shams-i-Tabriz unexpectedly. Shams (whose name
also means "the sun") appeared suddenly one day while Rumi was
studying. The raggedy dervish seized all of Rumi's scholarly writings
and, according to one account, threw them down a well. Shams offered
to make them reappear if Rumi wanted, or he could help him open his
heart. Rumi chose the heart. This collection of poems bears Shams's
name because Mevlana felt that they were the result of his guidance or,
even more intimately, the voice of Shams coming through him.

Heart Awareness

This body prayer comes from an ancient Sufi practice. Feel the
heart as a mirror or clear pool of water. With each gentle breath in and
out, feel the mirror becoming clearer. After a few minutes, feel the focus
of breath and sensation in the heart as a sacred space, an altar, a creative
spaciousness. What images or sensations might appear there from the
One Being?

Textual Notes

1. *Light Shall Be, Genesis 1:3–4.* The Hebrew word *îâomer,* usually translated as "said," also has several more expansive meanings. It points to a power that declares, manifests, and reflects its own inner nature outside. In this tradition, to declare something with such power is a step in manifestation—its reality becomes engraved on the vibratory slate of the cosmos, so to speak.

In verse 4, the word *îara,* usually translated as "saw," may also mean to direct a straight ray of intelligence toward something. This word is closely related to the one for light. That is, the quality of the Universe itself that recognized the light was in fact drawn forth by the new existence of light. The word *tôb,* usually translated as "good," means more exactly ripe or appropriate for the moment and thereby healthy, integrated, capable of conserving energy and setting aside corruption. The word *îabeddel,* usually translated as "divided," refers to an interior activity that causes things to become distinct or individual. For notes on *hoshech,* the primordial dark, please see the body prayer "Layers of the Deep" in chapter 2.

2. *Your Radiance Suckles Every Blade of Grass.* This excerpted version is based on earlier literal translations of an El-Amarnah tomb text by John A. Wilson in James B. Pritchard's collection (1955, pp. 370–71) and by Adolf Erman (1927, pp. 289–91). In the first stanza, I have retranslated and given an expanded version of the sacred names Re, Har-akhti, Shu, and Aton based on their underlying roots and meanings using the studies of E. A. Wallis Budge (1895, 1911a, 1911b), an early Egyptologist, and the Hebrew-Egyptian etymological comparisons of Fabre D'Olivet (1815) as references.

3. *The "I Am" Illuminates, John 8:12.* The Aramaic word *nuhreh* is directly related to the Hebrew *aor.* The addition of *n* to the root adds a sense of newness and youth to the illumination, yielding light that leads or guides somewhere, like a lamp or beacon. The word *alma,* usually translated "world," refers to all primal matter, vegetation, development, and the collection of them into masses, unions, and conjunctions, each being a "world" (similar to the sense we saw in the Mandaean hymn in chapter 2).

4. *Metaphors of Light, Quran, Sura 24:35.* The word *masalu* (in line C) can be a parable or a symbol, a line of meaning drawn between one thing and another. The word usually translated "niche," *mishkât,* can be any space that envelops energy or consciousness, that sculpts and focuses

it as a lamp shade does light. It also points to the image of shrouds or veils within veils, or the skin of an onion. The lamp itself, *misbâh,* may also indicate other, more physical layers of the veils. The glass, *zujâjah* (line D), is the exterior of this dynamic form, both protecting the light inside as well as obscuring it, depending on one's personal history or development through life.

As the metaphor continues to develop and expand in all directions (like light itself), it leaps across the cosmos: We are taken in line E from the glass to the stars (*kawkabûn*), a word based on a root pointing to burning and combustion. This burning radiates both a fragrance and an ethereal atmosphere (*durriyyuny*). The light of the stars also comes from somewhere, and following the metaphor of fragrance, we come to the blessed tree (*shajaratim*) in line F. The roots of this word point to any combination of movement and growth that brings a being back to face its original Self.

At this point (line G) the metaphor of the olive tree (*zaytûhâ*) enters. The roots of the word also point to a luminous ray, flash of light, grace, or brightness. The word connects to the illuminated essence of every being that one can see at moments when its purpose for existence shines out. This "tree of life" is neither of "East nor West": in an alternative meaning, it has nothing to do with either liberation or bondage—it shines because of its nature to shine. It does not need to be ignited from the outside.

Then comes the beautiful phrase in line H, *nûrun alâ nûr*—light from light from light. The only place the metaphor can end is in the end of metaphor, that is, in the Only Reality, the One (*Allah*, embedded in the word *yahdillâhu,* line I). Ultimately the One provides the only context for all metaphors: The Being behind the Universe has a clear desire (*yashaa*—usually translated as "whom he wills") that unfolds its ongoing story. This desire is heard as a call by those who are receptive to it (as Jesus also pointed out—"those with ears to hear"). The signs of the call are everywhere, all of manifestation serves to connect us to it. The last word *alîm,* usually translated as "know," may also mean to comprehend or to embrace a thing. What Oneness embraces here is *kulli shayîm,* the entire particle reality of the cosmos.

5. *Unity's Disguises.* The collected sayings of Muhammad, while not considered in the same class of sacredness as the Quran, nevertheless have become an important source of guidance and precedent for Muslims. This saying complements the verse of light by noting that a metaphor can reveal or hide truth, just like a veil (*hijaba*). The latter

word can mean anything that covers, wraps, screens, obscures, outshines, eclipses, or shelters. The number seventy thousand may relate to a sense of endlessness. The word contrasted here with *nur* is *zulm,* the ultimate extinction of light, the deepest darkness imaginable, the vanishing, cessation, or disappearance of intelligence. However, the Being of Beings itself is beyond both brilliance and eclipse, glare and shadow. To think that the Only Being is only in light and not in darkness is also a veil.

6. *The Back of the Mirror.* This version is based on a literal translation of number 4 in the collection by R. A. Nicholson (1898, pp. 14–17). I have added the titles for this and all selections from Rumi, Hafiz, Shabistari, and Sa'adi. Classical Persian poetry has no titles, only numbers related to the volumes in which they were collected.

Chapter Four

TIME AND TIMING

The Universe creates vibration and pulse as
well as the alternation of light and dark. This
further gift of diversity allows us to create
what we call time. The pulse from the heart
of the Universe also calls us to be in tune with
its own timing, with the unfoldment of its
purpose—and our own.

THE FIRST DAY   Hebrew

An expanded translation of Genesis 1:5

Wa-îkerâ Elohîm la-âôr îom,
w'la-hoshech karâ laîlah,
wa-îehî hereb, wa-îehî-boker,
îom ahad.

KJV: And God called the light Day, and the darkness he called Night.
And the evening and the morning were the first day.

> *To further engrave their character*
> *so that the story might continue,*
> *the Universe Being compressed the fate of Light and Dark*
> *into two gatherings:*
>
> *the first,*
> *a mass of definite, luminous manifestation and*
>   *intelligence—*
> *a fireball of straight rays of all spectrums*
> *moving with purpose—*
> *formed the quality of Primordial Day*
>
> *the second,*
> *a mass of indefinite, endarkened manifestation and*
>   *unknowing—*
> *circular energies moving out and back from center—*
> *formed the quality of Primordial Night.*
>
> *These forces alternated once:*
> *all events and forms congealed through the Grace of Primal*
>   *Night,*
> *all events and forms expanded through the Grace of Primal*
>   *Day,*
> *the Dark brought the possible to a close through density,*
> *the Light opened up again the expansive course of destiny.*
>
> *Once over and back again,*
> *forever after entwined,*
> *this first round of closing and opening,*

congealing and expanding,
off and on,
also marked the beginning of
a different sense of universe time.
(There were no seconds, minutes, or years,
but this we know:)
It was the first period of
manifest luminous phenomena
in our Cosmos—
the First Universal Day.

BODY PRAYER: DENSITY AND DESTINY

For textual notes on words translated but not included in this body prayer, please see the notes at the end of this chapter.

It should be clear that the "day" and "night, " *îom* and *laîlah,* talked about here are not, in the cosmological sense, periods that add up to twenty-four of our hours. The addition of *m* to the root IO (of *ior,* "primordial light") means a gathering or massing of this intelligence, illumination, and straight, radiant energy. The word *laîlah,* from the root LL or LIL, points to all circular movement that draws toward and away from a center, as well as any force that binds or envelops things in such a vortex.

There are at least two aspects of this opening and closing. First, the entire primordial cosmos opened and closed with a period of spontaneous lucid creation—the fireball—and a period when such radiant creation was consolidated and solidified. For instance, the birth of galaxies was a one-time event that happened ten to fourteen billion years ago. The conditions for this creation cannot, as far as we know, be re-created. From the standpoint of the galaxies, we are still in the period of consolidating and using the energy and elements that their creation seeded. We are still in the first "night."

Second, this process of opening and closing, radiating and consolidating, continues to repeat itself with each new creation, according to the Native Middle Eastern tradition. The first "day" on earth might have begun as the planet attained a fixed orbit and rotation in relation to the sun. Our journey toward and away from light began to repeat itself regularly rather than constantly create itself anew. The regular pulse of light for a certain period created a way to measure duration and what we call time.

Celebration of Night

At twilight take some moments to face the horizon and breathe with the fading of the light. Visualize yourself, and the other beings in your region, rolling away from the light (rather than the sun "setting") and toward darkness. As you breathe with the gathering darkness, begin to feel the effects of the day consolidating, congealing, and coming to a close. This is easier to feel in nature, as each plant prepares to use the energy and elements gathered during the day. For a moment at least, allow yourself to relax, to stop pushing, and consciously to enter the darkness.

Before going to sleep at night, complete this process by releasing the feelings and thoughts attached to any events, circumstances, and relationships you have received during the day that do not carry you toward your destiny. This can easily be done by placing the head on the earth or the floor and breathing a few times with gentle emphasis on the exhalation.

At dawn or the next morning, as you roll again toward the sun, take a few moments to breathe with the light and feel your destiny opening up before you. Gently emphasize the inhalation as you take a few breaths, feeling the sun in your heart.

THE RIGHT TIME AND PLACE   Avestan

A version of the Zoroastrian prayer recorded in Yasna 27:14, from ancient Persia, approximately 1700–1500 B.C.E.

Ashem vôhû vahîshtem astî. (1)
Ushtâ astî. (2)
Ushta ahmaî hyat ashaî vahîshtaî ashem. (3)

Dastur M. N. Dhalla translation: Righteousness is man's best acquisition. (1) / It is happiness. (2) It is his happiness / When he is righteous for the sake of Best Righteousness. (3)

> *To do rightly by the cosmos depends on timing:*
> *right doing, right being at*
> *the right time and place.*
> *This right guidance, found in every heart,*
> *finds its source in the universal Heart.* (1)
> *This rightness is ultimate good,*
> *ultimate happiness and joy.* (2)
> *The joy comes naturally to and through a life*
> *lived in moment-by-moment contact*
> *with the truth behind all nature,*
> *for its own sake and not for anything else.* (3)

BODY PRAYER: A BREATH
FROM THE HEART OF THE UNIVERSE

Starting about 1700 B.C.E., the Persian prophet Zarathushtra Spitama brought a universal message of One Being based on freedom and toler- ance, which influenced the development of Hinduism, Buddhism, Judaism, Christianity, and Islam. For almost a thousand years, Zoroas- trianism was the dominant religion of the Iranian plateau, and while there was a brief interruption during the Alexandrian conquests, the Zoroastrian Parthian Empire rivaled that of Rome during the time of Jesus. The Parthians gave way to the Sassanians, who were also Zoroas- trians, in the third century C.E. and lasted until the Arab Islamic con- quest in the seventh century.

From this time, the number of Zoroastrians declined drastically. A large remnant resettled in India in the ninth century, and this group is usually called the Parsis (people from Pars or Persia). Today there are about 125,000 Zoroastrians in the world. Many who had lived in Iran up until the twentieth century have moved to Europe or North America because of persecution from Islamic fundamentalists.

The Ashem Vohu is one of the central daily prayers of Zoroastrian- ism and affirms the wisdom that to be in right relationship with the nat- ural world, as a face of the Only Being, is the true source of happiness. The word *ashem* (based on *asha*) points to the sense of timeliness, right direction, and ripeness that guides the universe. The word *vohu,* usually translated as "good," points to the source of universal guidance and blessing, the heart of the cosmos.

Heart Awareness

Breathe easily and gently with your feeling in the center of the chest, and again feel the heart as a mirror. After a period of "cleaning the mirror" (as suggested in the last chapter), visualize the heart reflecting the purpose at the heart of the Universe, as though connected to it by a ray of light. Slowly intone the sound "ah-shem" into your own heart, with the chin toward the chest, keeping the neck relaxed. Then raise the head slowly as you intone "vô-" and continue raising it as you intone "-hû" upward, feeling a renewed connection between your own heart and that of the universe. Beginning with your own best note as felt in the heart, you may happen upon your own melody for this chant.

TOMORROW MEANS THINGS DEPART   Aramaic

A translation of Matthew 6:33–34 from the Peshitta version of the Gospels

Isho'a said:

*Bwhawdêyn lûqdam malkutêh Alaha wa zadîqûtêh
wa kulhêyn hâlêyn miththâwsphân.*

KJV: But seek ye first the kingdom of God, and his righteousness; and
all these things shall be added unto you.

> *If you're going to be anxious and rush around about
>   anything,
> do it first about finding the "I can" of the universe
> and how it straightens out your life.
> Line up your starting place with that of the cosmos:
> search and ask and boil with impatience
> until you find the vision of the One Being
> that empowers all your ideas and ideals,
> that restores your faith and justifies your love.*

> *All the rest—the universal and endless "things" of life—
> will then attach themselves to you as you need them.
> You will stand at the threshold where
> completeness arrives naturally
> and prostration leads to perfection.
> Pouring yourself out makes the universe do the same.*

*La hâkêyl thêtzphûn damchâr hû gêyr mhâr yâtzph dîlêh.
Sâphêq lêh l'yawmâ bîshtêh.*

KJV: Take therefore no thought for the morrow: for the morrow shall
take thought for the things of itself. Sufficient unto the day is the evil
thereof.

> *Don't torture yourself standing watch over things,
> accomplishments, or states of mind
> you want still to possess tomorrow.
> It doesn't work that way.*

Tomorrow means things depart.
Time and the elements wash them away
just as they came, with abundance,
as the future stands by watching.

Each day completes itself with
its own share of unripeness.
Every illumination carries enough
inappropriate action
without carrying any forward.

THE DAY IS NEARLY OVER   Arabic

A meditation on the Holy Quran, Sura 103, 'Asr

Bismillahir rahmanir rahim. (1)
Wal 'Asri (2)
'innal insâna lafî khusrin (3)
'illallazina 'amanu wa 'amilus sâllihâti (4)
wa tawâsaw bil Haqqi wa tawâsaw bis Sabr. (5)

N. J. Dawood translation: In the Name of Allah, the Compassionate, the
Merciful. I swear by the declining day that perdition shall be the lot of
man, except for those who have faith and do good works and exhort
each other to justice and fortitude.

> *We begin with the light of Unity,*
> *the womb that bears compassion and mercy.* (1)

> *Unity also includes the root of everything solid,*
> *the origin of everything compressed;*
> *the feeling of being pushed from outside in—*
> *the steepness of a mountain, the hardness of a rock,*
> *the bits and pieces we sense as matter,*
> *the bits and pieces we experience as time.*
> *"Time and again . . . Day after day . . ."*
> *the awareness we have*
> *when late afternoon light*
> *reminds us that the day is nearly over,*
> *again.* (2)

> *Because of this, if you count material gain,*
> *human existence always comes up a loss.*
> *Energy contracts to form a being,*
> *a vortex of "I-ness" envelops the Self.*
> *This creates a temporary shelter, a hostel for the night.*
> *But we miss the journey*
> *if we hold on to the shelter:*
> *its nature is to fall away behind us*
> *as we travel farther,*
> *just as do the moments of time.* (3)

Time's loss doesn't affect those whose
lives arise from the mother-principle, the giveaway:
who radiate beneficence without counting the cost,
whose actions are fully formed, a work of art,
because they are always opening softly
to the divine One. (4)

Time's loss also doesn't affect those who
come together simply and with feeling,
to point out and celebrate
the presence of Holy Wisdom all around,
who recognize the sacred ground of being,
the home of truth within embodiment;
who share the glory of patience and of limits
as they function like channels
for the sacred fire to flow. (5)

BODY PRAYER: GROUND AND PATIENCE

Sura 'Asr is one of the short suras sometimes used in the Islamic daily prayers. It reminds us that loss is a function of the cosmos. No forms, including human ones, are intended to last forever or to think themselves omnipotent. For textual notes on words translated but not included in this body prayer, please see the notes at the end of this chapter.

In the first line, the Arabic word *asr,* usually translated as "time" or "time through the ages," also means what is pressed down, sold, compressed as though from the outside, bounded, limited, or restricted. As we have already seen, all of these are naturally associated with the effects of time in Native Middle Eastern cosmology. There was no sense of "unlimited natural resources" or denial of mortality, both of which have plagued modern consciousness.

In the last section, the Quran says that coming together in community (*tawâsaw*) to cultivate and share wisdom helps counteract the stress of time. In particular, the Quran mentions two sacred qualities that can be named and celebrated. The first is *haqqi* (based on *haqq*), usually translated as "truth" but deriving from an older Semitic root meaning "the breath of wisdom from underneath." In its Egyptian form this is *hek* (used in the sacred name Hek Mat); in its Hebrew form this is *hokhmah*, Holy Wisdom, who reappears later in chapter 6 of this work. The second quality is *sabr* (derived from *sabur*), which is usually translated as "patience." It also refers to all fixed boundaries, limits, and disciplines that serve as useful channels to focus the fire and flow of the cosmos.

Sound and Embodiment

Both *haqq* and *sabur* are numbered among the "ninety-nine names of Allah"—qualities of feeling that are part of the universal One. Most, if not all, of these sacred words of power have ancient derivations and may be among the oldest spiritual practices in the Middle East. Rather than layering on a quality as if one were putting on a piece of clothing, it is more helpful to use these words of power to connect those qualities and feelings already within our cells and selves to their source in the cosmos. In the most profound sense, there is nothing "outside," a point that the Quran makes again and again.

1. For developing a grounded sense of wisdom, for sensing what is practical and possible for the moment, not inflated or grandiose, try the following body prayer: Intone the phrase *Yâ Hâqq* several times (the traditional number is thirty-three). The word *ya* is a form of address: We call to the quality as something living in ourselves. Feel the sound going down through the body, and release the muscles of the pelvic floor as you feel the double *q* sound. This practice may also be done walking in a rhythm of four, either speaking or simply breathing the phrase. After a few minutes of the practice, continue to breathe the phrase, then release the sound and breathe only with the feeling, making a gradual transition to "normal" consciousness. Gradually this sacred phrase will transform what is "normal."

2. For developing gratitude for limits, or for slowing down to maintain energy in a project or relationship over a longer period of time: Intone slowly on one note the phrase *Yâ Sâ-bûr,* feeling each part of the sound vibrate through the body. Our consumer society encourages an opposite tendency: throwaway goods, throwaway relationships, throwaway lives. There is enough appropriate loss in the Universe without adding what is inappropriate. Again, after several minutes, simply breathe with the phrase, and then with the feeling of the phrase, reach deep within to connect to the places that need "staying power."

THE PAST FLIES AWAY   Persian

From The Secret Rose Garden *by Sufi poet Mahmud Shabistari, thirteenth century*

> The past flies away,
> coming months and years do not exist:
> Only the pinprick of this moment
> belongs to us.
>
> We decorate this speck of a moment—time—
> by calling it a flowing river or a stream.
>
> But often I find myself alone
> in a desert wilderness,
> straining to catch the faint echo of
> unfamiliar sounds.

Time, Patience, and Love   Persian

From the fourteenth-century Sufi poet Hafiz

At dawn,
the nightingale spoke to the rose:
"Don't look down on my passion for you,
for while hovering around this garden, I have seen
many like you blossom and die."

The rose, smiling, replied:
"This truth does not bring me tears,
but what a way for a lover to speak!"

From now until time's end,
you will never know the perfume of love
until you have swept dust from the
doorstep of the tavern of ecstasy
with your forehead.

If you want to taste red wine from
a cup encrusted with jewels,
expect to pierce many pearls
with the hair of your eyebrows
before you have a sip.

Yesterday at dawn
I entered the garden of Identity.
The morning breeze wafted a blessing
across the hair of a hyacinth.
"Where," I cried in ecstasy, "is the cup that
satisfies all the thirst in the world?"
A voice replied,
"Poor man, you'd have better stayed in bed
than tempt fate with such questions."

Love's talk doesn't touch the tongue—
O cupbearer—
stop interrogating me!

With his own tears, Hafiz has poured
both wisdom and patience into the sea.
Love's pain made any cover-up
or delay impossible.

Textual Notes

1. *The First Day, Genesis 1:5.* The Hebrew word *îkera,* usually translated "called," can also mean to engrave a sign or character, to compress something into a firm course or fate, and to name. To the extent that the *shem* (vibration, atmosphere, light) of every being was beyond one particular name, this act of engraving by the cosmos compressed the more expansive energies of Light and Dark, considered in the last chapter, into their more particular characters of Day and Night, *îôm* and *laîlah.*

The phrase *îehî hereb wa îehî boker,* usually translated "there was evening, there was morning," refers to two further refinements of this opening and closing. The root of *hereb* points to a process whereby things and energy congeal, become denser, and move toward an end in that form. Correspondingly, *boker* points to an expansion, renewal, and new beginnings.

2. *The Right Time and Place.* This version retranslates the key sacred term (*asha*) and is based on comparisons with several previous literal translations, including Jafarey (1988, pp. 42–43), Boyce (1979, p. 38), and Dhalla (1942, p. 2). Zoroastrian scholar Ali A. Jafarey comments on this prayer:

> *Righteousness [asha] is the universal law that stands for order, evolution, progress and the perfection as ordained by God for the cosmos. One become righteous by doing the right thing at the right time, in the right place and with the right means to obtain the right result. It means precision in every thought, word and deed. It means constant improvement and continuous renovation. It brings enlightenment, true happiness, provided that happiness is shared by others. (p. 43)*

3. *Tomorrow Means Things Depart, Matthew 6:33–34.* The word *bwhawdêyn,* usually translated "seek," can indicate any rushing, harsh, anxious movement, including searching and boiling. The word *lûqdam,* usually translated "first," comes from the root QDM, which points to the primordial, originating time of the universe, the earliest "before." *Malkutêh* is another form of the "I can" energy of the cosmos—the ruling principles, ideals, and visions of the One Being, *Alaha.*

The Aramaic word *zadîqûthêh* is based on an old Hebrew word, *tzadak,* which, like the Ashem Vohu prayer, refers to a sense of straightness, faithfulness, mercy, and honesty—all attained by restoration of a right relationship with the cosmos.

The phrase *ḳulhêyn hâlêyn,* usually translated "all these things," literally refers to the sum total or universal "thing-ness," including all vessels, vehicles, tools, accomplishments, and mental and emotional states—anything one might attempt to possess.

The word *miththâwsphan,* usually translated "shall be added unto you," is based on an important Middle Eastern mystical root, SPH, which points to whatever is added to complete, perfect, or achieve consummation in a thing or being. It represents dynamic wholeness, an ability to embrace all points of view and states of feeling. It also points to one who becomes a threshold or an open doorway, or one who pours out or prostrates the small sense of self in order to receive the Self of the One. Later this same root is used to name the *Sufi* mystics in the Middle East. Here Jesus says that when we pursue a right relationship with the universal One and allow this relationship to realign our life, we produce a condition of receptivity in which anything we need to help us complete our purpose in life will be supplied by the universe.

In verse 34, the Aramaic *hâḳêyl thêthphûn,* usually translated "take thought," points to a tortured state of watching over and trying to hold on to things. The word *mchâr* (first used in the form *damchâr*) is usually translated as "tomorrow." It comes from a root that points to what passes away or into disuse due to the effects of time and the elements. In Aramaic "tomorrow" literally means "what passes away" or "things depart." And, according to Jesus, tomorrow watches while time and the elements cleanse each new day of what no longer belongs.

Following this theme, Jesus again uses a word with the SPH root, the one for completeness, but turns the metaphor inside out. Each illuminated period (*yawmâ*) or each day carries its perfect complement (*sâphêq*) of unripeness or inappropriate action (*bîshtêh*). This last word is usually translated as "evil" but really refers in Aramaic to any action that is not done in its right time, that is, either too early or too late. The implication here is that even unripe action has its place in the broader sense of all-embracing completion, which the universe brings forth each day.

4. *The Day Is Nearly Over, Quran, Sura 103, 'Asr.* In the third line, the word *insâna* refers to humanity or human existence. It is made up of two older roots: IN, which points to an individual existence created by a vortex of contracting energy, and SN, which points to the light given off by a polished gemstone. The word *ḳhusrin,* usually translated as "loss," also refers to anything that is only temporary or that diminishes in volume, like a shelter or momentary refuge.

In the next section, the word *amanu* comes from *iman,* a central concept usually translated as "faith." The word also points to a matrix of meaning, a mother-principle that includes all determined, unshakable, and beneficent actions, energy that gives without expecting to receive. The words *amilus sâllihâti,* usually translated as "righteous deeds," refer to all effects that spread from a soft, open connection to the Only Being and that are fully formed, complete from beginning to end. Developing both of these qualities of being—beneficence and openness—mitigates the wearing effects of time, says the Quran, because they focus not on grasping but on giving.

5. *The Past Flies Away.* This version is based on previous literal translations by Florence Lederer (1920), E. H. Whinfield (1880), and Johnson Pasha (1903).

Little is known about the life of Sa'duddin Mahmud Shabistari. He was born near Tabriz, northwest Persia, in about 1250 C.E., the same town noted as the birthplace of Mevlana Rumi's teacher, Shams. Apparently Tabriz (near the current border of Azerbaijan and Armenia) had a long-standing reputation as a home for tricksters and unscrupulous dervishes. Even as late as 1893, British traveler Edward Browne reported and translated the following saying among Persians: "From a Tabrizi thou wilt see naught but rascality: even this is best, that thou shouldst not see a Tabrizi." Shabistari is said to have written *The Secret Rose Garden* in reply to questions asked him by a Sufi doctor of Herat named Dmir Syad Hosaini.

6. *Time, Patience, and Love.* Version based on literal translations of number 48 from the Diwan of Hafiz, translated by Justin Huntly McCarthy (unpublished manuscript) and H. Wilberforce Clarke (1891).

Hafiz lived about a century after Shabistari and Mevlana Rumi. Born in about 1320 in Shiraz, Persia (the same birthplace as Sa'adi), he is said to have died about 1390. In between he suffered the loss of both his wife and his son, whom he mourns in his poems. According to some writers, he was a closet Zoroastrian mystic, and his references to wine, taverns, and cupbearers have coded meanings.

According to others, he was an Islamic Sufi, albeit very unorthodox. According to this opinion, all his images have references to the wine of divine ecstasy, to the meetinghouse for sacred practices, and to the spiritual guide. It seems equally clear that Hafiz was a free spirit who embarrassed everyone. He uses metaphors based on his own experience of love, disappointment, inebriation, ecstasy, and the natural world. His life of emotion itself became a guide, one that led him to connect further with the Feeling behind all feeling. Even confusion, impatience, and boredom are his teachers, as we shall see in subsequent selections.

Chapter Five

SACRED
SPACIOUSNESS

The Universe creates newness and diversity
by creating possibility itself. The power of
sacred space and spaciousness created our
planetary atmosphere. Because atmosphere
makes sound a possibility, our ears and vocal
cords wrap themselves around this reality just
as our eyes wrap themselves around the reality of light and dark. In this tradition, the
power of hearing and the power of the word
are creative—by them one can hear or speak
something into existence.

An expanded translation of Genesis 1:6–8

Wa îâomer Elohîm îehî raķîwh'a bethôķh hamaîm
w'îhî mabeddil beîn maîm la maîm. (6)

KJV: And God said, Let there be a firmament in the midst of the waters,
and let it divide the waters from the waters.

> *Again the Universe's intelligence*
> *tapped a more complex future for inspiration.*
> *It invoked a new process:*
> *one more rarefying, spacious,*
> *and possibility-enlivening,*
> *right in the middle*
> *of the primordial, compressed*
> *Dark Wave-Matter.*
> *By imagining more opening and expansion,*
> *the cosmos called forth Spacious Choice—*
> *the mother of all listening, receptive Universe habits—*
> *from the center of the primal cosmic Flow.*

Wa îahash Elohîm aeth ha-raķîwh'a
wa îabeddel beîn ha-maîm âsher mithahath la raķîwh'a
w'beîn ha-maîm âsher mewhal la-raķîwh'a waîehî 'chen. (7)

KJV: And God made the firmament and divided the waters which were
under the firmament from the waters which were above the firmament:
and it was so.

> *By calling forth the future possibility,*
> *the Universe began to assemble*
> *the waves and particles needed to embody*
> *this Spacious Choice as the firmament or atmosphere*
> *which receives sound in our vicinity.*
> *This plotline caused more change in the whole universe.*
> *The contracted Dense Flow–Dark Matter*
> *remained a mystery locked inside itself,*
> *compressed on the far side of Spacious Choice.*

Expansive Flow remained on this side—
the "Great Beyond" of the sky that embodies
the living metaphor of extension and exaltation.

Wa îkerâ Elohîm la rakîwh'a shâmaîm
wa îehi hereb wa îehi boker îom shenî. (8)

KJV: And God called the firmament Heaven. And the evening and the morning were the second day.

To further engrave this distinction,
the Universe gave Spacious Choice in our locale
the embodied form of one of its first archetypes:
the character of infinite vibration or shem—
the wave reality of name, sound, and light,
the atmosphere that creates, surrounds, and
unites all beings in a mutual communion of breath.

Once over and back again,
this second round of opening and closing
marked the second large manifestation
of luminous happenings and intelligent action
by the Universe in our vicinity since the beginning:
the creation of the earth's "personal" space.

BODY PRAYER: SACRED SPACIOUSNESS

To contemplate the wisdom embedded in the Hebrew text of Genesis brings up the questions, Was its author (or authors) reworking and passing down very ancient stories? If so, on what were these stories based, considering that no humans were around during the "beginning times" described? Was it pure "imagination," and if so, how does one account for its clear correspondences to habits of the universe that scientists have only recently discovered and articulated?

The most consistent explanation from a new scientific view would be that some cellular memory of early storytellers gave them access to images for the broad sweep of how the universe evolved. Since humans are not simply self-contained particles inhabiting an inert universe but are intimately interlaced with its evolving story, it could be imagined that long periods of communion with the natural world would evoke a knowledge of its basic habits and tendencies. Isolated from such communion, we tend to see such knowledge as special "wisdom." We enshrine it in sacred scriptures, which then often become the basis of disputes. However, all scriptures are inspired by the human relationship to the cosmos and nature. According to a modern Sufi, Hazrat Inayat Khan (1910), "There is only one sacred manuscript, the sacred manuscript of Nature, which alone can enlighten the reader."

In this portion of the Genesis story, we confront immediately the mysterious word usually translated as "firmament." In the Hebrew text, this is *rakîwh'a,* a process that rarefies or attenuates things and makes them more expansive. All its meanings center on what we call space, in particular, an emptiness that is creative. The addition of this spaciousness to the dark wave-matter of the primordial universe created the density differences we usually call our atmosphere.

In verse 8, we see the primordial archetype of "wave reality," or *shem,* becoming embodied as the personal space and vibratory atmosphere surrounding our planet. Neither infinite contraction nor infinite expansion, this atmosphere makes possible not only life but also sound. The density difference created by *rakîwh'a* serves as a sort of dome that allows sound to resonate and be heard. Our ears and vocal cords were ultimately shaped by this earlier development of wave reality in our region. Sky embodies the archetype of freedom, expansiveness, and choice. At the same time, it presents an obvious but often overlooked message about the communion of all species: There is only one sky, we all breathe one breath. It is difficult to get around this point without completely denying a relationship with nature. Unfortunately this is generally what modern culture has done.

For textual notes on words translated but not included in this body prayer, please see the notes at the end of this chapter.

Celebration of Sky and Space

When feeling contracted, compressed, or without the space to choose a different reality: Sit or lie comfortably in nature with as much expanse of sky in view as possible. Breathe for a moment as though from the whole sky, and allow yourself to gaze at and take in the amount of space that surrounds you. Then gently close the eyes and sense the air passing over the pores of your skin. Imagine that you are air and space, inside and out, with only a thin layer of skin in between. Imagine the same amount of space inside you as you sensed outside. Breathe a regular breath and feel the rhythm of heartbeat and breathing resonating in the inner space.

Breathe slowly the sound "ra-kî-wha," and focus on creating sacred spaciousness for new possibilities and choices to appear. These new choices may not appear immediately. Often we need practice to overcome the neurotic modern habit of filling our entire lives, inner and outer, with things and busyness.

HEAR THE SOUND　　Hebrew

A meditation on Deuteronomy 6:4

Shem'a israêl (A)
Adonai elohaînu (B)
Adonai echad. (C)

KJV: Hear, O Israel: the Lord our God is one Lord.

> *Hear the sound,*
> *Hear the tone,*
> *Hear the name*
> *of the unnameable.*
> *Be thunderstruck by its flash.*
>
> *Listen all beings:*
> *you who manifest*
> *the substantial ray of the One;*
> *who appear in the form*
> *of the Only Being's radiance.* (A)
>
> *Sacred Diversity is ours:*
> *the Nameless One expresses itself*
> *in the complex tangle of our lives,*
> *where being and absence exist together.* (B)
>
> *Sacred Communion is ours:*
> *the Nameless One is the center*
> *where all lines meet,*
> *where there is only one Being.* (C)

BODY PRAYER: THE HARMONY OF THE UNIVERSE

This passage is one of the most sacred in Judaism and contains worlds of meaning. My expanded translation can at best be called a meditation for that reason. The first stanza elaborates on themes contained in the word *shema,* which is derived from the root SHM.

Some Jewish mystics have pointed out that the word *israel* points not only to a name for the Jewish people but to all humanity. It is composed of multiple roots pointing to all beings as streaks or rays of manifestation from the Oneness, the Sacred "That" or *El.* The second stanza works with these alternative meanings.

The sacred name used here, *Adonai,* is really a substitute for the Nameless Name. *Adonai* points to an ultimate power of divisibility, the One as capable of showing itself in everything diverse and new. This "sacred diversity" is the same Oneness, *Elohaînu,* and points to Elohîm, The One That Is Many. If Adonai could be called the power that creates "one from the One," then it also must be said that this power brings us to the first point, the center where all lines meet (*echad*). Following any "one" to its depth brings us back to One.

Sound and Embodiment

Following on the previous body prayer, intone slowly the sound "Shem-âh." Feel it in the area of the heart and let it resonate throughout the entire inner space of the body. The intention with these sounds is to allow the Universe Being to wake up the awareness of choice in your life. You might also try cupping the hands behind the ears, a traditional gesture for a body prayer using *shema.*

It is necessary here to maintain a sense of the boundaries of the skin, that is, not to dissolve completely. To counteract the latter tendency, feel your bones and their connection to the earth. This can easily be done by briefly sitting (or lying) with your hands underneath you, enlivening the sensation of solid connection within and underneath. To conclude the practice, feel the entire body receiving sound from all around, as though being bathed in a universe of sound. Somewhere in this universe is a note that will bring out the melody of your purpose in life.

BY THE HEART AND BY THE TONGUE   Egyptian

An expanded version of a hymn to Ptah, third millennium B.C.E.

First lines of J. H. Wilson translation: There came into being as the heart and there came into being as the tongue [something] in the form of Atum. The mighty Great One is Ptah, who transmitted [life to all gods], as well as [to] their *ka*'s, through this heart, by which Horus becomes Ptah, and through this tongue, by which Thoth becomes Ptah.

> *By the heart and by the tongue*
> *all things came into being.*
> *By the heart and by the tongue of*
> *the Opening Mouth, the Space-maker,*
> *who is called Ptah,*
> *arose the creating principle,*
> *the universal mind*
> *called Atum.*
>
> *The great one is Ptah, cosmic Space,*
> *who gave life to all* ka-*spirits*—
> *the limited soul reality*—
> *of the gods, those shining archetypes.*
>
> *By the heart of Space,*
> *the Mind's conception*
> *extends throughout the Universe:*
> *then Horus, this conception, becomes Ptah.*
>
> *By the tongue of Space,*
> *the completion of Mind through Speech*
> *extends throughout the Universe:*
> *Then, Thoth, this completion, becomes Ptah.*
>
> *So it came to pass that*
> *Ptah's heart and tongue*
> *gained power over all bodies.*
> *This Sacred Opening dwells in every atom*—
> *of archetypes, humans, animals,*
> *creepers, plants, and dust.*

The manifested cosmos relies
on the commands of Space.

The eyes see, the ears hear, the nose smells:
they all report to the heart.
When the tongue announces
what the heart conceives, only then
does anything take a step
from nonexistence into being.

All work and crafts,
the movement of arms and legs,
every stirring tendril
conforms to this process of Ptah:
space unfurls
heart reveals
voice clarifies
life creates.

BODY PRAYER: HOW SPACE CREATES

A hallmark of Egyptian mythology is that, rather than eliminate archetypes (gods and goddesses), it chose to move them around in the cosmology according to which were popular at the time. Various "gods" are
credited with creation, depending upon which scripture one reads. Be
that as it may, this hymn to Ptah reveals an essential feature of the way
Native Middle Eastern cosmology sees things coming into being. This
process has become the basis for several renditions of a "law of manifestation." I would prefer to say that the universe has certain habits that
tend to encourage the creative process mentioned almost five thousand
years ago.

Heart Awareness

Contemplation on taking a new direction: Begin with sensing the
heart area and re-create the clear spacious boundaries set by the feeling
of breathing and heartbeat (cultivated in the first body prayer in chapter
1). If necessary, proceed to "clear the mirror" (as described in the last
body prayer in chapter 3). Nothing new can arise if one's entire life and
awareness has no space for it. As much as possible breathe with a sense
of fullness, remembering the sense of blessing that has infused the journey of the universe from the very beginning.

Breathe the sound "ptâh" in and out, focusing on a sense of opening from the heart. If you are looking for a new direction, allow the
space to evoke the various possibilities your life may present at this
moment.

If you are considering several possibilities, bring each of them into
your awareness of inner sacred space and notice how they affect your
heartbeat and breathing. Take a moment between each alternative to
"clear the mirror" again. Notice the changes, if any, and do not immediately attempt to interpret them. Often this practice must be done several
times in order to begin to understand the wisdom coming through one's
own body sensations. They are a bit like dreams in that regard—there is
no one, stereotypical list of what these sensations mean. This deeper wisdom connects to the sacred guidance that is throughout the universe at
all times and that can come equally through our own nature as through
the nature that surrounds us in its wild state.

ETHPHATAH! BE OPENED!   Aramaic

A version of Mark 7:32–35 from the Peshitta version of the Gospels

KJV: And they bring unto him one that was deaf, and had an impediment in his speech; and they beseech him to put his hand upon him. And he took him aside from the multitude, and put his fingers into his ears, and he spit, and touched his tongue; and looking up to heaven, he sighed, and saith unto him, Eph-pha-tha [*sic*], that is, Be opened. And straightway his ears were opened, and the string of his tongue was loosed, and he spake plain.

They brought Isho'a a man who could not speak or hear,
     asking that he lay a healing hand upon him.
Isho'a took the man aside, so the crowd could not see, and
     placed his fingers gently into the man's ears.

As they breathed together, Isho'a drew closer,
spat on the ground, and touched the man's tongue,
uniting his sensing self with the other.

As Isho'a focused on the One Source of all sensation and
     knowing,
he raised his glance and awareness upward,
breathing one long and powerful breath
with shemaya—*the universe of vibration.*

Releasing his hands from the man's ears, he said forcefully,
"Ethphatah!"

which means "Be opened, expand, clear the way—
allow yourself to be penetrated by the waves of space
that give and receive all sound,
hearing, and speech."

At that instant, the man's ears were opened, his tongue
     loosened, and he spoke clearly.

BODY PRAYER: BE OPENED

One of the arguments for an original Aramaic text of the Gospels, according to the Aramaic-speaking churches (which include the Syrian Orthodox and Assyrian Church of the East), is that even the so-called original Greek version contains several Aramaic words. Other literally rendered idioms (such as "poor in spirit" and "meek . . . inherit the earth") are clearly based on a lack of understanding of the original Aramaic expression, much like the American expression "to buy a pig in a poke" does not translate literally.

This version is based on an expansion of the Aramaic word of power *Ethphatah,* clearly related to older Egyptian ptâh. This invocation of the space-clearing dimension of the universe, which is also connected with name, hearing, and sound, continued to be used by the desert mystics in the Middle East. It reappears as the Arabic *Fatah,* "the Opener of the Way," which is another of the ninety-nine names or qualities of Allah. Chanting this word in the same fashion that Jesus used with the deaf man continues to this day.

Sound and Embodiment

For opening a way or strengthening a new choice: Following on the previous body prayer, this new choice will have come from a contemplation of sacred space and from allowing the often still, small voice of the Only Being to enter one's heart. There is a place where the desire at the heart of the Universe intersects with one's own desire. This need not always involve a goal that is "spiritual" or profound. As the Sufi Mevlana Rumi once said, "Whether you love the One or love a human being, if you love enough in the end you will come into the presence of Love itself."

Place the fingertips of both hands lightly on the heart. Breathe the sound "Eth-phâ-tâh" as the hands and arms open (inhale on "eth" and exhale on "pha-tah"). The eyes should be open. Then begin to speak the word, feeling the sound in the heart and focusing on opening a way for the Universe to work through your life.

If you are focusing on a particular goal, it may get either stronger or weaker after doing this body prayer. If you are willing to receive either answer, you are in a good position to benefit from the practice.

As a focus on sound, this body prayer is also good for "letting the voice out": Feel the resonance that develops as the power of the Universe breaks through any old messages you may have internalized that say that your voice should not be heard or should not be creative.

If an inspiration comes, remember to thank the Source. This can be done using one of the sacred words in Arabic from the next translation: *al-ham-dû-lil-lâh*, which can be translated, "May all I am and do return to praise the One!"

The Opening

Meditation on the Holy Quran, Sura 1, Fateha

Bismillahir rahmanir rahim. (1)
Alhamdulillahi (2a) *rabbi-l'alamin* (2b)
arrahman irrahim (3)
maliki yaumadin. (4)

A. Yusuf Ali version: In the name of Allah, Most Gracious, Most Merciful. Praise be to Allah, the Cherisher and Sustainer of the Worlds. Most Gracious, Most Merciful. Master of the Day of Judgment.

> *Upon hearing the Irresistible Voice of the Love's Wellspring*
> *   and Goal,*
> *we are led to affirm that* (1)

> *Whatever the Universe does, small or large,*
> *through any being or communion of beings,*
> *that helps further its purpose,*
> *this act celebrates the Source of our unfolding story.*
> *The essence of all praiseworthy qualities*
> *constantly returns to the One Being.*
> *Give praise and celebrate!* (2a)

> *This Being of beings mysteriously nurtures and sustains,*
> *grows and brings to maturity*
> *all worlds, universes, and pluriverses,*
> *all aspects of consciousness and knowledge,*
> *all story lines and lesson plans.* (2b)

> *This Source is the Original Womb of Love in all its*
> *   aspects.* (3)

> *It says "I can" on the day when all elements part company*
> *   and return home,*
> *when the threads of interweaving destiny unravel*
> *and the invoices come due.*
> *This Universe Being accepts the mission to resolve the*
> *   unresolvable*

at the time when time ends
just as it said yes to the birth movements that began it. (4)

Iyyaka n'abudu wa iyyaka nasta'ain. (5)

A. Yusuf Ali translation: Thee do we worship and thine aid we seek.

> *Cutting through all distractions, addictions, and diversions,*
> *all conflicting taboos, theologies, offenses, and*
>   *misunderstandings,*
> *we will act only from this Universe Purpose,*
> *we will develop abilities only in service to the Real,*
> *we will bow to and venerate only the deepest Source of all*
>   *Life,*
> *and we will expect help only from this direction,*
> *The ration of what we need, freely given by the One.* (5)

Ihdina sirat almustaqim (6)
sirat alladhina an'amta 'alayhim
ghayril maghdubi 'alayhim wa laddalin. (7)

A. Yusuf Ali translation: Show us the straight way, the way of those on whom Thou has bestowed thy Grace, those whose portion is not wrath, and who go not astray.

> *We ask you to reveal our next harmonious step.*
> *Show us the path that says, "Stand up, get going, do it!"*
> *which resurrects us from the the slumber of the drugged*
> *and leads to the consummation of Heart's desire,*
> *like all the stars and galaxies in tune, in time, straight*
>   *on.* (6)

> *The orbit of every being in the universe is filled with*
>   *delight.*
> *When each travels consciously,*
> *a sigh of wonder arises at the expanse, the abundance.*
> *This is not the path of frustration, anger, or annoyance,*
> *which happens only when we temporarily*
> *lose the way and become drained, roaming too far*
> *from the Wellspring of Love.* (7)

TEXTUAL NOTES

1. *The Earth's Personal Space, Genesis 1:6–8.* The word *iabeddel* (usually translated as "divide" used in verses 6 and 7 and previously used in verse 4) means to separate the natures of something in order to create diversity, individuality, or peculiarity. The word *mithahath,* usually translated as "below," refers in this relation to what is less spacious, denser, or more closed. Its opposite is the next word, *mewhal,* usually translated as "above"—a sense of exaltation, breaking the bounds of confinement. This latter word is still used in its Arabic form (*hal*) to describe temporary states of ecstasy Sufi mystics experience from spiritual practice.

2. *By the Heart and by the Tongue.* This version is based on literal translations of the Egyptian text, dated between 2700 and 700 B.C.E., by John A. Wilson as contained in James B. Pritchard's collection (1955, p. 5) and by J. H. Breasted (1933, p. 35). I have retranslated and given expanded meanings for the key sacred names based on their underlying roots and meanings using the works of E. A. Wallis Budge (1895, 1911a, 1911b), an early Egyptologist, and the Hebrew-Egyptian etymological comparisons of Fabre D'Olivet (1815) as references.

3. *The Opening, Sura 1, Fateha.* Just as the *bismillâh* phrase contains the essence of the Quran, so does its first sura, in more expanded fashion. One translation or commentary cannot do it justice. Here the sura helps summarize the first stage of our journey through sacred diversity.

After beginning with the *bismillâh* phrase, affirming the positive and receptive sides of divine love, the sura emphasizes praise. My second stanza focuses on the multiple meanings of the word *alhamdulillâhi,* which points beyond mere verbal praise to the way in which the essential purpose, or *hamd,* of every being is constantly dedicating itself to the One Being. My third stanza focuses on the words *rabbi-l'âlamîn,* sometimes translated "cherisher and sustainer of the worlds." The root RB points to all action that gathers, grows, and brings something to full fruition. The word *âlamîn* indicates not only "material" worlds but all collections of matter, meaning, learning, and knowledge.

Then, as though to emphasize their central position, the words *rahmân* and *rahîm* are repeated, reminding us of the Womb from which all life has come. The phrase *mâliki yaumadîn,* usually translated "Master of the Day of Judgment," is based on the same Semitic root we encountered earlier that points to the "I can" of the cosmos. The "day" is also related to the word we saw used in both Genesis and the saying of Jesus. It is an illuminated period of time. Here what the sura spotlights is an archetypal unraveling of causes and effects, the return of all elements to their source. From this standpoint, the Universe will "back out" of time in the same way it "came in," as described in Genesis. On another level, this sense of timelessness, the unraveling of complexity, a pristine sense of discrimination, is an experience that many people have had and that is cultivated by mystical practice in the Middle East. It is an awareness *now* as much as an eschatological statement about the proverbial *later.*

The next half of the sura offers a prayer that bids the One Being to use us in whatever way it chooses. The phrase *iyyâka n'abudu wa iyyâka nastaîn* affirms the intention to cut through all distractions, diversions, and clinging patterns of mind, to serve and receive sustenance only from the Source. The next phrase, *ihdinas sirâtal mustaqîm,* contains several words of power. The word *ihdinas,* usually translated as "show," comes from another of the "ninety-nine names" in Arabic—*hadi,* which also means to guide, show a path, or hear a voice that gives direction. The word *mustaqîm,* usually translated as "straight," is related to the sacred name *qayyoom,* which points to all energy that rises, wakes up, stands up, and continues that way forever. It is the everlasting "wake-up call" that cuts through mental and emotional muddles.

Finally, the path of the Universe Being (which we have just asked to follow) is described further. The path is filled with delight and abundance (*ladhina*) as well as a sense of wonder and grace (*an'amta*), which every being carries from the Source. The path is not about frustration or annoyance (*maghdubi*); it is not, in fact, about losing our way (*dhâlin*). The way is not meant to be difficult or obscure; it becomes that only when we wander too far from the heart of the matter, from the *rahmân* and *rahîm,* the Wellspring of Love with which we began.

PART TWO

Voices of Interiority and Presence

Interiority, or inner presence, reflects the way in which everything in the universe organizes a self and exhibits a dimension of subjective spontaneity. From the primeval fireball to the early galactic clouds to the planets in their infancy, each revealed an ability to act as a unique self and moved toward its own destiny. By this principle, the universe is a collection of subjects, not objects. Nothing is inert or dead. This wisdom helps us learn how and what we sense, feel, imagine, and experience. On the deepest spiritual level, these voices deal with knowing our self.

Chapter Six

WISDOM'S SEED — THE BREATH FROM UNDERNEATH

In the Native Middle Eastern tradition, we begin to develop a sense of depth or interiority by recognizing that something greater than ourselves is moving with intention through our lives. When we confront that within us which experiences, we enter the presence of *Hokhmah,* Holy Wisdom, the breath of awareness from underneath and within. This "I am" has gifts to give, including the fulfillment of needs we often try to satisfy by looking only outside.

THE ESSENCE OF SEED — DAY THREE

An expanded translation of Genesis 1:9–13

Wa-îâomer Elohîm îkkawoû ha-maîm mithahath ha-shâmaîm el-makôm
   echad w'thera ha-îabasha wa îehî khen. (9)
Wa-îkerâ Elohîm la-îabasha âretz w'l'mikweh ha-maîm karâ îammîm wa
   iara Elohîm khi-tôb. (10)

KJV: And God said, Let the waters under the heaven be gathered
together unto one place, and let the dry land appear: and it was so. And
God called the dry land Earth; and the gathering together of the waters
called he Seas; and God saw that it was good.

> [In the following rounds of expression of the Universe's lumi-
> nous intelligence—that is, the Primordial Days—the scene of
> the action remains in our vicinity, the earth. Archetypes and
> tendencies that were brought into being first in principle now
> become embodied in form and action. This explains why the
> earth is seemingly created "twice"—first in Genesis 1:1 and
> now here in verse 10. Yet every action in and on the earth
> affected the unfolding of the story of the whole cosmos. To
> reflect this shift in the plot, the language of our story also
> becomes less ethereal and shifts into narrative prose.]

> Next, part of the Flow that was of a lower vibration than the
> primordial atmosphere began to settle and find its own level,
> driven forward by the purpose of the whole Universe. The
> Flow settled toward a mode of being that was no longer
> unbounded and unpredictable but that now could maintain
> its own integrity over time. Its previous state of ecstasy
> became a new station of embodied action and character.
> Using this settled Flow as a basis, the Cosmos individuated a
> sense of inner fire [*îabashah*], an inflamed, warm, burning
> presence from within. (9)
>   This further differentiation created the embodied char-
> acters of what we call earth [*âretz*]—a radiant energy that
> finds a fixed limit, a definitive end in mass and substance—
> as well as that of sea [*îammîn*]—the energizing into form of
> Flow "squared" or compressed into itself. The great waters of
> earth reflect the great flow of the Cosmos and its great ques-

tion: "What happens next?" By this development, the archetypes of "land" and "sea" were initiated here: Their character was launched, no matter what their personality might evolve to be (that is, what stuff composed them). The Universe recognized that this was a timely and ripe way to proceed with the unfoldment of its destiny. (10)

Wa îâomer Elohîm thadesha ha-âretz desha hesheb mazeriha zerah hetz pherî
hoshe pherî le-mînoû âsher zareh ôb'ô hal-ha-âretz wa îehî khen. (11)
Wa thôtza ha-âretz desha hesheb mazeriha zerah le-mînoû w'hetz hosheh
pherî âsher zareh ôb'ô le mînehoû: wa-îara Elohîm khi-tôb. (12)
Wa îehî hereb wa îehî boker îom shelîshî. (13)

KJV: And God said, Let the earth bring forth grass, the herb yielding seed, and the fruit tree yielding fruit after his kind, whose seed is in itself upon the earth: and it was so. And the earth brought forth grass, and herb yielding seed after his kind, and the tree yielding fruit, whose seed was in itself, after his kind: and God saw that it was good. And the evening and the morning were the third day.

At this point, the tendency of the Universe toward interiority called into possibility the primordial essence of *seed-cell*—a being that unfolds continuously from a center within it. Seed came with sprouts, like center with circumference. Some of these "children" followed directly in the path of their ancestors: They stayed within the boundaries of what had been done before. Others diverged from the limits of previous expectations. Spontaneously they tried out new scenarios based on their own self-organization. Some offered material growing substance [*'hetz*] to the senses of other beings by gathering and assembling elements into fruit. All primordial seeds bore progeny of themselves and did not mix their interior essence with other types (11).

By establishing the habit of seed, the Universe accelerated the possibility for growth to happen: In all places where such experimentation could proceed, beings with their own interior seed of self began to take shape. In fact, in a mysterious way, they had already taken shape. With this new activity of the Universe, they now recognized themselves as part of a pattern that led somewhere. They participated in the action of the Cosmos as a whole in shaping the next part of the story. In this way the future again called to the past.

The Universe acknowledged that this was a timely and ripe way to proceed for the moment with the unfoldment of its destiny (12).

Once over and back again, opening and closing, this marked the third aeon of intelligent action in the Cosmos (13).

BODY PRAYER: THE SEED OF THE SELF

For textual notes on words translated but not included in this body prayer, please see the notes at the end of this chapter.

The key words in verse 11, *thadesha ... desha hesheb,* usually translated as "bring forth" and "grass," are both based on the root DSH, which points to everything that gives seed or germinates. The root is related to RSH, which we saw earlier in the first word of this story, *berêshîth,* the "in the beginningness" of Genesis 1:1. The words here point to an embodied center that unfolds movement, a seed that sprouts and grows from an inner self or origin. According to this tradition, each seed, each primordial living cell, unfolded from a center that mirrored the one-time unfolding of the whole universe.

Depths of the Self 2

This body prayer is for developing interiority, an ability to feel a solidity of self, or to organize experiences.

Our modern world does not encourage depth. It encourages being driven, led, or swept away by our perceived needs, which are often compulsively programmed into us based on someone else's priorities. Without apportioning blame to education, religion, business, government, or unhealthy family dynamics, one can simply say that, in the modern era, we are not encouraged to be in touch with our own inner, unrehearsed nature any more than we are encouraged to contact the wildness of nature outside us. As that outside nature rapidly deteriorates to the same degree that human institutions do, there is a certain urgency for us to contact the depth of our self.

As mentioned previously, the seed of the subconscious self in the Native Middle Eastern tradition is called *nephesh* in Hebrew (*naphsha* in Aramaic, *nafs* in Arabic). Most of the selections in this chapter center on developing a relationship to this sense of our own inner, self-organizing depths. Of course, there are many psychological models for working in this way. The Native Middle Eastern tradition contributes its own model and practices, and the body prayers are offered as possible doorways to begin what is understood to be a lifelong journey.

While in nature, consider the entire unfolding story of the cosmos that led to your being alive at this place and time. Breathe with the force and power of the cosmos, and consider the sense of purpose that empowered it. This takes a certain amount of surrender, of opening one-self to a sense of guidance and timeliness in unison with the desire of the Only Being (see body prayers in chapters 4 and 5). From this place, ask about the timing of working with your inner depths, the *nephesh* or sub-conscious self, now. If a feeling of spaciousness occurs, breathe into the depths, into the so-called darkness of the original womb of feeling. Notice all sensations of the body and breathe with the intention of growth and support.

To help focus this intention, you might use the word *deshâ* (to grow from a center) on the breath. As you continue to follow the breath, feel into what *feels* in you: Who is the experiencer? There may be voices waiting to be heard, parts of your self, your inner family, your inner nature, that have not been heard. Ask them with respect to identify themselves. Sometimes the responses come in words, sometimes images, sometimes body sensations. Once they come, thank them and thank the Source. The process unfolds from here.

SACRED POWER AND SACRED SENSE   Hebrew

An expanded translation of Proverbs 1:7

Irât IHφH re'ashîth dâ'ath Hokhmah wa-musr 'awiylîm bazû.

KJV: The fear of the Lord is the beginning of knowledge: but fools
despise wisdom and instruction.

> *When we feel awe for the Life behind all life (IHφH) . . .*
>
> *When we feel a fear of the manifested power of the*
> *Universe's energy,*
> *(that which turns form to no-form and back*
> *again) . . .*
>
> *When we feel terror and reverence for the Source of nature's*
> *power,*
> *past without beginning, future without edge . . .*
>
> *Then we begin to touch the Experiencer behind all*
> *experiences.*
>
> *This respect for eternity's strength is the prime archetype,*
> *the first psychic structure*
> *that organizes our inner life*
> *toward opening the senses*
> *and understanding Divine Wisdom (Hokhmah):*
> *The breath of life from underneath,*
> *the Sense behind all senses,*
> *that within which grasps meaning out of the swirl of*
> *existence.*
>
> *In other words,*
> *the reverence of Sacred Power naturally unfolds*
> *the understanding of Sacred Sense.*
>
> *Only the foolish—*
> *those who allow their limited desires to control them,*
> *who are addicted to their own small power and*
> *think they can extend it everywhere,*

who close their senses to the natural world—
only these despise self-control:
> *the power of limits,*   ·
> *which creates, fashions, and instructs*
> *everything that has a body:*
> *the divine architect of Holy Wisdom.*

For All Time Wisdom Rules   Assyrian

A version from the Sayings of Ahiqar *in Aramaic, fifth–seventh centuries B.C.E.*

First lines of H. L. Ginsberg translation: Two things [which] are meet,
and the third pleasing to Shamash: one who dr[inks] wine and gives it
to drink, one who guards wisdom, and one who hears a word and does
not tell.

> *Shamash approves of two things and blesses a third:*
> *First, the one who drinks wine and shares it.*
> *Second, the one who guards Wisdom.*
> *Third, the one who hears a word but does not speak it.*
>
> *Wisdom is also precious to the gods, the shining ones.*
> *She rules the psychic world of vision and ideal for all time.*
> *She was established in the shining realm,*
> *wave reality, by the order of the Holy One.*
>
> *More than anything, watch your mouth.*
> *A word is a bird—once released, it's gone.*
> *First number the secrets of your mouth,*
> *then unpack your words in solitary bundles.*

BODY PRAYER: SILENCE

This is part of a much longer text that contains the story of Ahiqar, who appears to have been an oracle or priestly counselor in the reign of Sennacherib (704–681 B.C.E.). After he retires, Ahiqar sets up his nephew as his successor, who unfortunately turns the new Assyrian king, Esarhaddon, against Ahiqar and attempts to have him killed. However, Ahiqar asks for a favor owed him by one of the king's high ministers, whom Ahiqar had earlier hid during a similar intrigue. The minister hides Ahiqar until the king misses his counsel; Ahiqar is "rehabilitated," and the ungrateful nephew gets his comeuppance. Ahiqar's proverbs reflect his seventh-century Assyrian street sense combined with a praise of Wisdom, which here, as in Proverbs, is personified as a female archetype that has existed from the beginning.

Another recurring theme associated with *Hokhmah* is the warning against telling secrets, or "loose tongues." Since Hokhmah reflects the wise breath of interiority, her nonintellectual, intuitive dimension feeds all beings with sense, not concepts or words. Perhaps because her secrets cannot be spoken, keeping a secret may have become associated with her.

Celebration of Silence

It is virtually impossible to develop interiority without developing a relationship to silence and to being with one's self without distractions. One of the best ways to do this is to spend a day or two in nature, walking, breathing, and taking in the presence that imbues every living being. Take some minutes to gaze at and breathe intimately with several beings you encounter: a mountain, a flower, a stream. Begin by breathing and gazing with eyes open, then after several minutes allow the eyes to close and continue to breathe in a feeling of connection with the being. Can you feel this being inside you as well as outside?

By not talking you are doing two things: First, you open other abilities to communicate with what is around you—you are developing, in fact, greater "social" skills. Second, you conserve the enormous amount of energy that talking uses and that small talk consumes in much greater proportion than meaningful, heartfelt conversation does. The energy saved can be directed toward our relationship with our inner self. This is not an invitation to become a hermit, which few of us are called to, but to moderate the outwardly directed, addictive pace of modern life, which distracts us from the voice of nature, whether inside or outside.

Thunder Speaks: Mind Embraces All Opposites, Part 1   Coptic

A version of sections of the gnostic text Thunder, Perfect Mind

First lines of George W. MacRae translation: I was sent forth from [the] power, and I have come to those who reflect upon me, and I have been found among those who seek after me.

The Voice

The Power sent me.
I appear in the minds I make restless.
I am found within by those who look for me.
If I disturb your mind with images, why not look at them?
If you can hear me in a sound, why not listen?
Whoever waits for me—here I am, embrace me!
Don't deny you've seen me,
Don't shut my sound out of your ears—or your voice.
You cannot fail to "know" me, anywhere or anytime.
I am both what knows and what denies knowledge.
Be aware, this moment—
don't claim ignorance of this mind.

For I am first and last,
honored and dishonored
prostitute and saint,
experienced and virginal
. . . .
I am the silence not grasped by the mind,
the image you can't forget.
I am the voice of every natural sound,
the word that always reappears.
I am the intonation of my name—hu-khm-ah—
the breath returning from form to its source.

The Bodies Who Come After

I am knowledge and ignorance,
I am timid and bold,

shamed and shameless.
I am strength.
I am fear.
I am war and peace.
Listen to me:
I am infamous and renowned.

Listen to my poor voices,
Listen to my rich ones.

Don't look down on me in the earth under your feet:
I compose the bodies of those who come after you.
Don't look away from me in the shit-pile:
I am the remnants of great civilizations.
Don't laugh inwardly at me when I am
disgraced, homeless, uneducated.
Don't isolate my voice as "another" victim of violence.
I am compassionate, but also cruel.

Be aware, this moment!
Do not indulge in obedience or self-control
because you love one or hate the other.

Do not turn your back on my weakness
or fear my power.
Why despise me when I am afraid,
or curse me when I am inflated?

I am she who shudders in all your fears and
who shakes in your moments of power.
I am the one in you who becomes sick and
I am the one who is completely healthy.
I am no sensation and I am the Sense,
the Wisdom of all.

BODY PRAYER: THE INTONATION OF MY NAME

The text usually called *Thunder, Perfect Mind* is part of a collection of scrolls from a presumably gnostic library found in Nag Hammadi, Egypt, in 1945. It is written in Coptic, a language derived from ancient Egyptian. Without going into an extensive background on this find, which is available in other works, one can say that the books discovered show a variety of cosmologies, beliefs, and spiritual practices, many of them related to the early Jesus movement. Most of these beliefs and practices were later branded unorthodox and heretical. As Elaine Pagels demonstrates convincingly in her work (1979), what these books exhibit, and what was purged from the development of orthodox Christianity, were (1) a more collaborative approach to authority in early Jesus movement circles (the position of bishop or priest was often shared or rotated); (2) an interpretation of Middle Eastern cosmology that emphasized God the Mother as much as God the Father; and (3) alternative definitions of the "true church" that had more to do with personal spiritual experience than with orthodox religious belief.

Past commentary on *Thunder, Perfect Mind* has emphasized its beautiful, paradoxical "I am" statements ("I am the first and last, honored and dishonored . . ."). Some scholars have tried to infer the text's relation to Greek philosophy. In this version I have emphasized its perfect expression as the Native Middle Eastern voice of Hokhmah—the breath of interiority and "I-ness" from the core of all beings. In this regard, the use of paradox and antithesis clearly connects to statements by the voice of Holy Wisdom in Proverbs. As important as the feminine archetype is, I find even more important the text's expression of the voice of our own interiority, the seed at the center of our inner self.

Sound and Embodiment

In this body prayer, we use the sound of the name *Hokhmah* to strengthen a connection to our interior wisdom and source of experience. Begin by breathing the name with the sound "hûkh" on the inhalation and "mâh" on the exhalation. Then elongate and emphasize the sounds even more as you intone them on a note that feels as though it begins to vibrate in your body. Begin with "hoo," feeling the source of the breath and life behind all beings. Then proceed to "khm"; be gentle with the *k* sound so that the throat doesn't constrict. Feel a resonance deep in the body, the embodiment of the life-breath-knowing within you. Finally intone "mâh," feeling the breath returning to the source and to all beings, carrying wisdom from its experience of embodiment.

Try intoning all three parts of the name on one breath. This may require you to release any clinging to the beginning, middle, or end of the process. After some minutes, breathe again with the sound in whatever way the breath settles. Then after some moments release the word itself and breathe only with the feeling that remains. Follow the feeling where it wants to lead, perhaps to a better relation to the "I am" within you, the source of what feeds and empowers your life.

WISDOM'S GIFT   Aramaic

An expanded translation of Matthew 26:26 from the Peshitta version of the Gospels

Kaddîm lâsîn shqal Isho'a lachmâ wa-barekh wa-qisba wa yahab
     l'thalmîdâw wa amar: (A)
sabu akhol hânâ pegrî. (B)

KJV: And as they were eating, Jesus took bread, and blessed it, and
brake it, and gave it to the disciples, and said, Take, eat; this is my body.

> *Then, while they ate, Isho'a embraced and picked up the*
>   *bread,*
> *sign and symbol of the earth's support and understanding.*
> *He did this as though becoming one with the loaf, absorbing*
>   *himself into it.*
> *He breathed into this* lachma—*daughter of Holy*
>   *Wisdom—with blessing.*
> *He divided it, just as a seer might divide something in order*
>   *to prophesy from the shapes that the will of the One*
>   *causes to form.*
> *He gave these pieces to his students and said:* (A)
>
> *Take and eat,*
> *Surround and enjoy,*
> *Convert and consume,*
> *Envelop and devour:*
>
> *This is my dead body.*
> *This is my corpse.*
> *This body* (pegri) *extends itself and wanders this world.*
> *It eventually loses strength and heat.*
> *Read the signs yourself:*
> *My future, your future is to be food—*lachma, *Wisdom's*
>   *gift—*
> *for what comes after you.* (B)

WISDOM'S BREAD   Aramaic

A translation of John 6:35 from the Peshitta version of the Gospels

Isho'a said:

Inana lachma d'chayye.

KJV: "I am the bread of life."

> *Simple Presence is Wisdom's daughter, the food of human
>   energy.*
>
> *The ego fully aware of its ephemeral nature
>   fuels our passion for the fresh and verdant.*
>
> *The depth of Identity is the ground of our life force.*
>
> *The germ of individuality's seed grows fruit of natural vigor.*
>
> *The eye of desire's hurricane feeds the life of all bodies.*
>
> *The self conscious of its Self energizes our animal existence.*
>
> *The "I am" is the bread of Elemental Life.*

BODY PRAYER: FOOD FROM WITHIN

The Aramaic word *hayye,* usually translated as "life," refers to life force, energy, the power that feeds our animal existence, the fuel for our human passion. Generally we are taught by our culture to look outside for this life energy, to fill an inner void with things that never really satisfy. At the same time, it is the life force, the presence, the freshness in food, relationships, and work that feed us—a connection to what feels energized in our psyche. When we connect with the "I am" within ourselves, we go directly to the source of our life force, the presence within that can enter, renew, or leave any outer relationship.

Simple Presence

When tempted to pursue something outside that feeds us, but that may ultimately leave us famished, return again to a place of simple presence. Sit comfortably, eyes closed, and feel the rise and fall of the breath. With each breath, reach out to whatever feelings or sensations arise, and feel the breath illuminating each sensation with awareness. Follow the feelings and body sensations associated with the need to be filled. Notice without judgment where the interconnections are felt between need and sensation. To help focus, you might also breathe the word *inana* (the "I am") in and out; notice the effect of the sound on what seems to be needed, or wanted, at the moment. The clarity about what needs to be filled does not appear overnight. Our reality does not come in the neat packages that we find in supermarkets.

LIKE SEED AND FRUIT   Persian

A version of a poem by the thirteenth-century Sufi poet Mahmud Shabistari, from The Secret Rose Garden

Look around you!
This world is tremendously mingled:
Angels, devils, Satan, Michael—
all mixed up like seed and fruit!
Atheist with fundamentalist,
materialist with mystic.

All cycles and seasons,
years, months, and days
converge at the dot of now:
"In the beginning" is "world without end."

Every point in this circle becomes
the first stroke for a million new forms.
Every point follows its own orbit,
but sooner or later
revolution meets itself,
coming and going.

Textual Notes

1. *The Essence of Seed, Genesis 1:9–13.* In verse 9 the Universe again "speaks"—that is, it engraves its purpose by manifesting a development that leads to increased diversity, interiority, and communion. The Hebrew word *îkkawoû,* which is not translated at all in the King James Version, indicates that this calling forth by the Universe was tending toward a purpose or driving toward a goal. The phrase *ha-maîm mitha-hath ha-shamaîm,* usually translated "waters under the heavens," refers, as we have seen in the previous passages, to a vibratory state of flow that was less than that of the primordial manifested atmosphere.

The effect of this settling—as each part of the flow finds its own optimum level—is pointed to by the Hebrew words *el-makôm echad,* usually translated as "one place." This solid "place" is the counterpart of the word *mewhal* in verse 7 (a state of expansion that is unstable). Later, in its Arabic form, the word *makam* is used in the Sufi tradition to indicate the embodiment of a mystical state, one that a person is able to live from and with on an everyday basis. According to scientists, all of the planets in our system went through this process of "settling down" into a more embodied state. Swimme and Berry comment:

> *In a liquid, semi-liquid, or gaseous state, each planet rearranged itself according to the ordering established by the gravitational interaction. The heavier elements such as iron and nickel settled in the core, the middle mass elements formed around these, and the lighter elements such as oxygen and silicon formed a layer still further out, and the lightest of all, such as hydrogen and helium, formed the outer layers. (1992, p. 82)*

The word *îabasha,* usually translated as "dry land," actually carries no reference to "land" at all; the word refers to an inner burning and continuous combustion, a radiant ferment that empowers the next step in the process. This inner fire seems to be a natural result of the expanded wave energy finding a way to live in form—the pulsation of the fireball within a body. The embodiment of an expanded spiritual experience or state can, if worked with in a conscious fashion, lead to a more integrated sense of one's real self or interiority, of one's heart's purpose.

Again, without looking for exact correspondences, there seems to be a relation here to the earth's own process:

> *When Earth reached the state where the heaviest elements were at*
> *the center and the lightest at the surface, the geological ordering*
> *would have ended had it been guided by the gravitational attrac-*
> *tion alone. But breaking up this static order was the radioactive*
> *energy. The unstable elements created by the stellar explosion*
> *broke apart and released their energy. This heat, arising through-*
> *out the planets, kept them in a boil. (Swimme and Berry 1992,*
> *p. 82)*

In verse 10, just as the primordial atmosphere of the planet characterized in embodied form the wave reality of *shâmaîm*, so also the new
developments become the embodied characters of particle reality (*aretz*)
and flow (*îammîm*, based on the same root as *maîm*).

The phrase *mazeriha zerah* (in verses 11 and 12), usually translated
as "herb yielding seed," refers to something that leaves a material enclosure and spreads, disperses, and radiates, that diverges from a previously
set pattern. Unfolding from a center involves built-in spontaneity in this
universe, it seems. The word *hetz*, usually translated "tree," refers to any
vegetable substance offered to the senses of another being. It represents
the entire principle of vegetation rather than a specific tree, a distinction
that has profound implications for a later phase of the Genesis story.

Even the first living cells on this planet, the prokaryotes of four billion years ago, which did not exchange genetic material with others,
showed this spontaneity from their own interior depth. Swimme and
Berry comment:

> *Throughout the whole of the early seas, cells gave birth to new*
> *versions of themselves, but they did so in a way that produced off-*
> *spring slightly different than themselves. Once every million*
> *births, a cell was created that was new. . . . This phenomenon—*
> genetic mutation—*is a primal act of life. Mutation explains a*
> *great deal of life's story in much the same way that gravitation*
> *explains a great deal of the galactic story. (1992, p. 88)*

2. *Sacred Power and Sacred Sense, Proverbs 1:7.* The word *irat*, usually translated as the "fear," can also mean terror, reverence, awe, vener-
ation, and respect. The next word is the most sacred name in Judaism,
so sacred that for many centuries it has not been pronounced. Many
traditions lie behind this. One, according to D'Olivet, is that the name
originally was not pronounced with any consonants at all. To make compressed and limited what was meant to be expanded and unlimited (as in

pronouncing the name Jehovah or Yahweh, as many Christians do) con-
stitutes a curse and not a blessing. A certain knowledge of the mysticism
of sound is necessary to pronounce the name at all.

Be that as it may, the meaning of the word is sublime and multilay-
ered. A few meanings are given in this translation, and more will appear
in later translations. Suffice it to say here that the roots of the word can
be rendered several different ways, starting with HH, indicating the life
behind all elementary life. To this is added the action of life manifested
(I) and the power that shuttles back and forth between being and nothingness (U). Here I use the transliteration *IHφH* to mark the place of the
name.

Historically there has been some comment from gnostic quarters
that "the fear of IHφH" meant that IHφH was doing the fearing or
respecting and that this action allowed Holy Wisdom, *Hokhmah,* to
make an appearance. While this interpretation has a certain appeal in
upsetting the usual translation, which depersonifies Holy Wisdom, it
really only substitutes one dualistic and anthropocentric interpretation
for another. I have chosen to place both terms on the same footing as cosmological and psychological forces, both of which are powerful within
us and among us. For the purposes of redressing the balance a bit, I have
referred to Holy Wisdom in her grammatically gendered form in these
notes and in some of the later translations from Proverbs.

The third word of the verse, *re'ashîth,* again returns us to the beginningness, the primal origins of *berêshîth.* Conscious interiority begins
with a sense of awe for the force behind the Universe, says this passage.
Holy Wisdom, or Hokhmah, is not only an archetypal quality (worthy
of being capitalized) but also the first voice within our own sense of
depth or inner self. Her name may be translated in perhaps as many
ways as IHφH, but we can again start with the breath of manifested Life
(the first H or *heth*), which enters the middle of collected manifestation
(KHM) and leaves as pure, intelligent Life (the second H or *hey*). One
could also say that it is the breath of life and the perception of sensation
that are embedded underneath, or in the middle of being. It is Sacred
Sense.

The word *musr,* usually translated as "instruction," carries more
the sense of correction, discipline, self-control, and even punishment. It
points to anything that gives something a proper outline, direction, or
training which allows its true nature to come out. It is related to the later
word in Arabic, *musawir,* another of the ninety-nine names of Unity.
The word *ylîm,* usually translated as "fools," refers specifically to any

being that suffers from an excess of expansion and that surrenders its movement to an inflated sense of its own perceived desire without connection to the desire behind the Universe. The word also points to the grandiosity of a being that overextends itself and refuses to recognize a universe whose creative power of manifestation and sensation is based on limits.

3. *For All Time Wisdom Rules.* This version is based on a much longer Aramaic text of *The Words of Ahiqar,* translated by H. L. Ginsberg from a fifth-century palimpsest papyrus discovered in the debris of Elephantine, Upper Egypt, in 1906–1907, as contained in Pritchard, ed. (1955, pp. 427–28).

4. *Thunder Speaks, Part I.* This version is based on the previous literal translations from the Coptic of George W. MacRae (1979, pp. 231–55) and Bentley Layton (1987, pp. 77–85).

5. *Wisdom's Gift, Matthew 26:26.* To say that there are many interpretations of what happened when Jesus broke bread at his last Passover celebration is an understatement. My expanded re-creation of this event from the Aramaic is based on new translations of several key words in Matthew's report.

The Aramaic word *shqal,* usually translated as "took" (as in "took bread"), also means to poise, to weigh, to embrace or envelop, to absorb oneself into in a special gesture of unification. The word *lachmâ* is related by its roots to *hokhmah* as the embodiment of the breath of wisdom, understanding, and nurturance. It is also the word for "bread"— food for all aspects of life, not simply the so-called physical. (For more on this, see my previous discussion of the fourth line of the Lord's Prayer [1990] where *lachmâ* also appears.)

To bless something in Aramaic (here *barekh*) means to breathe into it with energy and feeling. The word *qisba,* usually simply translated as "brake," points to a very special sort of breaking or dividing, one that was associated with the action a seer used to divine or prophesy based on the shapes the pieces made by "chance."

Jesus' own words are very enigmatic. The phrase *sabu akhol,* usually translated "take, eat," has several alternative meanings, which I have included in this version. The word *pegrî,* usually translated as "body," refers specifically to a dead body or corpse, a form that has lost its inner strength and heat.

6. *Like Seed and Fruit.* This version is based on previous literal translations by Florence Lederer (1920), E. H. Whinfield (1880), and Johnson Pasha (1903).

Chapter Seven

"I Am":
The Great
"Within"

The interiority of natural life on earth, as well as of each individual being, organizes itself with simple things, often taken for granted: the sensuous pleasure of sunlight or moonlight, the movement of flow within our body, the voices of need, desire, and struggle within. Following the experience back to the Experiencer, the sensation back to Sacred Sense, opens a door to developing an integrated self, the seed of a soul that contains the whole universe.

An expanded translation of Genesis 1:14–19

*Wa-îâomer Elohîm îehî maôroth bi-rekîwha ha-shamaîm le-habeddil beîn
    ha-îom w'beîn ha-laîlah w'haîoû le-âothth w'l'môhadîm w'l'îamîm
    w'shanîm.* (14)
*W'haîoû li-maôroth bi-rekiwha ha-shamaîm l'hâîr hal-ha-âretz wa îhî
    khen.* (15)

KJV: And God said, Let there be lights in the firmament of the heaven
to divide the day from the night; and let them be for signs, and for seasons, and for days, and years (14). And let them be for lights in the firmament of the heaven to give light upon the earth: and it was so.

[In the next round of the Universe's intelligence action—the
next Big Day—the sense of light and time developed in the
interiority of beings in the same way they had developed in
primordial, archetypal form earlier as an expression of diversity (chapters 3 and 4).]

From the standpoint of the seed-self of beings—their interior
awakening consciousness—light began to collect itself in sen-
sible bundles or centers in the middle of the Great Spaciousness. Living beings became aware of the effects of energy
surrounding them and organized their interior selves to
respond to it. So the lights surrounding the selves of living
beings helped organize their intelligence.

This further individuation touched off several more
possibilities. If light was experienced as localized, one could
turn oneself toward it or away from it. This interaction further organized an "I" and "Thou," a sense of inside and outside in the first living beings. Beings also began to feel a sense
of "timeliness" as they experienced pleasure in pulsing toward
or away from the light. The centers of light also created divisions of time—that is, the pause between when a being perceived them and when it did not.

These interactions also affected the interior life of the
light clusters. The entire nature of being in our vicinity began
to shift as a result (14–15).

Wa-îahash Elohîm aeth-sheni ha-mâoroth ha-ghcddolîm, aeth-hu-mâôr ha-
  gaddol le-memesheleth ha-îôm w'aeth-ha-mâôr ha-katon le-
  memesheleth ha-laîlah w'aeth-ha-khôkhabîm. (16)
Wa-îtthen âotham Elohîm bi-rekîwha ha-shamaîm l'haîr hal-ha-âretz. (17)
W'li-meshol ba-îôm w'ba-laîlah w'l'habeddîl beîn ha-âôr w'beîn ha-hoshekh
  wa-îera Elohîm khî-tôb. (18)
Wa-îehî hereb, wa-îehî boker, îôm rebîhî. (19)

KJV: And God made two great lights; the greater light to rule the day,
and the lesser light to rule the night: he made the stars also (16). And
God set them in the firmament of the heaven to give light upon the earth
(17), and to rule over the day and over the night, and to divide the light
from the darkness: and God saw that it was good (18). And the evening
and the morning were the fourth day (19).

> From the standpoint of the evolving interiority of living
> beings here, these lights above or around them (depending
> on how you stood), illuminated their further activity and
> growth. But this was not just a matter of revealing a process
> already fixed, of throwing a light on in a room completely
> arranged. As forms whirled toward their own unknown ends
> and purposes, the light bundles touched them with rays of
> heat, color, cosmic waves, and much more for which we still
> don't have a name. The rays of light changed forever the evo-
> lution of form.
>
> The closest radiant bodies had the greatest impact, of
> course, and came to represent, like a symbol in a poem, the
> local reality of day and night. Local day and night pointed to
> a much larger cycle of opening and closing: the Universe's
> continued periods of intelligent ebb of cause and mysterious
> flow of effect. In relation to the unfolding process on earth,
> the Universe arranged for a harmonious separation of light
> and darkness, so that periods of active growth and receptive
> assimilation could alternate.
>
> Again the Universe recognized that this was a timely
> and ripe way to proceed with the plot of its cosmic story
> (16–18).
>
> Once over and back again, opening and closing, this
> marked the fourth great cycle of the Universe's illuminating
> action (19).

Body Prayer: Gathering Bundles of Light

Many of the words in these verses have already been the subject of previous textual notes. For textual notes on words translated but not included in this body prayer, please see the notes at the end of this chapter.

In verse 14, the word *maôrth,* usually translated as "lights," is based on the word *âôr* used in verse 3 but modified to mean that which embodies the sensation of light or that which organizes the perception of light into bundles of light. Toward the end of the verse, the word *âothoth*, usually translated as "signs," also points to any character, type, or symbol—essentially whatever establishes a relationship between an "I" and something outside, a "Thou." Part of our Sacred Sense does this constant organizing and making of meaning so that we are not overwhelmed by the enormous wealth of sensation that the universe presents.

Heart Awareness

Find a place in nature, or at least a quiet place where you can contemplate a plant or a flower and its relationship to light. Within yourself, return to breathing in the heart, closing the eyes and clearing the mirror that takes impressions. Then open the eyes with a soft focus and allow your being to absorb the impression of the plant before you. Notice not only its visual details but its capacity and desire to turn toward the light. Particularly powerful times to do this are dawn and dusk.

Feel yourself absorbing and remembering the qualities of the plant that are still part of your being. Then with eyes closed, internalize even more the feeling rather than the visual image of the plant. Become the plant for a few moments and find the place within you that resonates with it in all its unfoldment: seed, sprout, fullness, and fading. Follow the feeling where it leads you in your developing relationship to the soul-self (*nephesh*) within. Breathe gratefulness toward the plant and the source of its creation as you complete this body prayer.

THE "I" JOINS THE JOURNEY Hebrew

A translation of Proverbs 8:22–24

IHΦH qananî re'ashîth darekhô qedem miphalîw meâz. (22)

KJV: The Lord possessed me in the beginning of this way, before his works of old.

> *The Life behind life, eternally now in past and present,*
> *possessed me at the beginning of beginnings:*
>
> *As the first principle of setting up an ordered existence,*
> *this Universal Life Force absorbed me,*
> *Hokhmah, Sacred Wisdom*
> *—Breath from Within and Underneath—*
> *into itself.*
>
> *Cosmic appetite combined with the power of density,*
> *the desire to compress and condense,*
> *and I—the first Interior Experience—joined the journey*
>   *from the very start.*
>
> *This was the first and most ancient mystery:*
> *how the power of growth can be contained*
> *and fixed around a center,*
> *the identity of the self.*
> *This is the axis on which the cosmos turns.* (22)

Me'olam nisakthî merôsh miqademî aretz. (23)
B'âyn thehomôth chôlelthî b'âyn mayanôth nikhbadey mayîm. (24)

KJV: I was set up from everlasting, from the beginning, or ever the earth was. When there were no depths, I was brought forth; when there were no fountains abounding with water.

> *From the first gathering of sensing and feeling,*
> *I was poured out like a libation, a consecration of the*
>   *cosmos.*
> *At that ancient pivotal moment,*

before particles and form were even imagined,
I flowed out, baptizing all in sacredness. (23)

This was even before there was a primordial abyss—
that dark kernel of purpose formed in the Universe's heart.
Even before this I danced into existence.
When everything we call reality was still a "Not!"
when even the abundant springs of flow and chaos
had not yet begun to flow,
I hoped, I waited,
I twisted and turned, I struggled
my way through the birth canal of the Holy One. (24)

BODY PRAYER: FLOW, STRUGGLE, AND DANCE

For textual notes on words translated but not included in this body prayer, please see the notes at the end of this chapter.

In verse 24, the word *b'âyn,* usually translated "when . . . no," could literally be translated "before being" or "when there was nothingness." The word *th'homôth,* usually translated as "depths," can also be translated as abyss, flow, chaos, or the depths of universal existence. The word *chôlelthî,* usually translated "brought forth," can also mean to turn in a circle, whirl, twist, reel, or be in the labor of childbirth. The Hebrew word for circle dance, *cholla,* is based on this and can also mean to bear a child. Behind this is the root CHL, which refers to any effort to extend the self, to develop or to stretch. As an interior reality, this is also hope and expectation.

The word *mayanôth,* usually translated as "fountains," is related by root to *môhadîm,* the inner pulse of flow and circulation within a body, which is used in Genesis 1:24. *Nikhbadey,* usually translated "abounding," also points to a sufficient amount, whatever is necessary for the moment. Combined with the word *mayîm,* the primordial flow, the whole phrase points to the origin from which even chaos pours out and pulses in the appropriate amount for the unfoldment of the cosmos, just like the pulse of fluids within our body.

Celebration of the Body's Flow

To further support a relationship to the Holy Wisdom and Sacred Sense that comes through the body: Begin again with natural, relaxed breath, and begin to sense your way into the "involuntary" pulsations of the body: heartbeat, lymphatic flow, peristalsis in digestion, the pulse of the spinal fluid. Anywhere a body sensation arises, thank it for the blessing it pours out. Feel the flow, even when the body struggles or seeks better health, as part of the dance of life. Allow each pulsation to lead you to that which senses, both the wisdom of the body and the doorway to the subconscious self. Thank each sensation as a gift of the Sacred Sense.

Thunder Speaks: Mind Embraces All Opposites, Part 2   Coptic

A version of sections of the gnostic text Thunder, Perfect Mind

First lines of George W. MacRae translation: [I am . . .] within. [I am . . .] of the natures. I am [. . .] of the creation of the [spirits]. [. . .] request of the souls. [I am] control and the uncontrollable.

The Within

I am the "within."
I am the "within" of all natures.
In the beginning, all spirits claim my creation.
In the end, all souls request my presence.
I am control—and uncontrollable.
I bring things together, I scatter them.
I persist, I fall apart.
I am the one felt as "below,"
but all rise in my presence.

I am the verdict: guilty and innocent.
I make no mistakes,
but all errors have their root in me.
I look like lust, but within I am restraint.
I am easy to hear, difficult to grasp.
I am mute and verbose together.
Hear my gentle voice or
learn the hard way, from experience.

I am the one who cries out
and gets a bad reputation.

I prepare the bread, the understanding,
earth's food for all needs.

I am the Hokhmah of my name:
earth-wisdom,
breath of the mother,
source of all livingness in form.

My voice is all around.
My ears listen everywhere.

BODY PRAYER:
SELVES SPEAKING FOR THEMSELVES

Depths of the Self 3

The process of establishing a relationship with the inner self or
selves, begun in previous chapters, may continue by allowing each aspect
of the self to have its own "I"—its own name, atmosphere, voice, and
expression. Begin by connecting again with your source of guidance, the
guidance behind the entire universe. Then breathe gently into the
depths of the body and ask with respect that any voices of the subconscious that have something to say present themselves and give their
names. Often this will feel like coaxing a frightened or angry child into
the light. Orders and threats have no place here, only love and acceptance. One way to begin is by breathing deeply into either the right or
left side of the body and identifying one or the other with the male or
female aspects of your subconscious.

After a name is exchanged, you might proceed by asking each self
to express its needs. It is important here to listen without judgment, but
also without any compulsion to act on everything you hear. An inner
family of selves, all aspects of the *nephesh* in this tradition, may be
formed in this way in order to clarify your inner life. Keep the boundaries of each session definite, set by your own focus, breathing, and body
awareness. Begin with a shorter period of time and then lengthen it as
your ability to focus increases. Consciously end each session with thanks
for what has been shared and a willingness to continue the relationship.
Then take some moments to integrate the feelings and sensations in
your body and bring your awareness present before proceeding to anything else.

ROAD, COMPASS, FUEL   Aramaic

A translation of John 14:6 from the Peshitta version of the Gospels

Isho'a said:

Ina(i)na ur'cha wa shrara w'chayye.

KJV: I am the way, the truth and the life.

> *The "I am" is the path, the sense of true direction, and the
> life force to travel.*

> *Simple Presence uncovers the hidden possibility, opens the
> circle of indecision, and gets us moving.*

> *The self conscious of its Self shows a way, solves the mystery
> of choice, and unleashes our animal energy.*

> *The nexus of individuality reveals a secret track, scents
> which way to go, and spurs the adrenaline.*

> *The depth of Identity illuminates what's ahead, liberates
> choice, and connects us to nature's power.*

> *The ego fully aware of its limitation declares a road,
> provides a compass, and fuels the journey.*

> *The eye of I's momentary swirl is the knowing, the
> confidence, and the vigor.*

THE DOOR BETWEEN THE WORLDS   Aramaic

A translation of John 10:9 from the Peshitta version of the Gospels

Isho'a said:

Ina(i)na thar'a.

KJV: I am the door.

> *The ego, aware of its moment-by-moment existence,*
> *conveys us between realities.*
>
> *Simple Presence shuttles us back and forth, from limitation*
> *to freedom.*
>
> *The eye of diversity's vortex can turn us from one face of life*
> *to another.*
>
> *The depth of Identity is the gatekeeper for a vast variety of*
> *possible and impossible experience.*
>
> *The self conscious of its Self opens a passage between times*
> *and spaces.*
>
> *The "I am" is the door between the worlds.*

BODY PRAYER: THE DOOR OF I

The Aramaic word *thara,* usually translated as "door," also points to everything that makes a transition from one form of reality to another, that turns us from one mode of being to another, that converts, distills, or infuses something into something else. The more profound use of the ancient root of this word, THR, probably includes the Egyptian sacred name *Ha-Thor,* she who presides over death and rebirth, as well as the later word, *darvesh,* in the Sufi tradition—the one who sits in the door-way between realities.

Simple Presence

To explore further the body sensations and emotions that center around the "I": Return again to a place of simple presence. Sitting comfortably, eyes closed, feel the rise and fall of the breath. With each breath, reach out to whatever feelings or sensations arise, and feel the breath illuminating each feeling with awareness. Explore the different arenas of your life, the places and ways you are known by others, and by yourself. Where in yourself is the door that allows you to make the transition, to keep all the aspects of yourself integrated and whole? Who sits in the door? Consider each image and sensation as a gift, with gratitude for an increasing sense of the universe's "I am" within.

In the Doorway   Persian

From The Diwan of Shams-i-Tabriz *by the Sufi poet Mevlana Jelaluddin Rumi, thirteenth-century Anatolia*

> My eyes gleam because there is Another inside:
> if water scalds you, there was fire behind it—understand?
> But I have no stone in my hand, no argument here.
> A rose garden is known for its sweetness, not thorns.
> So what you see in my eyes comes from another universe.
> Here's a world, there's a world—
> I'm seated in the doorway.
> Only those who sit between can deliver wordless lectures.
> It's sufficient to give this hint:
> say no more—stop talking and
> reverse the use of your tongue!

DROPS AND SPECKS   Persian

From The Secret Rose Garden *by Sufi poet Mahmud Shabistari, thirteenth century*

> *Penetrate the heart of one drop of water—*
> *you'll be flooded by a hundred pure oceans.*
> *If you examine carefully a speck of dust,*
> *you'll see a million unnameable beings.*
> *The limbs of a fly are like an elephant.*
> *A hundred harvests reside in a germ of barley seed.*
> *A millet seed holds a whole world.*
> *An insect's wing unfolds an ocean.*
> *Cosmic rays lie hidden in the pupil of my eye,*
> *and somehow the center of my heart*
> *accommodates the Pulse of the Universe.*

Textual Notes

1. *How to Organize a Self, Genesis 1:14–19.* At the end of verse 14, the phrase *w'l'môhadîm w'l'îamîm w'shanîm,* usually translated as "seasons, days, and years," also points to the way in which consciousness becomes organized. *Môhadîm* points to a body sensation of time's passage; this is related to the periodic pulsation of fluids that conveys a feeling of being in rhythm. *Iamîm,* based on the same root as *îom,* points to the effect of light on the larger mind or nervous system of a being. *Shanîm* points to an inner sensation of change over time, the sense one may have that one is not the same as yesterday. The way that light organizes our consciousness, and vice versa, according to Genesis, produces a change in the very nature of our existence.

2. *The "I" Joins the Journey, Proverbs 8:22–24.* The word *qanani,* translated in the King James Version as "possess," can also mean to create, absorb, assimilate into oneself, redeem, and acquire. This variety of seemingly disparate meanings coalesces around the root QN, which points to the power of ardor with density, compression, and tension, a centralizing force, a nest, or enclosed home of awareness. The word *re'ashîth* again returns us to that archetypal "beginningness," the primordial origin of mystery that is the object of so much contemplation in this tradition.

The word *darekhô,* translated as "way" in the King James Version, can also mean a journey, course, or path—that is, something that unfolds rather than is completed immediately. The phrase *qedem miphalîw meâz,* usually translated as "works of old," points to a pivotal moment, a point on which everything turns, at which time something wonderful, mysterious, and miraculous happened. This mystery is hidden in the germ of everything, according to the root PHL. The word *meâz* points to a definite, fixed point in space or time, one that never recurs in the same way.

In verse 23, the word *olam,* translated as "everlasting" in the King James Version, refers to another archetypal moment, the ancient first gathering of sensing and feeling that enabled a sense of "past" to appear. What was before we could feel a "before"? For life itself, and for our own life, this is *olam.* The word *nisakthî,* usually translated as "set up," can also mean to pour out, appoint, or consecrate, pointing to a sacred flow that initiates awareness and that is likely mirrored in all baptismal rites.

3. *Thunder Speaks, Part 2.* This version is based on the previous literal translations from the Coptic of George W. MacRae (1979, pp. 231–55) and Bentley Layton (1987, pp. 77–85).

4. *Road, Compass, Fuel, John 14:6.* The Aramaic word *ûrchâ,* usually translated as "way," is related to AUR, "the light" (Hebrew, IOR). In this case, it is the light that uncovers a path, shows a hidden possibility, reveals a practical, manifested way that was not previously known. The word *shrara,* usually translated as "truth," points to a solution or liberation, the opening of a circle, something solid and in accordance with universal harmony, with the measured tempo of the song of the cosmos. It is similar to the sense of right direction associated with the Zoroastrian Ashem Vohu prayer. The word *hayye,* which we encountered in the last chapter, is again the life force or primal energy that pervades the universe and nature.

5. *In the Doorway.* This version is based on a portion of the literal translation of number 36 in the collection by R. A. Nicholson (1898, p. 145).

6. *Drops and Specks.* This version is based on previous literal translations by Florence Lederer (1920), E. H. Whinfield (1880), and Johnson Pasha (1903).

Chapter Eight

THE SOUL'S
JOURNEY

In the Native Middle Eastern tradition, the
journey into the depths of self begins with the
discovery of who is doing the traveling. First
we might differentiate various parts of the
self, then hear their voices and call them
together. Often these voices are as disturbing
and surprising as the sound of thunder. We
each journey on our own from here. There is
no one right way to proceed. We can draw on
Hokhmah—Sacred Sense and Holy Wisdom—which helps guide the self's process
and integrate its demands into the life of the
whole being. We do not so much follow the
self as lead it to follow us, all the while deter-
mining who the real "I" might be.

THE PREFERENTIAL OPTION FOR A SOUL—
DAY FIVE   Hebrew

An expanded translation of Genesis 1:20–23

Wa îâomer Elohîm îshertzoû ha-maîm sheretz nephesh haîah w'hoph
*   îwhopheph hal-ha-âretz hal-phenʾeî rekîwha ha-shamaîm.* (20)
Wa îberâ Elohîm aeth-ha-thanînîm ha-gheddolîm w'aeth khol-nephesh ha-
*   haîah ha-romesheth âsher shartzoû ha-maîm le-mînehem w'aeth khol-*
*   hoph khanaph le-mîne-hou wa-îara Elohîm khitôb.* (21)
Wa îbarekh aôtham Elohîm l'amor phroû w'reboû w'milaoû aeth-ha-maîm
*   ba-îamîm w'ha hoph îreb ba-âretz.* (22)
Wa-îhî herb wa-îhî boker îôm hamîshî. (23)

KJV: And God said, Let the waters bring forth abundantly the moving
creature that hath life, and fowl that may fly above the earth in the open
firmament of heaven. (20) And God created great whales, and every living creature that moveth, which the waters brought forth abundantly,
after their kind, and every winged fowl after his kind: and God saw that
it was good. (21) And God blessed them, saying, Be fruitful, and multiply, and fill the waters in the seas, and let fowl multiply in the earth. (22)
And the evening and the morning were the fifth day. (23)

> In the next shining moment of Universe activity . . .
>   The cosmos again called forth—it inscribed a possibility
> in the mutable character of unfolding reality—and enlivened
> the primal flow with a swirling, liberating energy. In a cen-
> trifugal fashion, this swirling caused the interiority of living
> beings to separate and distinguish various new psychic struc-
> tures. These new ways of developing an "I" took living beings
> farther away from being extensions of one undifferentiated
> whole and farther toward their own aliveness and feeling.
>   Two inner realities evolved at this time. First came the
> subconscious soul-self (*nephesh*), which behaved like a living
> being with its own primal energy. It could inhale and exhale,
> be inspired and effusive, be affected by what was outside as
> well as initiate action from within. It was empowered by an
> impassioned, rising fire, which caused it to grow and try to
> fulfill its own purpose.
>   The second inner reality (*'hoph*) was the instinctual self,
> an even more obscure part of the "I," but one whose move-

ments were swift, easy, and soaring. It responded quickly to changes in atmosphere, space, and vibration. No effort was needed for instinct's participation in maintaining the integrity and survival of the evolving self. (20)

During this cycle, further experimentation continued on the theme of "new and unique," including some interior soul-selves with very large bodies, which swam along together in the primal psychic flow, and some instinctual selves that traveled together in large flocks. These inner "animals" guided early souls.

These new aspects of the self did not exist in isolation but began to generate their own offspring, which left the bodies of their parents and sprung off toward their own destiny. Each self pursued its own inspiration and expressed it in action; by this in- and out-breath, it affirmed its unity as part of the one soul of the Universe.

The preferential option for an individual soul already existed as one among many, and the call of the Universe from the future activated it everywhere. In other words, the Universe again found that this unfoldment of the cosmic story was good—ripe and appropriate for the present moment. (21)

After it achieved the individual soul-self and instinct, the Universe Being breathed radiantly toward the waters of flow. It quickened the tendency already developing there for this new form of living individuality to give birth, to multiply abundantly and with diversity. This helped fill any gaps in possible evolution and complete the interiority of the new selves (who were still all connected, even though an "I" had developed). (22)

Once over and back again, breathing in and breathing out, these luminous events marked the fifth period of intelligent Universe action, the fifth Cosmic Day. (23)

BODY PRAYER: THE SOUL OF LIFE

The word *îshertzoû,* usually translated as "bring forth abundantly," points through its roots to a circular movement that causes new generation to occur by the process of separation or individuation. What is individuated first from the cosmic flow (*maîm*) is *nephesh haîah,* usually translated "creature that hath life," but this is a clear reference to the living subconscious or soul-self, which is the subject of so much attention in Hebrew, Aramaic, and Arabic sacred scripture. The roots of the word *nephesh* can be rendered in at least three ways as: NPH, that which breathes in, can be inspired or infused from the outside; PH, the reaction to the in-breath, the sense of expansion and effusion moving from inside to outside; and ASH, the primordial embodied fire, that which generates ardor and passion for a goal. This three-part nature of the soul-self in the Native Middle Eastern tradition causes it to act as a living being in its own right.

The second new creation in the interiority of living beings is *w'hoph îwhopheph,* usually translated as "fowl that may fly." The roots of this word point to an interior activity of material sentience and sensation that is quick, unbounded by particle reality (*hal-ha-âretz*), and whose natural element is wave reality and atmosphere (*rekîwha ha-shamaîm*). I have translated this as the instinctual self (sometimes called animal instinct), an intelligence that operates at the level of our so-called involuntary nervous system. This instinctual self, when we don't block out its action with mental chatter, is extremely sensitive to atmosphere, vibration, and sound. It reacts quickly and with support (like training in the martial arts) can become astoundingly fast.

Depths of the Self 4

After beginning with a remembrance of the Source (using the sound *b'shêmy, bismillah,* or another of the practices), consciously breathe with each aspect of the subconscious self that you have been able to feel or identify. With the inhalation, feel the sound "neph" (*ph* pronounced like *f*) and focus on the infusion of new energy. With the exhalation, feel the sound "phâh" and focus on passing along life energy. In the brief natural pause after the exhalation, and without extending the pause, feel the sound "âsh" and honor the fire and passion that each aspect of the *nephesh* carries to fulfill its purpose for existence. After a few minutes with each part of the self, breathe thanksgiving to all parts and to the Source.

At the end of the session, breathe with the self of your bodily instinct. See if there is anything that you are neglecting in the health of your body. Thank the instinctual self for all that it does to keep you together, body and soul.

Wisdom's Dinner Party   Hebrew

A translation of Proverbs 9:1–6

Hokhmôth bântheh bêytha châtzbah amîdey-ha shibah. (1)

KJV: Wisdom hath builded her house, she hath hewn out her seven pillars:

> *From the primordial, chaotic "within,"*
> Hokhmah—*the breath of nourishing insight—*
> *has created a separate place to live:*
> *By enclosing her unknowable, inner mystery,*
> *Holy Wisdom has created an address for her temple.*
>
> *She has done this by dividing the Dark,*
> *pushing from outside until the*
> *foundations of her dwelling—the necessary basic "selves"—*
> *join together by their own mutual attraction:*
> *this natural union creates the first conscious "I am."*

Tâbchah tîbchâh mâskhah yêynah âph-'arkhah shulchânâh. (2)

KJV: She hath killed her beasts; she hath mingled her wine; she hath also furnished her table.

> *She has resisted her inner resistance to having limits:*
> *killed the beast, sacrificed and cooked it for nourishment.*
> *From her own intoxication of the "All,"*
> *she has mixed spiced wine of spirit-soaked Mind,*
> *which can be drunk and digested by the "small."*
> *She has spread out a table to nourish the selves*
> *by ordering matter and light, form and vibration*
> *in a reliable and harmonious way.*

Shalchâh na'rôtheyhâ thîqrâ 'al-gapêy m'rômêy qâreth. (3)

KJV: She hath sent forth her maidens: she crieth upon the high places of the city.

From the first bursts of desire
coming from this new union of her soul-selves,
Wisdom sends out messengers, children of her own being.
From the new center of her unfurling reality—
the enclosure of dynamic relationship we call soul—
she proclaims and pleads, she calls together more selves,
she engraves more order on her interior reality:

Mîy-pethîy yâsur hênâh ch'sar-lêb âmrâh lô (4)
L'khû lachmû b'lachmî wa shthû b'yayin mâskhethî (5)
'Izbû phetâyîm wîcheyû wa-îshrû bederekh bînâh. (6)

KJV: Whoso is simple, let him turn in hither: as for him that wanteth understanding, she saith to him, (4) Come, eat of my bread and drink of the wine which I have mingled. (5) Forsake the foolish, and live; and go in the way of understanding. (6)

"You who are open, susceptible, ready to learn,
You who are simple enough to take a new direction—
right this way, change here, this moment!"
To those who lack heart,
whose vital passion is diminished,
whose center of courage is blocked,
she radiates certainty, command, and praise,
she promises: (4)

"Absorb my understanding of radical wetness—
of greening, growing, vital force.
Eat my bread of freshness and beauty:
in the form offered here, it's all digestible.
Drink wine distilled from my experience, my embodied
*   breath,*
the power that stands under and supports you.
This liquor offers the intoxication of your soul. (5)

"Free your open-heartedness and feel the energy of life!
Release the power of your simplicity—
your 'getting ready for'—and start actually living!

Find the direct way,
follow a path that goes somewhere.
Begin a journey that leads to the education
and understanding of your soul." (6)

THUNDER SPEAKS: MIND EMBRACES
ALL OPPOSITES, PART 3   Coptic

A version of sections of the gnostic text Thunder, Perfect Mind

First lines of George W. MacRae translation: Why have you hated me in
your counsels? For I shall be silent among those who are silent, and I
shall appear and speak.

APPEARING, DISAPPEARING

Why am I hated wherever the powerful meet?
I am silent with those who are silent,
I stand up with those who speak out.

. . . .

I am the one who has caused hate and love everywhere.
Some call me Life, some Death.
Some Law, some Anarchy.
You have pursued me and
you are my captive.
I have been scattered and gathered.
Shamed, shameless you appear before me.
I honor no holy days and
they all belong to me.
I have no god and my god is great.

You would like to forget me,
but I am everywhere in your mind.
I am uneducated, but everyone learns from me.
You despise me,
but you cannot remove me from your mind.
You try to hide from me,
but my gaze sees you everywhere.
For whenever you hide, I appear.
Whenever you are truly present, I hide from you.

EMBRACE ME

Embrace me from the place in you
that understands and that grieves,
from the place that seems ugly and in ruin,
from the self that steals from its neighbors
though they are really no better off.

From the self that feels shame,
embrace me shamelessly.
From the middle of shame and shamelessness,
the place where grandiosity and depression merge,
find a center that brings sense and order
to all my dismembered members in you.

Advance together to me:
you who know my unity and disunity,
the One Self or my separate selves.
Bring the "great," the spiritual Self
to live among the small, the animal selves.

Advance together to childhood:
the small, the simple, the poor
living with
the great, the complex, the rich.
Don't isolate "great" from "small,"
"rich" from "poor" within you.
By one you know the other,
and none can live in health divided.

Why, then, do you curse me in one form
and honor me in another?
You have wounded some of mine, had mercy on others.
Do not separate me from the First Ones
who were here before you.
Do not cast anyone or anything away
because you think them primitive.
I know the First Ones and
those who followed in their ways know me.

BODY PRAYER: CALLING THE SELVES TOGETHER

Depths of the Self 5

After remembering the Source, breathe with the sound of "hû-khm-mâh" as in the body prayer in chapter 6. Using the sound to invoke a feeling of life-giving support, call the various aspects of your subconscious to a table at which they can share. Call together even those aspects that do not get along. Allow the "rich" and the "poor" to come to the same table together. Allow each aspect to express its own needs and desires. Again, listen without judgment but also without any compulsion to fulfill everything. Listen with the ears of Hokhmah. Find the place of simplicity, openness, and susceptibility in each aspect of the self. Open to the possibility that in this simplicity lies the power to fulfill the true purpose of your being.

In concluding the practice, breathe thankfulness toward each aspect of the self and to the Source. With all such work—which separates, articulates, and, hopefully, clarifies the inner territory—take some time afterward to breathe, stretch, and reintegrate all parts of the self into a unified whole. Sometimes we encounter voices of our *nephesh* that can be surprising and disturbing. As a psychic reality, Hokhmah (the sometimes severe nurturance of the soul) and Binah (the education of the soul) embrace and include them all. Again, being outdoors in nature reminds us of the simple, integrated presence that each being brings to existence.

THE CREATOR OF RIPENESS Aramaic

A translation of John 10:11 from the Peshitta version of the Gospels

Isho'a said:

Inânâ râ'hyâ thâba.

KJV: I am the good shepherd.

> *Simple Presence leads our flock of needs to fulfillment, at the right place and the right time.*
>
> *The self conscious of its Self guides our material existence to complete fruition.*
>
> *The ego fully aware of its ephemeral reality shares the cares of living in a body.*
>
> *The eye of desire's hurricane supplies comfort and protection for life's brittleness.*
>
> *The peaceful center at the middle of "Who am I" leads our anxieties to the right pasture for the moment.*
>
> *The depth of Identity consoles us as we wander toward health.*
>
> *The "I am" is the shepherd who creates ripeness.*

FIND A SELF, LOSE A SELF   Aramaic

A translation of Matthew 10:39 from the Peshitta version of the Gospels

Isho'a said:

Man deshkach naphshêh nâwbdêyh (A)
wa man dnâwbedê naphshêh metlâthy neshkahîh. (B)

KJV: He that findeth his life shall lose it (A): and he that loseth his life for my sake shall find it (B).

> *Whoever blindly chases the subconscious self*
> > *as mirrored in things outside, in the surrounding*
> > > *world,*
> > *will be isolated from it:*
> *Whoever tries to fulfill all its demands will end up divided.*
> *Whoever unconsciously peels the onion of animal desire*
> > *will find only separate, clamoring voices.*
> *Whoever gains only the instinctive soul that scatters and*
> > *gathers*
> > *will ultimately lose connection with it.* (A)

> *However,*
> *whoever gives the subconscious self its own place*
> > *with awareness, by directing a focused feeling within,*
> > > *will follow the self consciously.*
> *Whoever discriminates among its demands and finds their*
> > *roots*
> > *will end up fulfilling them.*
> *Whoever separates its voices clearly*
> > *will find the center's profound repose,*
> *Whoever loses the basic soul-self's inflation*
> > *—and connects self to Source—*
> > *will gain its true nature.* (B)

Body Prayer: Who Follows Whom?

In these few words, Jesus gives some very profound and subtle teachings about the *naphsha,* the subconscious self. First, in working with the naphsha, it is important to realize that, although its voice is very important, it is not the voice of guidance or the voice of the Source of the whole cosmos. Its needs and demands, even when very powerfully expressed, are material to work with creatively, not to obey blindly. The true heart of feeling does not come from a place of compulsion.

The Aramaic words *deshkach . . . neshkahîh,* usually translated as "find," also mean following a direction or inclination to possess something material, to accomplish a duty, to pursue a desire that has no end to its layers, or figuratively to peel something that has no core (like an onion). The Aramaic words *nâwbdêyh . . . dnâwbedê,* usually translated as "lose," may also mean to separate, isolate, individualize, or to sprout through an interior activity of division.

Using the more physical "following" energy (*deshkach*) to obey the demands of the *naphsha* can only lead to its isolation. Its real desires have to do with fulfilling its purpose, not possessing objects or people. The compulsive needs for outward things and relationships are layered on top of the self's deeper needs for contact, love, and inclusion in the purpose of the whole being, needs that can be fulfilled only by oneself and the One Self. However, by separating, isolating, and clearly hearing all the voices of the *naphsha,* its needs for contact, love, and inclusion begin to be met. When the voices of the *naphsha* are heard, it does not need to shout or imitate the voice of Source. When included, its needs are fulfilled and followed in that they are integrated with the purpose of the whole being.

Despite the influence of some aspects of modern psychology, the subconscious and its needs are not "God." According to this tradition, the work here is not so much to "follow our feelings," but to have our feelings follow us, a process that involves slowly developing better internal communication, so that we know who "us" is.

In the *Gospel of Thomas,* another of the scrolls in the Nag Hammadi collection, Jesus is quoted as saying, "If you bring forth that which is within you, that which is within you will save you. If you fail to bring forth that which is within you, that which is within you will kill you." This is a succinct comment on all forms of addictive and compulsive consumption and behavior. Generally we need to shift from thinking that the presence of these voices in us is "bad" to looking at them as an opportunity to communicate with our soul-self. If we, as individuals and a species, continue to ignore this opportunity, however, it will present itself with more and more deadly urgency.

Depths of the Self 6

Begin again with whatever invocation of the Source you have chosen, and breathe with the parts of the *naphsha* that have demands and desires you have not heard before or that overwhelm you blindly in moments when you are not conscious of their source. Sometimes these messages from the *naphsha* are very powerful, washing over in waves of compulsive behavior, which can seem inevitable or undeniable. See it as some part of the self trying to get your attention. There is always a deeper need underneath, perhaps one you cannot fulfill immediately or at all. When you come to the bottom, there may be anger, sadness, or fear concerning a past event, but it is ultimately a need for love, acceptance, and inclusion.

Cultivate the quality of inner, attentive, and understanding listening. Affirm the reality of the need as it is felt. Notice where its sensations are felt in your body, and follow them, affirming the wisdom that is there at the bottom of the thread of feeling. If you have clearly distinguished which voice of the self needs attention, make a list of its likes and dislikes. Consciously seek to fulfill some of the ones that are not harmful to your being or that of others.

Gradually a relationship is established and more cooperation is felt. The inner territory becomes less polarized, less a matter of a massive conflagration between good and evil and more one of ripe and unripe for this moment. At some point you may begin to ask whether the aspects of your *naphsha* would like to experience a more direct relationship to the Source—an invitation to Wisdom's party, as we saw in Proverbs. When the time is ripe, the pathway will open. To conclude this body prayer, thank all aspects of the self and thank the Source.

GAMBLING THE SELF   Persian

From The Secret Rose Garden *by Sufi poet Mahmud Shabistari, thirteenth century*

The stakes are high for real prayer.
You must gamble your self
and be willing to lose.
When you have done this,
and your self shakes off
what you believed your self to be,
then no prayer remains,
only a sparkle of the eyes.
Knower and known are one.

If you penetrate the center of time and space,
you can bypass the addictions of the world:
You can become the world yourself.

THE MOON AND THE SEA   Persian

From The Diwan of Shams-i-Tabriz *by Mevlana Jelaluddin Rumi, thirteenth-century Anatolia*

> At dawn, the moon appeared
> > and swooped down from the sky to take a look at me.
> Like a falcon hunting up a meal,
> > the moon grabbed me and away we went!
> I looked for my self, but my self was gone:
> > in the moon, by grace, my body had become like soul.
> Luminous, I journeyed on as soul, but all I saw was
> > that moon—
> > until the mystery of Self and self was completely clear.
> Nine types of heaven, nine vibrations, all mingled in
> > that moon;
> > and the boundaries of my being disappeared in the sea.
>
> Waves broke.
> Awareness rose again
> and sent out a voice.
> It always happens like this.
> Sea turns on itself and foams:
> with every foaming bit
> another body, another being takes form.
> And when the sea sends word,
> each foaming body
> melts immediately back to ocean breath.
>
> Thanks to my beloved friend Shams 'l Haqq, Sun of Truth!
> Without his strength,
> I couldn't see the moon,
> I couldn't become the sea.

Body Prayer: The Moon

With profound subtlety Mevlana Jelaluddin Rumi here points to the experience in which the subconscious self (*nafs* in this tradition) becomes totally luminous and glimpses its reality as part of the soul of the whole universe. The "moon" here symbolizes the reality of a mind or awareness that has become clear of disturbances and can reflect the divine light. By opening to divine guidance, the *nafs*, or soul-self, may begin to see its own reflection as part of the One Being—its oneness and that One as part of the same reality. What actually reflects (like a mirror) is the heart-mind, a reality that can be both solar-positive and lunar-receptive, according this tradition.

Heart Awareness

After remembering the Source, breathe in, feeling a relationship to the aspects of self that you have already explored. If you feel a willingness on the part of the *nafs* to establish a better connection with the Source, then use the practice developed under "heart awareness" in previous chapters: Breathe easily and naturally with awareness in the heart. Clear the mirror, and, to the extent you are able at the present moment, feel a reflection of light, purpose, and love from the Only Being. Then direct the mirror downward toward the soul-selves and let them share in this experience of the Source. Allow some time for any feelings, sensations, inspirations, or images to arise. Allow for a thinning of the boundaries between self and Self that may outshine any of these. This prayer ends with thanks for anything received.

THE SOUL'S THREE FACES   Hebrew

A version of selected portions of the Zohar, Book of Radiant Life, *a collection of mystical Jewish commentaries assembled in the fifteenth century*

First lines of Gershom Scholem translation: The names and grades of the soul of man are three: *nefesh* [vital soul], *ruah* [spirit], *neshamah* [innermost soul, supersoul]. The three are comprehended one within the other, but each has its separate abode.

> The human soul has three faces: *nephesh, ruach,* and *neshemah. Nephesh* is the animating and animal self—that within which scatters and gathers. *Ruach* is the breathing self, conscious in the present moment—a portion of the Breathing Life of All. *Neshemah* is the illuminating self—light of the light of guidance from the One. The three are contained, one inside the other, although each has its own neighborhood of activity. . . .
>
> The animal self (*nephesh*) is intimate with the body: It nourishes and supports it. It is the "below"—the first instant of the arising of all sensation. Having fulfilled its purpose and conscious of itself, it becomes a throne, an accommodation for the breathing, conscious self—a place for *ruach* to rest—as Isaiah writes (32:15): "when the breath pours upon us from the first Source."
>
> When these two selves have fulfilled their purpose and prepared themselves, they are ready to receive the illuminating self (*neshemah*), which rests in the accommodation created by the breath. The illuminating self transcends the normal ways of sensing: it is the fulfillment of all sensation. Throne upon throne, vehicle within vehicle, one place to rest—one accommodation—rests upon another and again upon another.
>
> Studying and experiencing these faces of the soul leads to *Hokhmah,* Sacred Wisdom, Sacred Sense, and in this way the Source of Sacred Breath and Soul can bring together mysteries that seem separate and divisive.
>
> *Nephesh* is like the dark light at the bottom of a candle's flame, the part close to the wick that you can't see through but without which there would be no flame at all. When fully lit, the bottom of the flame provides a seat for the white light

above it (*ruach*), the only one we usually see. And when these two are burning fully, the white light creates a foundation for another light—one not completely seen or sensed yet present as a mysterious essence—the illuminating atmosphere or aura of the light (*neshemah*). All three reach completeness in conscious relationship to and partnership with each other. This is the light of the All-embracing.

Textual Notes

1. *The Preferential Option for a Soul, Genesis 1:20–23.* In verses 21–23, the new soul-selves multiply and diversify, and one could say that the interiority of living beings becomes much more complex as more differentiation occurs. The words that the Universe Being speaks are *phroû w'reboû w'milaoû,* usually translated "be fruitful and multiply and fill." These words point respectively to the actions of producing offspring and becoming fertile (*phroû*), of creating great numbers of beings through an interior process (*reboû*), and of filling any gaps, extending until each being is entirely formed (*milaoû*).

2. *Wisdom's Dinner Party, Proverbs 9:1–6.* The phrase *bântheh,* usually translated "hath builded," refers to an interior activity that creates a boundary or circumference around the self and that forms, embodies, or constructs something from the "me." What gets formed here is *bêytha,* usually translated "house," but also any container or separate inside space, an interior or a "within." The word *châtzbah,* usually translated as "hewn," comes from the root HWH, which points to any division that occurs by pushing from the outside until an irruption occurs. The phrase *amîdey-ha shibah,* usually translated as "seven pillars," refers to parts that come together and bond in a way that satisfies or fulfills a purpose—in this case to form the "I am" of an individual.

In verse 2, the phrase *tâbchah tîbchâh,* usually translated "killed her beasts," actually says "slaughtered her slaughter" or "resisted her resistance." Both words have the same root (TB): a force of resistance from the inside that conserves the central integrity of a being or that sets aside any corruption. It might also be translated "ripened her ripeness." The phrase *mâskhah yêynah,* usually translated "mingled her wine," is a beautiful expression that could also mean to fuse or compress (*mâskhah*) the intoxicating, spiritual power of pure mind or intelligence (*yêynah*). The phrase *arkhah shulchânâh,* usually translated "furnished her table," can also mean to spread out, order, or move into physical reality a harmonious (SHL) fixed extension of time and space (CHN), which supports the growth of the self.

In verse 3, the phrase *shalchâh na'rôtheyhâ,* usually translated "sent forth her maidens," can also mean to stretch out, extend, or sprout a new impulse or desire. The word *thîqrâ,* usually translated as "cried," can also mean to proclaim, plead, summon, celebrate, or praise. The phrase *'al-gapêy m'rômêy qâreth,* usually translated "upon the highest places in the city," can also mean an enclosure that protects and fills space around something centralized and sacred.

In verse 4, the word *mîy-phethîy,* usually translated as "simple," may also mean open, susceptible, or accessible. It is based on the root PHTH, which we encountered several times in chapter 4. The phrase *yâsur hênâh,* usually translated "let him turn in hither," points to turning aside in order to be instructed or corrected, to take a new direction in the present moment, right now. The phrase *ch'sar-lêb,* usually translated "as for him that wanteth understanding," actually talks about someone diminished or blocked in heart, courage, force, or passion.

The words *lachmû b'lachmî* in verse 5 are both derived from *lachma,* the elemental food, which includes bread for all levels of being, that which offers for consumption all natural vigor, radical moisture, everything verdant, young, or fresh.

The phrase *'izbû phetâyîm* in verse 6, usually translated as "forsake the foolish," may have several layers of meaning, as I have indicated. *'Izbû* may also mean to set free, release, or loosen. *Phetâyîm* is the same simplicity, openness, and susceptibility mentioned in verse 4. The word *wîcheyû,* usually translated "and live," is related to the same *chayy* or elemental power and life force we have encountered previously. The final phrase, *îshrû bederekh bînâh,* usually translated "go in the way of understanding," is repeated many times in Hebrew scriptures. *Ishrû* means to walk straight and directly, to go in the way that leads to ultimate happiness for the soul. It is based on the same root (ASH) that we encountered previously as the fire that empowers the basic soul-self (*nephesh*). The word *derekh* points to any journey, path, course, manner, or way. The word *bînâh* (which later becomes very important as a quality on the Kabbalistic tree of life) points to the understanding or intelligence that educates a soul from within.

3. *Thunder Speaks, Part 3.* This version is based on the previous literal translations from the Coptic of George W. MacRae (1979, pp. 231–55) and Bentley Layton (1987, pp. 77–85).

4. *The Creator of Ripeness, John 10:11.* Here we see *inânâ,* the "I am," as a force for guidance to the right action at the right moment. The Aramaic word *râ'hyâ,* usually translated as "shepherd," may also mean anyone who shares the same cares, pains, or anxieties as another, who rules or leads but is at the same time a comrade or neighbor. The Aramaic word *tâbâ,* usually translated as "good," is related to the Hebrew word we saw in Proverbs 9:2: a force that resists corruption, conserves a central integrity, and leads to healthy, timely action or ripe "fruit." It is

the opposite of *bîsha,* or unripeness, which we encountered in Jesus' saying about timeliness in chapter 4 (Tomorrow Means Things Depart, Matthew 6:33–34). It is a variation of the same word that begins all of the Beatitudes in Aramaic (see chapter 2, textual note 3).

5. *Gambling the Self.* This version is based on previous literal translations by Florence Lederer (1920), E. H. Whinfield (1880), and Johnson Pasha (1903).

6. *The Moon and the Sea.* This version is based on the literal translation of number 19 in the collection by R. A. Nicholson (1898, pp. 76–79).

7. *The Soul's Three Faces.* This version of a small selection of the Zohar is based on the literal translation of Gershom Scholem (1949, pp. 44, 96). In addition, I have retranslated the meanings of the key terms from the original Hebrew roots and, I hope, have clarified the meaning of the rest of the passage in relationship to them.

Chapter Nine

THE VEIL OF SEPARATION — "I AND YOU"

As the interior life becomes richer and more complex, it lives on a knife's edge between creative independence and destructive isolation. The "I" has the choice to remember or to forget its Source. Judgment—of self or other—increases with the distance felt between "you" and "I." And the search for ways to bridge this gap, to remove the veil, begins in earnest.

An Experiment in Independence —
Day Six, Part 1 Hebrew

An expanded translation of Genesis 1:24–26

Wa-îâomer Elohîm thôtza ha-âaretz nephesh haîah le-mîne-ha behemah wa-
remesh w'haîthô-aretz le-mîne-ha wa-îhî-khen. (24)
Wa-îahash Elohîm ath-haîath ha-âretz le-mîneha w'ath-ha-behemah le-
mîne-ha w'ath-khol-remesh ha-âdamah le-mîne-hou wa-îara Elohîm
khi-tôb. (25)

KJV: And God said, Let the earth bring forth the living creature after
his kind, cattle, and creeping thing, and beast of the earth after his kind:
and it was so. (24) And God made the beast of the earth after his kind,
and cattle after their kind, and every thing that creepeth upon the earth
after his kind: and God saw that it was good. (25)

> [Proceeding farther toward the call of its purpose, toward the
> horizon of its destiny, which seemed to recede with each
> step . . .]

> After the previous experimentation, the Universe evoked
> from particle reality the basic character of new soul-selves
> that could exist and thrive as individuals on earth. These new
> selves moved in the psychic realm by other than the previ-
> ously tried means of wiggling, creeping, paddling, floating, or
> winging: Legs and limbs were invented.
>
> This new reality had two effects for the interiority of
> living beings. First, individual soul-selves developed more
> speed in relation to particle reality. They could, without con-
> tacting the more communal wave reality, move faster and
> make more noise. Second, they could, through the new move-
> ments of gathering and piling up, amass more of the material
> "stuff" of the Universe, also without needing to contact the
> communal wave reality. Both of these new developments in
> interior life also created new consequences in outer form, for
> better or worse.
>
> As the story continued, each new means of movement
> led individual beings to seek the fulfillment of their own
> ends, often at the expense of others. All beings of the kind we
> have been talking about were composed of the assimilated,

whole substance of the Universe (*adamah*); not one was composed of anything else or came from outside. There was, and is, no "outside" to this universal ground of Being. This the Universe recognized again as a ripe way to act. (24–25)

Wa-îâomer Elohîm nahasheh Adam be-tzalleme-noû khi-de-mouthe-noû
w'îreddou be-deggath ha-îam w'be-hoph ha-shamaîm w'ba-behemah
w'bekhol-ha-âretz w'bekhol-ha-remesh ha-romesh hal-ha-âretz. (26)

KJV: And God said, Let us make man in our image, after our likeness: and let them have dominion over the fish of the sea, and over the fowl of the air, and over the cattle, and over all the earth, and over every creeping thing that creepeth upon the earth.

Then the Universe declared its radiant, burning willingness in another way. Speaking both as a collection of multitudinous experiments in being and simultaneously as a single individual, it said, so to speak:

By taking into account everything going on,
every tendency, process, destiny, and question,
let us draw out the assimilation of all this activity,
the distillation of the essence of Unity,
in a form that will endure, develop, and affect our destiny
in an even more powerful way.

Let this Universal Assimilation of the whole ground of
*   Being* (adam)
take on the veil or appearance of the Universe itself,
the shadow of the totality as projected from the Source
through the experiment of earthiness.

Let this adam, *universal collective humanity,*
have the complete powers of
differentiation, subjectivity, and communion
we have developed so far.

Let it unfold its course like a wheel covering ground
and have more power to persevere,
for better or worse, in its own destiny

than other embodiments of instinctive soul.
In its own nature, let this adam hold the key
to identifying with the Universe as a whole:
to conceive, imagine, and think
as We—I—the Universe does. (26)

[Remember that this was yet a projection of the entire Universe itself, an archetype not yet embodied, so to speak. Yet it was a powerful projection: We know that shadows can seem very real and can cause beings to act strangely.]

Body Prayer: The Challenge of Humanity

For textual notes on words translated but not included in this body prayer, please see the notes at the end of this chapter.

In verse 25, the important word *âdamah,* which is not translated in the King James Version, means the universal, immortal, and powerful (A) assimilation, collection, and whole aggregation (DM) of primordial creative life (AH). According to this cosmology, nothing used in our evolution came from anywhere but the Universe itself.

Several words in verse 26 deserve closer attention. The word *adam,* usually translated as "man," follows closely on *adamah.* It means the collective assimilation of the Universe's activity in a stable form—the collective archetype in this cosmology of the human being. It does not refer here to a masculine-gendered person.

The word *be-tzalleme-noû,* usually translated "in our image," also means "in the universal shadow of" or "in the veil of." It also points to an image projected by means of light. The word *khi-de-mouth-noû,* usually translated "after our likeness," is linked to the root DM and points to something that is assimilated, mingled with, or identified with the whole. It is a "blood bond" between humanity and the Universe Being in its entirety, including the way it conceives, thinks, and imagines.

The important word *îreddou,* usually translated "have dominion," points to a singular power to radiate diversity and differentiation, a power that spreads out, unfolds, and occupies space by its very nature, that moves with firmness and perseveres in its own will. The power given to the interiority developed by the human has all these qualities, again for better and for worse. This was the challenge the Universe set for itself.

As the interiority of human beings continued to develop and become more complex, the tendency increased for the small "I" to forget its Source. This, in short, is the entire history of humanity's psychic evolution up until now, and in accelerated form in the modern era.

At the center of each "I," we have the choice to isolate or to connect. Each moment is a choice about how to balance the needs of various voices in our interior reality with the purpose of the whole Universe, which leads us onward. In a moment we decide how "I" will respond to any situation, remembering or forgetting that we always have a choice to face the front or the back of the mirror.

Heart Awareness

Breathing easily and naturally, with awareness in the region of the heart, return to the image of the heart as a sacred mirror. Focus your awareness on the back of the mirror and the door it opens to the depths of the *nephesh,* or subconscious self, as you have experienced it so far. Then open your awareness to the front of the mirror and its ability to reflect the purpose at the heart of the Universe. Practice keeping an awareness of both dimensions of existence while you clean the mirror of impressions that do not lead to the fulfillment of your purpose, individually, as a unified "I," or collectively, as a group of growing "me's." Conclude this body prayer with thanks for the challenge of being human at this time.

THE OLD ORDER: EVERY MOUTH IS CRAMMED WITH "LOVE ME!"   Egyptian

A version of selections from the Prophecies of Nefer-Rohu, *written down in the Middle Kingdom about 2000 B.C.E., which describe the period at the end of the Old Kingdom, about one
hundred to two hundred years earlier.*

First lines of Adolf Erman translation: "Up, mine heart, that thou
mayest bewail the land whence thou art sprung. . . . Rest not! Behold, it
lieth before thy face. Rise up against that which is in thy presence. . . .
That which was made is as if it were never made, and Re might begin to
found (anew).

Try to stay together, my heart,
while you mourn the land
where you first began to beat.
To keep silent is impossible—stifling!
The Radiant One must build the foundations again.
The land is so devastated that not enough black earth
survives to fit under a fingernail.
The land is so devastated, and no one cares,
no one speaks out, no eyes are even wet.
The sun is covered,
the rivers are empty,
the fish ponds are polluted.
Land is fought over, seized, and returned,
seized and returned,
and no one can see or hear the end of it.
Nothing seems important, and everything seems sick.
People make arrows of metal,
beg to be fed with blood, and
laugh in a sick tone of voice.
Death doesn't cause anyone to weep
or fast or turn toward anything but themselves.
Every mouth is crammed with "Love Me!"
and ripeness has disappeared.
The earth is diminished
but bureaucrats abound.
The earth is bare

but taxes increase.
The less grain we raise,
the more they take from us.
The Radiant One turns away from humanity
and shines only an hour a day.
People can't tell midday,
because they don't see their shadow.
No one's face brightens when they see
the Radiant One, no eyes water with feeling.
Radiance is still there, as before,
but we don't face the right direction.

THUNDER SPEAKS: MIND EMBRACES
ALL OPPOSITES, PART 4   Coptic

A version of sections of the gnostic text Thunder, Perfect Mind

First lines of George W. MacRae translation: You honor me [. . .] and
you whisper against [me]. You [who] are vanquished, judge them [who
vanquish you] before they give judgment against you, because the judge
and partiality exist in you.

THE JUDGMENT

You praise me and plot against me
out of different sides of your mouth.
You cannot win. You are beaten.
Wisdom cries out as judgment.
If you cannot embrace the opposites within you,
you will be judged by your own environment.

Instead, first judge the one who judges within you—
the discriminating power
that calls this worthy and that worthless
within and among you.
If your inner judge condemns you,
who can set you free?
If your inner judge acquits you,
who can lock you up?

What is inside you is outside you.
Your outer appearance is created
by the same one who dresses you inside.
What you judge outside,
what you value, what you call living,
the voices you hear or ignore,
you also judge inside.
You create your inner life in
visible form all around you.

BODY PRAYER: THE INNER JUDGE

Depths of the Self 7

After beginning with a remembrance of the Source, allow your breath and awareness to connect with aspects of the nephesh with which you have developed a relationship. Using their support, request the presence of that aspect of the self which judges, and ask for its name. This inner judge offers both discrimination and self-criticism, both practical wisdom and cynicism, as well as other two-edged swords that we may feel as a combined blessing and curse. Begin to develop a relationship to this aspect of your soul-self. It also will have its likes and dislikes, its needs and goals. As before, become a good listener and don't react, even if you hear some things you don't like.

To support the strengths of this side of the self, you might use either the sound practice of intoning "Ho-khm-mah" (mentioned earlier) or the Arabic equivalent, "Ya Hâkîm" (the Judge). As you bring each session to a close, thank all aspects of the self for their cooperation, and thank the Source.

LIKE VINE AND BRANCHES   Aramaic

A translation of John 15:1 from the Peshitta version of the Gospels

Isho'a said:

Inânâ gpethâ wa aton shbîshtê.

KJV: I am the vine and ye are the branches thereof.

> *The depth of identity gives life,*
> *the depth of relationship receives it.*

> *The self conscious of its Self generates a current of vitality;*
> *the sense of "other" balances the circuit.*

> *Simple Presence is the artery through which health pulses;*
> *Simple Contact is the vein that restores universal*
> *healing.*

> *The ego hollowed by its own sense of mortality flows with*
> *breath;*
> *sympathy with another receives the flow in harmony.*

> *The eye of the whirlpool of subjectivity allows life to grow;*
> *the "thou" of the waves of objectivity allows life*
> *to age.*

> *The center of individuality's circle sends out rays;*
> *the space between any two of them forms "you."*

> *The "I am" is the vine of interiority;*
> *the "You are" is the branches of communion.*

COMMUNION'S GIFT   Aramaic

An expanded version of Matthew 26:27–28 from the Peshitta version of the Gospels

Shqal khâsâ w'âoraî wa îhab lhôn wa amar:
Sabu ishtâw minêh kulkhôn. (27)
Hânâw damî dadeyâtêqê ch'dathâ
dachlâp sagîyê mithashid l'shûbqânâ dachtâhê. (28)

KJV: And he took the cup, and gave thanks, and gave it to them, saying,
Drink ye all of it (27); for this is my blood of the new testament, which is
shed for many for the remission of sins (28).

> *Then he poised the cup, symbol of all the physical shelter*
>   *and accommodation of the body.*
> *As with the bread, he embraced and absorbed himself into*
>   *it; he burned with an inner fire, enlightening the*
>   *atmosphere with joy and life.*
> *Then he gave it to them and said:*
>
> *Everyone, take and drink,*
> *Surround and enjoy,*
> *Convert and consume,*
> *Envelop and undergo*
> *the depths of Sacred Foundation: (27)*
>
> *This is my wine (damî)—*
> *the juice of the Universe that satisfies*
> *all thirsts for communion.*
> *This is my blood, sap of the adamah,*
> *—the assimilated essence of the cosmos—*
> *the bond between all souls and bodies,*
> *all you's and I's.*
> *This renewable prescription fills every need.*
> *It flows out from its Source*
> *in ever greater amounts.*
> *It unties all the knots and*
> *embraces all mistakes with emptiness.*

Just like blood this universal effusion,
in whose likeness we appear,
releases us from the past,
heartbeat by heartbeat. (28)

BODY PRAYER: PRESENCE AND CONTACT

Simple Presence

Return again to an inner experience of simple presence. Sit comfortably, eyes closed, and feel the rise and fall of the breath. With each breath reach out to whatever feelings or sensations arise and feel the breath illuminating each with awareness. Place one hand lightly on your heart and allow the sensation of the heartbeat to come into it. Find a contact with your hand that is neither pressing nor holding away, neither reaching nor absent, but simply present. Allow this sense of simple contact to lead you to deeper layers of sensing the blood's pulsation, releasing the body, heartbeat by heartbeat, from the past. This is a doorway to the same action of renewal that flows through the whole universe.

This simple contact can be extended to include another. Our society does not have many good models of healthy touch. Sitting side by side with a partner, one of you begins by placing one hand lightly on the middle of the back of the other and "listens with the hand." If you are receiving the touch, focus on the sensation of your own heartbeat and feel the sensation supported by the touch. If you are giving the touch, focus on receiving the heartbeat of your partner into your hand and connecting with it through your awareness of your own pulsation. Begin to form a communion of blood and pulsation that bridges the gulf between "I" and "you."

"I AND YOU" Persian

From The Secret Rose Garden *by Sufi poet Mahmud Shabistari, thirteenth century*

"I" and "you" focus light
like decorative holes cut
in a lamp shade.
But there is only One Light

"I" and "you" throw a
thin veil between
heaven and earth.
Lift the veil and all
creeds and theologies disappear.

When "I" and "you" vanish,
how can I tell whether I am
in a mosque, a synagogue,
a church, or an observatory?

I Am Not   Persian

From The Diwan of Shams-i-Tabriz *by Mevlana Jelaluddin Rumi, thirteenth-century Anatolia*

Muslims! What can I do? I have lost my identity!
I am not a Christian, Jew, pagan, or Muslim.
I am neither an Easterner nor a Westerner,
*   neither a land nor a sea person.*
Nature can't fully account for me,
*   nor can the whirling cosmos.*
I don't exclusively belong to earth, water, fire, or air.
*   I am not of the invisible-ineffable, nor of the dust—*
I am not a process or a being.
I am not of this world or the next, and deserve
*   neither eternal reward nor eternal punishment.*
I am not of Adam or Eve,
*   not of the original Garden nor the final one.*
My home has no address; my tracks leave no trace.
I am neither body nor soul—What can I say?
I belong to the Self of the Beloved.

I have laid all "twos" aside:
this world and that world are one.
I search for One, I recognize One,
I see One clearly, and I call the name of the One.
That unnameable One, the breath of the breath,
is the first and last, the outside and the inside.
I identify no one except by "O That . . . O This!"
I am drunk on the cup of Love:
here-now and everywhere-all-the-time have vanished.
I can't handle any business except celebration.

If I spend an instant without you,
that instant makes my whole life seem worthless.
If I can win one moment with you,
I will crush both worlds under my feet
as I dance in joy forever.

My beloved Shams-i-Tabriz, I am living permanently
intoxicated:
I have no more stories to tell except ones about drunks and
parties.

Textual Notes

1. *An Experiment in Independence, Genesis 1:24–26.* The word *thôtza,* usually translated "bring forth," refers to an action that sets a certain character or choice in motion. That choice then grows, matures, and follows its own course. The word *behemah,* usually translated as "cattle," refers to movement and noise that occur when a being raises itself from the earth. The word *remesh,* usually translated as "creeping thing," refers to contractile movements that gather or pile up things. The phrase *le-mîne-ha,* which occurs in various forms throughout this account and is usually translated "after his kind," points to an exterior result in form that follows and develops from the previous definition of an interior reality or idea.

2. *The Old Order: Every Mouth Is Crammed with "Love Me!"* Version extracted from and based on Papyrus Leningrad 1116B, from literal translations by John A. Wilson in the collections of James B. Pritchard (1955, p. 445) and Adolf Erman (1927, pp. 112–14).

3. *Thunder Speaks, Part 4.* This version is also based on the previous literal translations from the Coptic of George W. MacRae (1979, pp. 231–55) and Bentley Layton (1987, pp. 77–85).

4. *Like Vine and Branches, John 15:1.* This "I am" statement is based on the multiple meanings of *gepethâ* and *shibîshtê,* the words usually translated as "vine" and "branches." *Gepethâ* refers to any channel or canal, any object hollowed out in order to allow something to flow through or in order to protect, enclose, or defend life. *Shibîshtê* refers to that which receives something as it returns to its original state, which balances "going away" with "coming back," or which restores something in harmony and proportion. All its images have to do with growth that is entwined and twisted together in a communal way.

5. *Communion's Gift, Matthew 26:27–28.* As in the previous passage from Matthew 26, the Aramaic word *shqal,* usually translated as "took" (as in "took the cup"), also means to poise, to weigh, to embrace or envelop, to absorb oneself into in a special gesture of unification. In Aramaic the word *khâsâ,* used for "cup," may also mean any temporary cover, accommodation, clothing, or physical shelter. By inference it points to the body. (It's also related to the later Arabic word we encountered in the Quranic sura about time; see chapter 4, textual note 4.) The word *âoraî,* usually translated "gave thanks," may also mean to light up or burn with joy and desire. It's related to *îâor,* the word for "light" used in the Genesis creation story.

Sabu, usually translated "take," may also mean to surround, envelop, or convert. *Ishtâw,* usually translated "drink," may also mean to enjoy, consume, or undergo a movement that takes one to the depths or foundations of something.

Coming to the key word, *damî,* usually translated "blood," it is important to note that the word also refers literally to any red wine, juice, or sap. Its roots are directly related to the *adamah* found in Genesis 1, the assimilated essence of the Universe out of which all life came. These roots point to a bond that brings together what was previously separate, that allows parts to mingle into a whole, or that assimilates individuality into the universal essence. The words *dadeyâtêqê ch'dathâ,* usually translated "new testament," may also refer to any renewing, abundant, or effusive command, prescription, or law, one that satisfies all needs or reconciles all opposites.

The word *sagîyê,* usually translated as "for many," may also mean "in a way that continues to grow or extend itself," as in the circumference of a circle opening. The word *mithashid,* usually translated "shed," may also mean to flow out or pour out, as from a reservoir. *Shûbqânâ,* usually translated as "forgive," may also mean to return something to its original state, to untie, or to embrace with emptiness. The word *chtâhê,* usually translated as "sins," may also mean tangled threads, failures, mistakes, or hopes frustrated in the past. These last two words are the same as those used in Luke's version of the Lord's Prayer. (For more on this, see the discussion in my earlier work, 1990.)

6. *"I and You."* This version is based on the previous literal translations from the Persian by Florence Lederer (1920) and E. H. Whinfield (1880).

7. *I Am Not.* This version is based on the literal translation of number 31 in the collection by R. A. Nicholson (1898, pp. 124–27).

PART THREE

Voices of Communion

Communion reflects that way in which
every wave and particle in the universe is
connected to every other. Every atom, person,
and action is related to every other, to a
greater or lesser extent. The tendency of
atoms to bond, of animals to herd, and of
human beings to form communities reflects
this principle. On a personal level, this wisdom helps us focus on our relationships with
every other being, and with the source and
end of Being. On the deepest spiritual level,
these voices deal with how we love and how
we die.

Chapter Ten

DESIRE AND LOVE

Increased diversity and increasingly complex
interiority lead to some very fundamental
differences—like those between male and
female. These differences are balanced by the
desire of living beings to return to more intimately bonded relationships. Compulsive
desire can override the other voices in one's
nature. But desire can also develop into love,
a more mysterious force that grows slowly
from the inside rather than through more
immediate—and often blinding—attraction.
Following desire or love to its source, without holding on to its object, can lead us to
the communion of the Universe.

Two Habits of Being Human —
Day Six, Part 2   Hebrew

An expanded translation of Genesis 1:27–28

Wa-îberâ Elohîm ath-ha-Adam be-tzallem-ô be-tzellem Elohîm barâ âothô
zakhar w'neqeba barâ âoth'am. (27)

KJV: So God created man in his own image, in the image of God created
he him; male and female created he them.

> The sixth "day" continued: From its own essence of total
> presence, the Universe established a principle of individuated
> collective unity, sometimes called the human. This new
> experiment in being was envisioned as having two basic
> modes, tones, or habits:
> One was innocent, obvious and apparent, growing and
> rising, engraving what has been established and embodying
> the memory of the origin of things.
> The other was innocent, subtle and deep, hollowed and
> cavernous, nurturing the new and embodying knowledge of
> space and the primeval void.
> These two habits of being formed the initial archetypes
> of male and female as contained within each human being.
> One being, two ways—forever destined to deal with the dif-
> ference, one way or another.

Wa-îbarekh âoth'am Elohîm wa-îâomer la-hem Elohîm phroû w'reboû
w'milâoû ath-ha-âretz w'khibeshu-ha w'redoû bi-deggath ha-îam
w'bi-hôph ha-shamaîm w'bi-khol-haîah ha-romesheth hal-ha-
âretz. (28)

KJV: And God blessed them, and God said unto them, Be fruitful, and
multiply, and replenish the earth, and subdue it: and have dominion
over the fish of the sea, and over the fowl of the air, and over every living
thing that moveth upon the earth.

> The entire principle of humanity was still "in its beginning-
> ness"—only in potential, not action—yet it already had a life
> of its own. The Universe breathed compassionately on this
> yet-unmanifest being so that it began to generate, multiply,

and fill space. It became the dominant and most attractive goal of the Universe to establish the human principle in embodiment, embracing the whole of manifest creation at the time.

The collective consciousness of the human, being a very centralized fire of the entire cosmos, could override and overrule its older interior structures—subconscious, instinctual self, reptilian intelligence, and all the other prior developments that it received as a heritage.

The attractive force of this accommodation for the human was dangerous. This being needed to be conscious enough of itself that it could also be conscious of the whole Universe; and the self-reflexive spinning and whirling required to create this was potentially a force for both harmony and chaos. Yet the Universe gave its blessing to such a force of desire.

BODY PRAYER: PARTNERSHIP AND DOMINANCE

As mentioned in the previous chapter, the word *be-tzallem,* usually translated variously "in the image," also points to a veil, shadow, or projection of the totality of the Being who is One-and-Many (Elohîm) into and onto the assimilated "stuff" of the universe (*adam*). That the expression is repeated twice shows how important the author of Genesis considered this concept of veiling and layers. Note that, just like the universe itself, the archetype, vision, or principle of humanity is created first; its embodiment comes later in Genesis 2.

The relentless use of the masculine gender by various translators contradicts the clear assertion that this veil or projection happened from the beginning in two modes: *zakhar* and *neqeba. Zakhar,* usually translated "male," points by its roots to everything that has to do with memory and remembrance, with action that grows, rises, engraves, or hollows out, with what is apparent and obvious. The word *neqeba,* usually translated "female," refers to that which has to do with nurturance of the new, spaciousness, and the creative void, with everything that is hollowed or cavernous.

Both words carry the meaning that the archetypes to which they point are innocent, pure, and free of interference by other modes of being or doing. According to this cosmology, these were the first archetypes of male and female. They seem to have nothing to do with which sex is dominant or what roles are appropriate to each. They have everything to do with a sensory feeling for what the differences in embodiment mean for fulfilling the purpose of the universe.

In verse 28, the word *îbarekh,* usually translated as "blessed," points to the sacred breath (*roûah*) and can also mean to breathe compassionately or to bend toward something with compassion. The next words refer to the attraction of the Universe toward a principle that could embody the complete awareness of its consciousness. The controversial word *khibeshu,* usually translated "subdue," refers to centralizing and internalizing (KHB) fire, heat, and light (ASH), thereby empowering something through the force of compression. This leads to the images of pushing or treading down with the feet. The images of feet and psychic movement are related to their evolution in the previous verses (24–26). That is, the ability of human consciousness to move with a greater amount of free will was here extended to include an ability to override its own subconscious self, instincts, and other interior abilities, which are a heritage from the interiority of older beings.

Depths of the Self 8

After beginning with a remembrance of the Source, allow your breath and awareness to contact the side of your body that you associate with maleness. Breathe from the One as a creative force that rises, engraves, and extends itself.

After a few minutes, allow your awareness to shift to the other side of your body, breathing from the One as a creative force that forms a matrix of spaciousness drawing out of the void what is new.

After a few minutes, breathe in both sides of the body and feel the partnership of the two modes of being. This partnership may not occur immediately. One side of being or the other may feel that it has, in the past, been ignored or slighted. Begin to build some bridges of understanding, as you did in other body prayers of "depth."

At the end of the body prayer, include the awareness of the other aspects of your subconscious self, instinct, and inheritances from older species. Consider that the energy of the human interaction, especially between the sexes, may become so dominant that these other needs and voices may fade into the background. Resolve to keep the rest of nature's voices alive inside you.

As with the others, this body prayer ends with thanks for each voice and thanks for the Source behind the Universe.

BIRDS, CROCODILES, ECSTASY, LONGING Egyptian

Versions of love songs from approximately 1300–1100 B.C.E.

First lines of Adolf Erman translation: The beautiful songs of thy sister,
whom thine heart loveth, who cometh from the meadow. My beloved
brother, my heart aspireth to thy love. . . . I say to thee: "See what I do.
I have come and catch with my trap in mine hand."

> *The sister, who is the beloved of all hearts,*
> *begins these songs*
> *as she returns from the forest:*
>
> *"O my beloved, my brother,*
> *My heart runs after your love,*
> *You have brought everything to life!*
> *Come along and see what I am doing!*
> *I have just returned from setting a trap:*
> *the bait and snare are in my own hand.*
> *Birds of outrageous beauty and plumage*
> *are traveling from perfumed lands far away,*
> *anointed with myrrh and scents.*
> *One has come and taken my worm,*
> *its fragrance from Arabia, its talons full of raw amber:*
> *Come, let us release him together.*
> *When I am alone with you,*
> *I want you to hear the cry of*
> *that poor bird anointed with spices.*
> *How much better it will be if*
> *you are with me when I prepare the trap.*
> *There's nothing better than going to the fields*
> *with the beloved!"*
>
> *The brother says:*
>
> *"My sister's love waits for me*
> *on the other side of a stream.*
> *A crocodile waits in the shallows.*
> *But when I go down into the water,*

when I wade through the current,
my heartbeat will master
the rhythm of the tide,
my feet will turn the waves to land.
My love for her steadies me—
it's my water magic!
As I see my sister coming toward me,
my heart dances
and my arms open to encircle her.
My sister comes to me!"

The sister says:

"The swallow is trying to distract me:
'It's dawn, aren't you coming to the forest?'
Bird—you will not disturb me today!
I have found my brother in his bed.
My heart is light today, for he told me:
'I will not go far—my hand is in yours—
and we will stroll together
through every beautiful place.'
He honors me,
he does not hurt my heart."

The brother says:

"I have not seen her for seven days
and now I am sick.
My body is heavy, I pass out easily.
If the chief doctor visits,
my heart isn't satisfied.
If the priests chant for me,
it's useless, their diagnosis is flawed.
Just tell me, 'Here she is!' and I'll revive:
her name picks me right up.
Letters from and to her restore my heart.
My sister is a better tonic than any prescription.
She means more to me than all the holy books.

If I see her, I start to recover.
If she throws me a glance, I get younger.
If she speaks to me, my strength returns.
When we embrace, all evil flees.
But I have not seen her for seven days!"

A Song About Love and Desire, Part 1 Hebrew

An expanded translation of the Song of Songs 8:1–5

Mî yîtenkâ ḳeâch lîy yônêq shaddêy 'imîy emtzaḳâ ba-chûtz eshâqkâ gam lo-
yâbûzû lîy. (1)

KJV: O that thou were as my brother, that sucked the breasts of my
mother! When I should find thee without, I would kiss thee; yea, I
should not be despised.

> *I want you added to my body,*
> *joined like an extension.*
> *I want you gifted to me like a baby cousin,*
> *attached and sucking at my breast—*
> *my field of abundance is enlarged by you.*
> *If I came to you outside—if we met in a field—*
> *I would overflow,*
> *I would give you something to drink.*
> *I would embrace and absorb you utterly.*
> *No one would rise above me*
> *and no one would look down on me.*

Enhâgkâ 'abîyakâ el-bêyth îmîy t'lamdênîy ashqkâ mîyayîn hâreqach mê-
'asîys rîmônîy. (2)

KJV: I would lead thee, and bring thee into my mother's house, who
would instruct me: I would cause thee to drink of spiced wine of the
juice of my pomegranate.

> *I would drive you on and lead you in,*
> *I would carry you away and cause you to enter.*
> *I would take possession of your will*
> *and bring you gradually, progressively*
> *farther inside—*
> *into the interior mansion of*
> *all my mothers and grandmothers,*
> *into the place where all the birthing happens.*
> *I would overflow for you with*
> *an abundance of spiced wine,*

the perfumed essence of my spirit,
the rarefied liquor of my intoxication.
I would possess you with spaciousness,
the melted wetness of my pomegranates,
the juice of those rising, expanding,
effervescing buds inside.

Shmô'lô tachat rô'shîy wi-y'mîynô t'chabqenîy. (3)

KJV: His left hand should be under my head, and his right hand should embrace me.

The north should be under my best part;
the south should make itself scarce,
embracing and draining into me:
The left submits to me, the right bursts me open.
I want to feel chaos beneath me,
prosperity clasping me, eternalized inside.

Hîshba'tîy ethkhem b'nôth yerûshâlâim mahtâ'irû w'mah-te'or'rû eth-hâ-
ahabâ ad shetechpâtz. (4)

KJV: I charge you, O daughters of Jerusalem, that ye stir not up, nor awake my love until he please.

Swear to me, daughters of Jerusalem!
Future sisters who revere peace,
let me captivate you with this insight:
The love that expands and spreads out
gradually, mysteriously, from a secret place,
that seeks to give rather than to possess,
should not be excited all at once, without awareness.
It should not be ignited without light,
aroused without clear sight or
stripped naked and fired on to
a complete loss of intelligence.
Not unless the depths of its foundation
are securely laid,

> *until it finds pleasure in bending*
> *and bowing to the wishes of the beloved.*

Mîy zô'at 'olâh mîn-hamîdbâr mîthrapeqeth 'al-dôdâh.
Tachath ha-tapôcha 'wôrartîykhâ shâmâh chîblathkhâ 'îmekhâ shâmâh
   chîblâh y'lâdathkhâ. (5)

KJV: Who is this that cometh up from the wilderness, leaning upon her
beloved? I raised thee up under the apple tree: there thy mother brought
thee forth: there she brought thee forth that bare thee.

> *Who is this, rising like a primal plant,*
> *growing with primordial energy,*
> *mounting the open spaces*
> *and grasslands that spread freely?*
> *Who is this restoring herself*
> *upon her beloved—*
> *leaning, resting, moving*
> *in a regenerating wave?*
> *Who is this mending*
> *the vessel of love she has chosen,*
> *healing the flower of her desire*
> *like a medicine,*
> *like a redemption of the moment?*
>
> *I first aroused you below the apple tree,*
> *I blinded you down in the chamber of dark fruit.*
> *Inside there I astonished and desolated you—*
> *within the light of that dark, fecund place.*
> *Inside there, you were linked to the ancestress.*
> *Inside there, you were brought forth in struggle*
> *by all the women who have carried on life.*

Body Prayer: Fire and Light

For textual notes on words translated but not included in this body prayer, please see the notes at the end of this chapter.

In verse 1, the word *eshâqkâ,* usually translated "I would kiss thee," may also mean to possess, be attached to, join in pleasure or delight, give something to drink or overflow. A different form of the word returns in verse 2 as *ashqkâ,* usually translated "cause thee to drink." It may also mean to cause to overflow or give abundantly and relates to both amorous desire and the inclination of things to seek and join. In the Native Middle Eastern tradition, this word represents the archetype of the desire of particles in the universe to be bonded or assert their connection of communion. The same Semitic word roots appear later in a sacred phrase in the Sufi tradition, *'ishq Allah:* The desire of the universe to come together, including the desire of sexual love, is also a name of the One Being.

In verse 4, the phrase *mahtâ'iru w'mahte'orrû,* usually translated "stir not up nor awake," both come from the same root ʿWHR, which points to a blind passion, an inner ardor and fire that produces disorder and leads to the loss of light and rational intelligence. It also points to nakedness or naked skin. The word *ahabâ* points to a mysterious force of life-giving love or friendship, which grows gradually from the inside and then spreads out to others. It expands from a desire to have to a desire to share itself unselfishly. The roots of this word also appear later in another Arabic sacred phrase: *ma'abud Allah* (about which more later). The word *shetechpâtz,* usually translated "until he pleases," could better be translated "until it chooses" or "until its foundations and depths are securely laid." The roots of the word also point to bending and bowing, to seeking the pleasure or desire of another.

Heart Awareness

When making love, allow the sense of simple contact mentioned in the last chapter to sensitize your connection to your partner. Allow the awareness in the heart, the depths of the love, to keep the light in the fire, the vision in the passion. Allow the feeling of the heart to spread throughout the whole body. When the foundations are laid, and there is strength at the bottom, love bends to the wishes of the beloved. Then the blinding fire of desire will find its own right moment. You will be linked to the ancient and sacred healing power of love and passion. These moments should not be assumed as a right but valued as an astonishing grace; they can be prepared for but not demanded.

A Prayer for Seed, Bread, and Water   Sumerian

A version of a hymn of Inanna and Dumuzi, third millennium B.C.E.

First lines of S. N. Kramer translation: Oh, wild bull, "eye" of the land,
I would fulfill all its needs, Would make its lord carry out justice in the
princely house.

> *Inanna says:*
> *Wild bull—pulsing, single-eye of the whole land!*
> *I want to fulfill all your needs:*
> *I want to force your master to wage justice*
>   *in the royal place inside.*
> *Leave no voice unheard,*
>   *leave nothing undone!*
> *I want to make your seed grow*
>   *to fullness in my mansion.*
>
> *Dumuzi says:*
> *Inanna, your breast is an open field,*
>   *your wide open spaces gush with greenery*
>   *like a freely spreading meadow flowing with grain.*
> *Your deep waters pour down on me*
>   *like bread from the source.*
> *Water flowing and flowing,*
>   *bread and understanding from on high.*
> *Release the flood for its desired goal;*
>   *I will drink it all from you.*

BODY PRAYER: CALL AND RESPONSE

Sumer was located in the extreme southeast of what is now Iraq. As a political force, its greatest impact lasted from approximately 3100 to 2100 B.C.E., although its science, economics, political organization, and religion continued to influence the Middle East for a much longer time.

Inanna and Dumuzi are the archetypal lovers of the Middle East. Their passionate love and separation, including Dumuzi's death and (sometimes) rebirth, influence later myths like that of Ast and Usari (Isis and Osiris). As we have already seen, Inanna was also identified with creation and green growth; Dumuzi was identified with herds and shepherding. Their sacred marriage united these two modes of living, as well as the relationships to nature that they represented. This small portion of a much longer hymn would have been chanted as part of a sacred marriage ceremony.

Sound and Embodiment

Some of the oldest chants of humanity involve call and response between two attracting but differing energies. As differences are clearly felt—in voice, tone, and atmosphere—each "pole" of the battery, so to speak, is cleared of corrosion and better able to connect with the other. This process can take place within a person, in the subconscious soul-self, as well as between people. Such old responsive chants can lead us beyond stereotypes of male and female since they work above and beyond mental conceptions. They can also open a doorway of feeling to earlier, simpler human responsiveness, when sexuality and eroticism were not commercialized and exploited as a way to sell, manipulate, and control.

Try chanting the names Innânâ and Dumûzî on one note and begin to hear them as a call and response between the female and male aspects of yourself. Begin softly, directing the sound inside. At some point, a melody may also appear if you are able to lose yourself in the process. A similar chant uses the names of Innana and Dumuzi's Egyptian counterparts, Ast Amentî (Isis in the Underworld, searching for Osiris) and Usarî Nepra (Osiris in the grain, waiting for rebirth). Both forces meet in the full moon—Aâh—which becomes a mutual name as they unite. The full form of the chant (which can be spoken or sung with an improvised melody) is:

> Ast Amentî, Ast Amentî, Ast Amentî, Ast Amentî, Ast Aâh!
> Usarî Nepra, Usarî Nepra, Usarî Nepra, Usarî Aâh!
> Ast Usarî, Ast Usarî, Ast Usarî, Ast Aâh!

As the Cosmos Opens and Closes   Aramaic

An expanded translation of Matthew 7:7 from the Peshitta version of the Gospels

Isho'a said:

Shalu wa nethihbw l'khôn. (A)
B'uhw wa theshkhûn. (B)
Qôshw wa nethphta'ch l'khôn. (C)

KJV: Ask, and it shall be given you; seek, and ye shall find; knock, and it
shall be opened unto you.

> *Ask intensely—*
>> *like a straight line engraved toward*
>> *the object you want;*
> *pray with desire—*
>> *as though you interrogated your own soul about*
>> *its deepest, most hidden longings;*
> *and you will*
> *receive expansively—*
>> *not only what your desire asked,*
>> *but where the elemental breath led you—*
>> *love's doorstep, the place where you*
> *bear fruit*
>> *and become part of the universe's*
>> *power of generation and sympathy.* (A)

> *Search anxiously—*
>> *from the interior of your desire*
>> *to its outer embodiment—*
>> *let the inner gnawing and boiling lead you to*
> *act passionately—*
>> *no matter how material or gross*
>> *your goal seems at first;*
> *and you will*
> *find fulfillment*
>> *of the body's drive to accomplish its purpose*
>> *and see its destiny.*

Like a spring unbound, you will
  gain the force
  of profound stillness after an effort—
  the earth's power to grow anew each season. (B)

Knock innocently—
  as if you were driving a tent stake or
  striking one clear note, never heard before.
Create enough space within
  to receive the force you release;
  hollow yourself—
  purified of hidden hopes and fears,
and it shall be
opened easily—
  a natural response to space created,
  part of the contraction and expansion
  of the universe;
and penetrated smoothly—
  as the cosmos opens and closes
  around your words of satisfied desire. (C)

BODY PRAYER: LOVE'S DOORSTEP

This expanded translation uses many of the multiple meanings of Jesus' Aramaic words to reveal the depths behind their apparent simplicity. The word *shalu,* usually translated as "ask," may also mean to pray intensely or to interrogate. The roots point to a stroke that unites or a straight line traced from one object to another. The word *nethîhbw,* usually translated "receive," also refers to the action of bearing fruit from an inner generative force, the same mysterious, growing love and sympathy (related to the Hebrew word *ahaba*) that we encountered in the Song of Songs. It is a force that leads the desire of attraction to find its origin in something much larger, the Source of Love.

In the next phrase, the word *b'uhw,* usually translated "seek," refers to an anxious searching or inquiry, one that figuratively boils over with impatience. It is an interior action that seeks to complete itself in a material sense. The word *theshkhûn,* usually translated "find," refers to nature's power of regeneration, to the embodied form of the sympathetic fire (ASH), which we have encountered many times previously. Here the action, which begins by looking outward, finds stillness and fulfillment through connection with what is behind appearances, the inner fire of life in all beings. One of the roots points to the image of a force that reaches stillness after being uncoiled or unbound.

In the last phrase, the word *qôshw,* usually translated "knock," may also mean to pitch a tent or to strike the strings of a musical instrument. The roots point to a sense of innocence, a willingness to be a beginner. They also point to a spacious, unconfused state inside that allows any decision made, action taken, or note struck to be done with simplicity as well as strength. The word *nethphtach,* usually translated "opened," is related to the one we encountered in chapter 5 as a word of healing.

Simple Presence

When overcome with a desire or need to take an action, return to a place of simple presence. Focus the feeling of the breath on all the sensations that arise, and follow them to their source. This may require sorting through layers of reactions and impressions from previous, similar situations. Stay with the sensation of breathing and the awareness of all the pulsations of the body and simply notice where your attention wants to stick or to skitter away.

A more difficult practice is this: With eyes open, following a goal, desiring, passionately engaged, leave space inside for the response of the Universe. Allow what is real and from the heart to separate from what is compulsive and habitual. Follow the real.

HER EYEBROWS HAVE
KIDNAPPED MY HEART Persian

From the odes of the thirteenth-century Sufi poet Sa'adi of Shiraz

The first breath of spring!
But do I smell a garden or
the aroma of two friends meeting?
Like calligraphy, which transports
our eyes from thought to beauty,
her eyebrows have kidnapped my heart.
Bird! My heart snared you once.
Why not return to nest voluntarily?

Nightly the candle and I both melt,
but my fire burns within.
All my focus is on road noises,
my eyes linger on the doorstep.
While the call to prayer resounds,
I hear only the caravan's bell.
Even if you hate me, return—
that would be some kind of relationship!

Love has strong-armed my patience—
my writing hand trembles!
When lovers separate,
soul and body do too.
Sa'adi, moaning, is your security
for this proposed contract of love:
Fire consumes my reed pen,
the ink you see here is smoke.

CUPS AND WINE   Persian

From the fourteenth-century Sufi poet Hafiz

You there, carrying that cup!
Fill it with the joy of youth—
bring me another cup of the wine of ecstasy.
Bring me medicine for the disease of love—
bring pure passionate intoxication,
the remedy of young and old.

Musician! Don't whine to me about the wheel of time—
it turned this way and not that for you.
Quiet! Just touch the strings in peace.
Too much wisdom is boring:
Let's bring the noose of wine for its neck.

When the rose starts to fade, say "Let it go!"
and drink the present moment, like the rose does.
If the dove's coo has vanished, who cares—
we can make music with the wine jug!

The sun is the wine, the moon is the cup:
Pour the sun into the moon if you want to be filled.
Drinking such wine can be good or bad—
drink anyway!

If you can't see the beloved's face except in dreams,
then what's wrong with a little sleep?
More cups of wine! Keep them coming for Hafiz:
Whether it's sin or salvation—keep pouring!

BODY PRAYER: SACRED DESIRE, SACRED LOVE

Sometimes it's difficult to tell desire from love. In these moments, it might be well to remember that both have addresses that lead to the doorstep of the One Being. A Sufi practice that works with this understanding is *'ishq Allah ma'abûd lillah.* As mentioned earlier, *'ishq* is based on the passionate desire of all particles in the universe to join, possess, or embrace one another. On earth this force is called gravity. It includes even the most blind amorous desire as well as physical coupling.

Ma'abûd is a complex word made up of a number of older Semitic roots compressed: M at the beginning indicates the means by which something happens or the embodiment of an action. AUB is love acting from the inside out or the person of the lover. AUD is love acting from the outside in, or the person of the beloved. Related to both of these last two is the later compound Arabic root ABD, to serve, worship, adore, or venerate, which we encountered earlier in Sura Fateha. The phrase *ma'abûd Allah* points to a quality of the One Being that is a nondualistic type of love, dependent not only on one's own feeling being projected outward but also on following the desire of the beloved and being able to receive love into the deepest part of the self. It is love and service combined. The variation of the phrase, *ma'abûd lillah,* means that everywhere this love appears it is not only *of* the One but *for* the One—that is, it returns to praise the Source.

Sound and Embodiment

Begin with relaxed breathing, felt in the area of the heart, and breathe the sound of the phrase. The first sound of *'ishq* is one not present in English—a bit like the diphthong "ah-ee" but pronounced faster and farther back in the throat, where the final *q* is clearly felt, allowing the sound to enter the heart deeply. The second *a* in *ma'abûd* is the same as the first in *'ishq* but is a bit less intense because of its placement. Both phrases may be repeated softly together in the heart: *'ishq Allah ma'abûd lillah.* After a few minutes simply breathe the phrase, noticing its resonance in both body sensation and emotions.

TEXTUAL NOTES

1. *Birds, Crocodiles, Ecstasy, Longing.* Versions based on Papyrus Harris 500 (British Museum 10060, recto iv 1–7, recto v 6–8), Cairo Ostracon 25218, lines 6–10 and Papyrus Beatty I, verso C iv 6–v 2 with literal translations by Adolf Erman (1927, pp. 243–48) and John A. Wilson as contained in the collection of James B. Pritchard (1955, pp. 467–69).

2. *A Song About Love and Desire, Song of Songs 8:1–5.* In verse 1, the word *yîtenkâ,* usually translated as "brother," may also mean a near relation, cousin, or friend. More figuratively it means anything added or joined to oneself as an extension that becomes part of one's identity. All the images in the first part of this passage play with suggestions around this theme. The word *yoneq* may mean a sucking child, or any young, tender shoot attached to the mother plant. It is related to the word *neqeba,* which we encountered just before in Genesis. The word *sheddêy,* usually translated "breasts," also refers to the fertility of nature as it displays itself in fields or mounds of abundance.

The words *imîy emtzakâ,* usually translated "when I should find thee," can also mean "if I should come to you or discover you." There is a near pun here with *mâtzâh,* which means to suck out and empty of moisture or milk. The word *ba-chûtz,* usually translated "outside," may also mean in a field or in nature. *Gam* means "together," "also," or "even."

The phrase *lo-yâbûzû lîy,* usually translated "I should not be despised," points to an action of rising above someone either physically or otherwise as humiliation, disdain, or scorn.

In verse 2, the word *enhâgkâ,* usually translated "lead thee," may also mean to drive on or forward, to lead by taking possession of the will of someone. It also means a sigh. The word *abîyakâ,* usually translated "bring thee," also means to go in, lead in, enter, or cause to come in. The roots point to a gradual, progressive action of going and coming. *Bêyth,* usually translated as "house," may also mean palace, tent, or any dwelling, receptacle, or interior space. The word *t'lamdênîy,* usually translated as "who would instruct me," refers more to bearing children and giving birth.

The phrase *mîyayîn hâreqach,* usually translated "spiced wine" (and related to the phrase used in Proverbs 9:2), also refers to the essence of spiritual intoxication and power (*yayîn*) that is rarefied, spacious, attenuated (*reqach*—related to the word we encountered in Genesis for the spaciousness of the primeval void). The word *mê'asîys,* usually translated "juice," also refers to anything melted, dissolved, flowing, wet. *Mesech* is also another Hebrew word for mixed or spiced wine. The word *rîmônîy,* usually translated "pomegranate(s)," points through its roots to an action that dilates, rises, expands, and effervesces.

In verse 3, the words *shmôlô* and *y'mîynô,* usually translated as "left hand" and "right hand," may also simply be translated "left" and "right" (a hand is not explicitly mentioned) or as north and south. The root of *shmôlô* points to putting things in disorder or chaos and to letting go or rejoicing. The root of *y'mîynô* points to accumulating things and prosperity. The word *rôshîy,* usually translated as "head," may also mean the beginning or origin (related to the word in Genesis 1:1), the best or leading part, or the main acting principle. The root points to the center at the middle of a circle. *Chabqenîy,* usually translated "embrace," may also mean to clasp, to hide or conceal oneself, to cleave or to burst open. The roots of this word are related to one of the words for love (*ahabâ*—used in the next verse): an eternal life force of existence that grows and bears fruit from a hidden or secret place inside.

In verse 4, the word *hîshba'tîy,* usually translated "charge you," may also mean to swear or confirm with an oath, or to captivate. The phrase *b'nôth yerûshâlâim,* usually translated "daughters of Jerusalem," also has other layers of meaning. *B'nôth* may be any child, future descendant, or pupil. It is linked to the word for the embodiment of interior intelligence (*bîna*), which we encountered earlier in Proverbs. Besides being the name of the city, *yerûshâlâim* also points to the fear of or respect for the flow of peace or harmony.

In verse 5, the word *'olâh,* translated in the King James Version as "cometh up," may refer to any action of ascending, mounting, rising, or being lifted up, to foliage or leaves that rise in the same way. The word *mîdbâr,* usually translated as "wilderness," also refers to any open space of grassland or pasture that spreads without restriction. *Mîthrapeqeth,* usually translated as "leaning upon," can also mean to rest, to restore or heal, to mend or recover. The roots point to a regenerating movement that acts as a medicine or remedy. The word *dôdâh,* usually translated "beloved," can also mean a chosen vessel of love or a flower.

The phrase *tachath ha-taphôcha,* usually translated "under the apple tree," may also be translated as below, down in, or under the wedding chamber or the boundary of glory. The roots of the word for apple tree are related to those for splendor, beauty, or glory (*tipharah*). The word *'wôrartîykhâ,* translated in the King James Version as "raised thee up," is the same word mentioned in verse 4, which means to arouse, excite, or inflame with blinding passion. *Shâmâh,* usually translated "there," carries more the sense "within," "inside there," and, more emphatically, "in that very place." It is related to the word that means to astonish or desolate. *Chîblathkhâ,* translated "brought thee forth," also means to bind or link, to labor in childbirth, to bring forth with pain, to destroy or ravage.

3. *A Prayer for Seed, Bread, and Water.* The literal translation on which my version is based is from S. N. Kramer as contained in J. B. Pritchard's collection (1955, p. 642).

4. *Her Eyebrows Have Kidnapped My Heart.* This version is based on selections from the Odes of Sa'adi from a literal translation of the Persian by R. M. Rehder in James Kritzeck's collection (1964, p. 236).

5. *Cups and Wine.* This version is based on number 72 from "Ghazals from the Divan of Hafiz," translated by Justin Huntly McCarthy (unpublished manuscript), and by H. Wilberforce Clarke (1891).

Chapter Eleven

LOVE AND DEATH

The desire of the Universe to pursue communion leads to various types of sacrifice—willing and unwilling—including the acts of
eating and being eaten. Ultimately, love and
death prove to be forces that are more interwoven than our culture wishes to acknowledge. The denial of death splits the modern
psyche. Simple presence heals the split
between love and death and provides a
refuge of creative peace. Deep bonding with
another invokes the death of who we thought
we were and the birth of something new.

Eating and Being Eaten —
Day Six, Part 3   Hebrew

An expanded translation of Genesis 1:29–31

*Wa-îâomer Elohîm hinneh nathathî lakhem ath-kol-hesheb zoreha zera âsher
   hal-phenêi khol-ha-âretz w'ath-kol ha-hatz âsher-b'ô pherî hetz zoreha
   zerah lakhem îhîeh la-âkhelah. (29)*
*W'l-khol-haîah ha-âretz w'l-khol-hôph ha-shamaîm w'lkhol-romesh hal-ha-
   âretz âsher b'ô nephesh hâiah ath-khol îerek hesheb lâkhela wa-îhî-
   khen. (30)*
*Wa-îara Elohîm ath-kol-âsher 'hshâh w'hinhêh-tôb mâôd wa-îhî-hereb wa-
   îhî-boker îôm-ha-shîshî. (31)*

KJV: And God said, Behold, I have given you every herb bearing seed,
which is upon the face of all the earth, and every tree, in the which is the
fruit of a tree yielding seed; to you it shall be for meat. (29) And to every
beast of the earth, and to every fowl of the air, and to every thing that
creepeth upon the earth, wherein there is life, I have given every green
herb for meat, and it was so. (30) And God saw every thing that he had
made, and, behold, it was very good. And the evening and the morning
were the sixth day. (31)

> [In order for the Universe's desire for the human to take
> shape, the short life span of various beings had to be
> extended: Eating and being eaten were instituted. This intro-
> duction of archetypal bread, food, or understanding (*lakhem*)
> meant that one being could assimilate the interior wisdom
> (*hokhmah*) of another in a tangible form. One being could
> pass on bundles of energy and understanding to another so
> that the desire for communion in the Universe would con-
> tinue to unfold.]

> As understanding and nourishment for the developing
> human self, the Universe offered the essence of *personality*—
> the changing melody of a being. This includes all fragile, new
> desires to produce, which bear strange and lavish experiments
> of unfolding diversity and contain the fire of life. It also fed
> the human consciousness with the essence of *character*—the
> more stable rhythm of a being. This includes a stronger capa-
> bility to sense, organize, and remember experience that can,

by being more reliable, raise bonded offspring, its own children. The essence of character also contains the fire of life and can produce seeds of unfolding diversity. (29)

To the remainder of the experiments in individuality, which all had their own living subconscious soul-self, including the quick instinctual selves and slower reptilian selves, the Universe fed only personality, new desires, and mutations. They could not eat, or assimilate for their understanding, the character of another being. (30)

While these developments were not completely balanced, the Universe recognized that to pursue a new direction made a completely balanced and ripe existence impossible. A fire had been lit, and the smoke was rising. Choices had been made that had to run their course. The developments were as close to relative unity as possible, that is, ripe for the moment.

Once over and back again, the wheel turned once more. This activity marked the sixth period of the supremely lucid activity by the Universe. (31)

BODY PRAYER:
EATING PERSONALITY AND CHARACTER

The developing human self (which was not yet embodied and wouldn't be until later in chapter 2 of Genesis) could assimilate the personality and character of other beings—both their new tendencies and the stronger memories of what they had been. Other interior soul-selves could only assimilate the life-giving newness, the personality of other beings. While they might have their own character, they could not "eat" that of another and incorporate it into their psyche. In this way, the human came to contain the interior character of all previous selves, according to this cosmogony. For textual notes on words translated but not included in this body prayer, please see the notes at the end of this chapter.

Celebration of Eating and Being Eaten

When we eat, we bring into a bonded relationship with ourselves the interiority, diversity, and communion of other beings. The personality of the universe, lavish in diversity, presents itself to us as the subtle differences in each vegetable, grain, or bean. Wildness and freshness, not uniformity, are nature's gifts. Fruit results from a longer, more bonded relationship to time and space. So, of course, do any animal products. All willingly or unwillingly give their life to us in a very literal sense.

For one meal, consider the gifts of diversity and communion that you receive by eating. Sense the personality and character of each being that feeds you and how this adds to your own sense of being totally human—that is, aware of the consciousness of the entire universe. This may take a little preparation. For one thing, you may need to discover what you actually *are* eating. For another, you may have to slow down to actually sense—in the same way in which you have begun to sense your own body—the body that is feeding you. As with talking, the prescription to sensitize our awareness to what is giving us its life may also dictate a change from our normal pattern. Eating simpler and less for a period of retreat can reawaken this sensitivity.

Another question to consider is the one raised by Jesus earlier: For which future beings will our bodies be bread?

CREATE AGAIN THE RISING WATERS   Babylonian

From a liturgy of lament of Inanna for her lost lover, Dumuzi, approximately 1800–1200 B.C.E.

First lines of Stephen Langdon translation: The heavenly queen who
brings the verdure in abundance, Innina who brings the verdure in
abundance. The sprouting things abundance where . . .

Inanna, who is always bringing us
green life in plenty, asks her consort,
who has departed to the underworld
and sleeps in the buried grain:
"Where did it go—all the abundance,
all the springing fruit of nature?
Brother, who has taken it?
Where has it gone?"

Dumuzi replies:
"My queen, this springing plant,
vigorous and rising like a bull,
I will restore for you,
I will raise it for you.
All that was taken away
will return again."

Inanna still wants to know:
"But whom shall I embrace?
It is you, husband, that I must embrace!
With whom shall I join?
With the one who has risen
from the great flood,
from the whirlpool after death!
I want to join with you!
With the one who created life
in my holy chamber.
I want to embrace you!
Return, my plentiful one,
return and create again
the rising waters,
create again the rising waters.

A Song About Love and Desire, Part 2 Hebrew

An expanded translation of Song of Songs 8:6–7

Shîmê-nîy kha-chôthâm 'al-lîbekhâ kachôtâm 'al-zerô'ekhâ (6A)
kîy-'azâh kha-mâwêth 'ahbâh. (B)
Qâshâh khî-sh'aôl qînâh. (C)
R'shâpheyhâ rîshphêy aêsh shalhebethyâh. (D)

KJV: Set me as a seal upon thine heart, as a seal upon thine arm: (A) for love is strong as death; (B) jealousy is cruel as the grave: (C) the coals thereof are coals of fire, which hath a most vehement flame. (D)

> *Engrave my essence*
> *like a seal on your heart.*
> *Let my memory resound*
> *through the core of your being.*
> *Let me shine and rise*
> *through the center of your passion,*
> *through the fringes of your action,*
> *through every part of you that*
> *becomes a traveler and leaves home.*
> *Engrave me like a monogram*
> *that alerts everyone:*
> *"This is the sign of integrity:*
> *The strength of the cosmos*
> *hides underneath."* (A)

> *For this love that expands us*
> *boldly faces death's contraction.*
> *This mysterious self-effacing power—*
> *a double-strong, fully physical force—*
> *is as audacious and potent as*
> *anything with juice and sap,*
> *as fierce and violent as*
> *the withering, the decay*
> *that returns us all to sameness*
> *with the universal Self.* (B)

This blinding passion,
this jealous, envious desire that
possesses and redeems us,
this tense, compressed ardor
is as confusing and mixed up
as the world after physical death.
It binds us as closely as
the whirlpool of sensation and calm,
the abyss of delirium and peace,
the netherworld of questions and answers
which we find on the other side. (C)

It sparks like lightning.
It spreads like the plague.
It burns like the fire
inside the fire inside the fire.
It radiates like the inside
of the first moment of the cosmos. (D)

Mayîm rabîym lo' yûkhlû l'khabôth eth-hâ-ahbâh
w'nhârôth lo' yîsht'phûh (7A)
Im-yîtên aîsh eth-kâl-hôn bêythô bâ-ahabâh bôz yâbûzû lô. (B)

KJV: Many waters cannot quench love, neither can the floods drown it:
(A) if a man would give all the substance of his house for love, it would
utterly be condemned. (B)

Not the many waters of the Great Dark,
the collected possibilities of chaos . . .
Not the rivers of Directed Light,
the vibrating stream of purpose . . .
Neither can contain or put out,
neither can overwhelm or drown
the secret power of expansive love.
Not the great passive flow,
womb of all chance . . .
Not the great active flow,
story line of the Universe . . .

Neither can understand or control
a love that wants to share life
more than it wants to possess it. (A)

If the individual mind tried to rent this love . . .
If it offered in trade all its ideas and compulsions . . .
Even if it tried to extend its whole being to join it,
it would still be completely humiliated.
The self-centered mind can't rise so far:
a love that grows from the inside
would still look down on it. (B)

Body Prayer: Love and Death

For an explication of the Hebrew words that lead to this translation, please see the notes at the end of this chapter.

Heart Awareness

Return to the sensation of breathing and feeling the heart as a mirror. Allow it to be as clear as possible for the present moment. Then consciously bring into the mirror two reflections and impressions: your love for another and the death of your individual body consciousness. Allow the feeling, sensation, and energy raised by considering your own death to act upon the love you experience, and meet it directly. Allow it to whirl and to clarify everything that is not of the deepest aspect of love, *ahbâh*. What happens to possessive desire, compulsion, and envy? Some of these travelers with love may vanish, and some may not, but they will likely be more conscious after this practice than before. And that strengthens the love.

Thunder Speaks:
Mind Embraces All Opposites, Part 5   Coptic

Concluding version of sections of the gnostic text Thunder, Perfect Mind

First lines of George W. MacRae translation: Hear me, you hearers, and learn of my words, you who know me. I am the hearing that is attainable to everything.

The "I Am" Alone Exists

Listen, then, those who can hear.
Also you angels and those who
appear in visions or deliver messages,
you disembodied spirits still around.
The "I Am" of all these sayings alone exists.
I have no one who judges me:
I embrace all opposites.

You may fool yourselves with
contrary thoughts,
imaginations,
traditions,
theologies,
commentaries,
and legal precedents
by which you break contact with me.
It may be forgetfulness,
a passion to acquire, or
a temporary intoxication,
to all of which human beings
become addicted
until they sober up, lie down, and die.

But you will find me there too.
The way you have treated me is
the way you have treated your own soul.
And this time you will not die.

You will live with me until you learn.

BODY PRAYER: FACING THE "I AM"

In this last section of *Thunder,* the voice of Sacred Sense and Wisdom leads us to contemplate the passing of our physical bodies and what holds our many selves together. This event separates the two sides of the mirror, so to speak, but both sides will have changed by their experiences together. This practice takes its theme from the old Sufi expression "die before death."

Depths of the Self 9

After beginning with a remembrance of the Source, allow your breath and awareness to touch with love and respect all the aspects of your subconscious soul-self that you have experienced so far through these body prayers. In a breathing communion with each, bring in the awareness of the passing of your physical body. How does this help clarify for each voice what is really important? What is essential for it to fulfill its purpose as part of your consciousness at this time? What will remain after individuality separates? Don't force anything. This process must be undertaken in the context of deep and abiding love for all aspects of yourself and for their courage. Toward the end of the process, consider the saying of a modern Sufi of this century, Hazrat Inayat Khan: "It is death which dies, not life." End this body prayer with a breath of thanks for all aspects of self and for the Source.

RESURRECTION   Aramaic

A translation of John 11:25 from the Peshitta version of the Gospels

Isho'a said:

Inana nûchâmâ wa chayyê.

KJV: I am the resurrection and the life.

> *Simple Presence is the energized repose of individual wisdom.*
>
> *The depth of identity remains tranquil and vibrant after embodied sensation dissolves.*
>
> *The self conscious of its Self envelops us with warmth and life after death.*
>
> *The ego fully aware of its limitation creates a calm, creative refuge after a journey of agitation.*
>
> *The eye of the tornado of "I" offers peace and power when the small selves unravel.*
>
> *The germ of individuality's seed still grows in tranquillity after the plant dies.*
>
> *The "I am" resurrects our purpose in life when the small "I" fades away.*

BODY PRAYER:
THE PRESENCE OF IMPENDING ABSENCE

The word *nuchama,* usually translated as "resurrection," may also mean repose, rest, a dwelling, or abode of peace or tranquillity. Specifically the roots point to an experience of deep, creative peace that occurs after a long period of agitation (NUH) and that stems from the Sacred Sense or Holy Wisdom residing in the "I" of every being (CHMA).

Simple Presence

To be consciously in the presence of a dying person may be one of the most profound body prayers. When there is nothing more that can be done for a person except to be with her or him, then simple presence can become the gift of each to the other. An unraveling of the unfulfilled aspects of the self occurs, which clarifies, purifies, and enlightens the "I" of the person. The idea of death seems to die, leaving only what is eternal. This opportunity may be sought out, but if not, it comes sooner or later to everyone.

In the presence of death itself, or remembering the passage of a loved one, return to the place of simple presence, breathing with each feeling and sensation and following each to its Source. Find a communion of breath and presence with the other and meet in the repose of existence, the deep peace after the agitation of selves and desires has subsided. Meet in the center of Life.

LOVE AFTER DEATH   Persian

From The Diwan of Shams-i-Tabriz *by Mevlana Jelaluddin Rumi, thirteenth-century Anatolia*

This is Love: to fly without limits;
to cut through all the veils—now!
The first instant—to reject the life you knew.
The last step—to give up feet entirely.
To see right through materialism,
To refuse to see addiction as inevitable.

"My heart," I said, "be grateful that
you have entered the circle of lovers,
that you look beyond what the eye sees,
that you feel the heart's twists and turns.
My inner self—are you out of breath?
My heart—what's all this commotion?
My bird of a soul—speak in your own language:
I can understand what's behind your song."

My soul-self answered:
"I remember now:
I was in the pottery studio . . . clay and water are
        mixing . . .
a new body being made, which is . . .
another workshop, another studio, my new home . . .
then I feel fire, something's baking. . . . I am trying to
        escape!
But they grab me. When I can no longer resist,
they begin kneading and molding me into shape,
just like all the other lumps of clay."

TEXTUAL NOTES

1. *Eating and Being Eaten, Genesis 1:29–31.* The word *lakhem,* translated "meat" in the King James Version, is the same archetype of food, bread, understanding, the "daughter" of *Hokhmah,* that we encountered earlier. It is what can be assimilated by living beings directly into themselves from Sacred Sense or Holy Wisdom. It is not specifically an animal product as the King James Version renders it.

We also encountered the word *hesheb,* usually translated "herb," in verse 11. It also means all creations, work, labors, sacrifices, or offers of the whole vegetable world. The phrase *zoreha zera,* usually translated "bearing seed," was also previously considered in verse 11. These are the primal mutations, the departures from what had gone before that seem to be completely foreign or strange in comparison to what bore them. Here we encounter the principle of lavish diversity in the universe: no two blades of grass are alike—one could not be considered the "child" or "fruit" of another. In other words, the aspect of bondedness does not exist in these beings. As a quality of human consciousness, this could be compared with *personality,* that which can excel in diversity and newness without a hold on the past.

In comparison to this is the word *hetz* (also returning from verse 11), which is usually translated "tree." It means a growing substance that has stronger and harder boundaries and for this reason works to assemble elements into beings that express its essence more closely, either as fruit or children. Both are in a closer relationship of bonding with their "parents" than those beings that simply bear more newness. As a quality of human consciousness, this could be compared with *character,* that which remains more stable, which establishes a certain strength and reliability that makes more bonded relationships possible.

In verse 31 we find a departure from the usual formula that ends the other "days." Instead of finding everything *tôb* (ripe, appropriate for the moment), we find it *tôb mâôd,* which the King James Version translates as "very good." The word *mâôd* also means "as much as possible," "to a high degree," or "filling its whole extent." It points to an action or process that, once chosen from multiple possibilities, must follow its course. The roots also point to a smoking fire—the smoke cannot be called back.

2. *Create Again the Rising Waters.* This expanded version from the Sumerian and Akkadian transcriptions is based on the text transcribed,

transliterated, and literally translated by Stephen Langdon in his collection of Babylonian liturgies (1913, pp. 99–102).

The reference to the rising waters indicates that Dumuzi has descended beneath the flood of death and lies sleeping in the submerged grain. In this version of the story, Dumuzi descends into the underworld at the summer solstice and rises again at the winter solstice.

3. *A Song About Love and Desire, Part 2, Song of Songs 8:6–7.* The word *shîmên-nîy,* usually translated "set me," is derived from SHM, a root we have encountered many times previously. As a verb, it can mean to engrave, to vibrate or resound, to set as a memorial or outward sign. The word *chôthâm,* usually translated "seal," can also indicate the sign of an impression made or a symbol that declares that a much greater being or power is hidden and acting behind it. The word *lîbekhâ,* usually translated "heart," should also be familiar by now. It is the center of courage, passion, audacity, desire, affection, or sense. It is what always stays "at home," so to speak. The word *zerô'ekhâ,* usually translated as "arm," also means strength or power, anything that leaves the center, spreads, and disperses. It is what "leaves home," and everything which that implies.

The word *azâh,* usually translated "strong," also means fierce, violent, bold, and firm. The roots point to the sensuous, material force of nature that is doubled by being added to itself, through two beings becoming one. The word is also associated with the vigor and fertility of nature, especially of animals like goats. The later Arabic equivalent of this word also becomes one of the ninety-nine names of Unity—*Azîz.* The word *mâwêth,* usually translated "death," also means to wither, decay, and return through an action of reciprocity to the sameness of universal existence from which a being came. We have previously encountered the word for love, *'ahbâh,* as the mysterious power that grows and unites from within, that wants to share itself more than possess something.

In the next phrase, the word *qâshâh,* usually translated "cruel," can also mean heavy, difficult, confusing, obstinate, hardened, and inextricable. The word *sh'aol,* usually translated "grave," also means the netherworld, the realm of the dead, the depths or abyss. Its roots point to a whirlpool, a place where calm and delirium alternate, as well as interrogating and answering questions. The word *qînâh,* usually translated "jealousy," refers to yet another side of the desire for communion in the universe; it can be eager and envious, it wants to possess and redeem, it is a confusing, tense ardor that often travels with *ahbah,* the deeper love.

In the last phrase of verse 6, the words *r'shâpheyhâ rîshphêy,* usually translated "coals of fire," come from the same roots meaning a spark, flame, lightning, fever, or plague. They are related, in a more material sense, to the primordial unfolding (RSH) in light and heat that began the cosmos. So is the next word *aêsh,* not translated in the King James Version, which refers to the fire as a growing, energizing life force in every living being. Finally, yet another side of this image is shown in *shalhebethyâh,* usually translated "flame." From its roots this word points to the radiance and fire that is contained inside any form and that was contained in the accommodation before the fire that began the cosmos.

In verse 7, the word *mayîm,* usually translated "waters," also directly points to the primal waters of flow that we encountered previously. The word *rabîym,* usually translated as "many," can also mean great, abundant, strong, or sufficient. The phrase *yûkhlû l'khabôth,* usually translated "quench," means to comprehend, apprehend, prevail over, or assimilate something to the extent that it is restrained, contained, repressed, or extinguished. *Ahbâh* again represents the deeper aspect of love. *Nhârôth,* usually translated "floods," refers to a flow different from *mayîm:* It is a stream, river, or current of light, that which guides, shines, and enlightens in a direct path. The word *sht'phûh,* usually translated "drown," can also mean to pour out abundantly, overflow, wash away, overwhelm, or persist without stopping.

In the final part of the verse, the word *yîtên,* usually translated "give," can also mean hire, as in renting a dwelling. The word *aîsh,* usually translated "man," actually refers more exactly to the intellectual individuality and possessions of a human being. The word *adam,* which we encountered in Genesis, means the archetype or principle of humanness; it includes both male and female. The word *aîsh* combines the roots AI and ASH, an individual center that grows, grasps, and apprehends for itself.

4. *Thunder Speaks, Part 5.* This version is also based on the previous literal translations from the Coptic of George W. MacRae (1979, pp. 231–55) and Bentley Layton (1987, pp. 77–85).

5. *Love After Death.* This version is based on the literal translation of number 35 in the collection by R. A. Nicholson (1898, pp. 136–39).

Chapter Twelve

HEALING —
A REMEMBRANCE
OF THE VOID

Encounters with love and death lead to the
ultimate communion: a return to and
remembrance of how it all began—the original state of the cosmos. In this remembrance,
we find a sense of honor for what has gone
before. We also find awe for the powers of
recovery, regeneration, and healing in all
their forms. This remembrance of the void
can also put into perspective how we think
about "work" and "rest," as well as how we
think about our own individual goals and
their fulfillment. Ultimately there is nothing
more that words can clarify. We know only
what we experience when we encounter the
Friend behind and within all friends.

Facing Future, Embracing Past—
Day Seven, Part 1   Hebrew

An expanded translation of Genesis 2:1–3

Wa-îkhuloû ha-shamaîm w'ha-âretz w'khol-tzbâ'am. (1)
*Wa-îkhal Elohîm ba-îom ha-shebîhî melakheth-ô âsher hasah waîsheboth
    ba-îôm ha-shebîhî mi-khol milâkheth-ô âsher hashah.* (2)
*Wa-îbarekh Elohîm ath-îôm ha-shebîhî w-îqaddesh âoth-ô khi bô shabath
    mi-khol-melâkheth-ô âsher barâ Elohîm la-hashôth.* (3)*

KJV: Thus the heavens and the earth were finished, and all the host
of them. (1) And on the seventh day God ended his work which he had
made; and he rested on the seventh day from all his work which he
had made. (2) And God blessed the seventh day, and sanctified it:
because that in it he had rested from all his work which God created
and made. (3)

> By this time, the Universe's call from the future—the mag-
> netic "shall become"—had completely activated all of the
> basic wave and particle tendencies that it had drawn out of
> the primordial "was" in the beginning. All of the principal
> interactions were set, the tendencies were seeded, and the
> essential character and habits (not really "laws") of the Uni-
> verse were established. Of course, the unexpected could
> always happen. One of the prime character traits the Universe
> had established so far was expectancy and the desire to fulfill
> and complete itself through the creative dreams of every
> being. (1)
>
> During the seventh and consummating period of its
> intelligent action, the Universe realized the fulfillment of part
> of its own dream. The establishment of ruling principles and
> visions was complete. The story line of the Universe, the
> direction of its own creative destiny, was fully initiated. A
> clear "I can!" had resounded from the heart of the Universe
> in response to the questioning void with which the whole
> process began. Nothing would return to the way it was, no
> matter what happened.
>
> Because this was so, the Universe permitted itself the
> most mysterious creative act of all. In addition to full engage-
> ment in the experiment of creative being and becoming,

which happened in the first six luminous periods, it also restored to itself the awareness of its own origins. When the Universe embraced what had been "before the beginning," something even more complete rippled through its being: empathy with everything that drops its form and returns to the other side of being, with all that "dies." (2)

The Universe again sent out a breath of compassion toward this new period of luminosity in which it remembered its own original state. This act of restoration, returning to Source, the Universe set aside as a pivotal principle. To clear space in the awareness and remember the primal "before" became central to the development of the further story of the cosmos, which previously was only a "what next?" The Universe recognized the essential role this focus on clearing space and touching the void now took and called all periods of restoration that commemorated it sacred (*kaddesh*). (3)

BODY PRAYER: THE ORIGINAL STATE

In verse 1, the word *îkhuloû,* usually translated "finished," means literally "shall become/were wholly finished." As we have encountered previously (as in the creation of light), this form of a verb indicates that,
through a progressive development, something has shifted from potential to action, that the future has activated a tendency in the here and
now, making it an accomplished fact. The Universe's "call of the future"
causes its story to unfold in a way that never exactly repeats itself. The
word *tzbâ'am,* usually translated "host," refers to an order or direction
that tends toward a purpose. It is the essence of a force or will that takes
on a certain character of movement to fulfill a goal, even if the specifics
of that movement have not yet unfolded.

In verse 2, the word *îkhal,* usually translated "ended," means more
specifically "completely activated" and is related to the word in verse 1.
The phrase *melakheth-ô âsher hasah*, translated by the King James Version as "his work which he had made," says more accurately a work,
composition, or creation (*hasah*) that embodies the primordial fire of life
(*âsher*) through the vision, ideals, ruling principles, and "I can"
(*melakheth*) of the cosmos. The word *îsheboth,* usually translated
"rested," means to restore itself or return to its original state or point of
departure (SHUB) in a way that completes and consummates something
with sympathy (TH). This word becomes the name for any period of
remembrance and return to the source: the *shabath,* or Sabbath.

For textual notes on words translated but not included in this body
prayer, please see the notes at the end of this chapter.

Celebration of the Day Before Creation

After completing a creative act or project, take some time to
breathe in a sense of peacefulness and accomplishment before going on
to something else. Feel a breath of fullness and completion in unison
with the breath of the universe, and bring into the mirror of your heart a
recollection of all the stages of work and effort right back to the original
inspiration. Then go back even before there was a vision or idea: What
was there? As you embrace the blessing of the original void, release the
form that the creation took and clear space to undertake the next step in
your own story.

This type of clearing and recollection can also be done at the end of
every day, week, or month. Consider the projects, relationships, and

actions that have come to fullness, as well as those that are yet incomplete in your being. Take some time to remember your own original state, as well as that of the universe, and allow this remembrance to revivify your energy and clarify what lies ahead. Sometimes you might feel a reluctance to let go of the past: Allow this recollection to honor what has gone before and your part in it. Make this period of remembrance your own Sabbath, a sacred space and time of renewal.

Many traditional melodies exist for the Hebrew sacred phrase *shalom havarim,* "peace to us." This *shalom* is not merely the "opposite" of war—it is a deeper peace, which really has no opposite and which asks us to remember the creative, full, ineffable silence with which the cosmos began. When we can recall this to our awareness, it is difficult to be in conflict with anyone.

The New Order: Everyone Breathes Like Everyone Else   Egyptian

A version of coffin texts from the Middle Kingdom, around 2000 B.C.E.

First lines of John A. Wilson version: The All-Lord says in the presence of those stilled from tumult on the journey of the court: "Pray, be prosperous in peace! I repeat for you four good deeds which my heart did for me in the midst of the serpent-coil, in order to still evil."

> *Radiance returns*
> *in the daily journey of the sun-boat,*
> *collecting the souls of the dead at twilight.*
> *The Radiant One interrupts the passengers,*
> *who are taking a rest*
> *in between the noise and stress*
> *of being in a physical body:*
>
> *"Please be calm—enjoy the peace!*
> *Let me tell you about four good things*
> *my own heart created for me*
> *when I was enmeshed in the struggles*
> *and strains of creating the world.*
>
> *"At the dawn of existence,*
> *I made the four winds so that*
> *everyone could breathe like everyone else.*
>
> *"I made the great flood that creates fertile earth,*
> *so that the poor might have the same rights as the rich.*
>
> *"I made every human being like its sister and brother.*
> *I did not give any orders for them to violate this principle:*
> *Their own hearts did that.*
>
> *"I made all human hearts able to remember death,*
> *so that they would honor those who had gone before.*
>
> *"From the One Radiant Essence came all the shining ones*
> *and human ones.*
> *The gods were my sweat, humans were my tears."*

Isaiah's Vision, Part 1 — Wings of Healing in Diversity's Temple Hebrew

An expanded translation of Isaiah 6:1–2

Wâ-'ereh 'et-Adônâi îsheb 'al-ķisê râm w'nîshâ w'shûlây-w m'lê'îym eth-ha-hêyķhâl. (1)

KJV: I saw the Lord sitting upon a throne, high and lifted up, and his train filled the temple.

> *Suddenly, I was struck by a ray of power,*
> *a vision of Adonai—*
> *that aspect of primeval cosmic Unity*
> *which emanates new life,*
> *which creates diversity and complexity,*
> *which gives and receives both*
> *unexpected gifts and the results they unfold.*

> *This Diversifying Universe appeared*
> *as if returned to its original state:*
> *the collection and meeting place of*
> *all straight lines and all curving spirals.*
> *At that pinnacle of reality*
> *all strong movements,*
> *expanding from a center*
> *like a ray filling space,*
> *united with*
> *all fragile movements*
> *spiraling around no center,*
> *carried away with themselves.*

> *A harmonious balance of*
> *these opposing energies clothed*
> *cosmic Diversity in power.*
> *The edge of the cloak*
> *woven by this dynamic peace*
> *filled space and time—*
> *it embraced and sheltered*
> *all individual beings.*

Within the sacred temple of Diversity,
all life gathered each moment in awe.

Shrâphîm 'ômdîym.
Mî'ma'al lô shêsh ḳ'nâphayîm shêsh ḳ'nâphayîm l'echâd bî-sh'tayîm
y'ḳhaseh phânây wû-bîsh'tayîm y'ḳhaseh raglây wû bîsh'tayîm y'ôphêph. (2)

KJV: Above it [the "throne"] stood the seraphims: each one had six
wings; with twain he covered his face, and with twain he covered his
feet, and with twain he did fly.

Around the original seat of Diversity
gathered all the healing powers of the cosmos,
those forces of regeneration and redemption
called seraphim or angels.

Each recovery power had six wings—
harmonious extensions from its core—
which could touch the inner soul-self of every being
like a mutual, interdependent skin.
These wings arose from the desire to embody
that created souls in the beginning.
Contact with this angelic skin
could remind a being of its source
and repair the illusion of separation.
Each two wings,
recalling the first split in the cosmos,
satisfied a particular need:

Two could transform the face and atmosphere—
the desire of the self to appear whole.
Their touch could return one's presence
to its original state.

Two could transform all motion and emotion,
whatever stirs and agitates the feeling self.
Their touch could reconnect all movement
to the unfolding wheel of celestial joy.

Two could transform the self's interior baggage,
burning away the superficial.
Their touch could renew the instincts
and cause a being to fly.

BODY PRAYER: THE GRACE OF WHAT'S NEEDED

This text, and others like it, was associated with an early Jewish mystical practice that centered on ascending to the *merkabah,* or throne-chariot of the One. Some of the noncanonical texts describe a paradoxical descent before one can ascend, a reference that has confused some scholars. For textual notes on words translated but not included in this body prayer, please see the notes at the end of this chapter.

In verse 2, the word *shrâphîm,* usually translated "seraphims," refers by its roots to all powers of healing, reparation, recovery, redemption, and regeneration, to the source of all medicine and remedies. This gift of the universe is the province of what we might call angels. Each healing power extended *shêsh k'nâphayîm,* usually translated "six wings." *Shesh* refers to a number that is in proportion, measure, or harmony with what is needed. *K'nâphayîm* can mean any extremity, edge, or border that, like a skin, extends and spreads out from the primal central force that defined the boundaries of all bodies or selves. The word is related to that for the soul-self, *nephesh.* The word *sh'tayîm,* usually translated "twain," also refers to that which leads to change and variation, to passing from one state to another, or to the initial divisions in the universe. The word *y'khaseh,* usually translated as "covered," can also mean to hide, clothe, conceal a fault and forgive, to fill in any gaps necessary. It is related to the word used for "throne," the place where all opposites are reconciled.

Depths of the Self 9

After beginning with a remembrance of the Source, allow your breath and awareness to touch with love and respect all the aspects of your subconscious soul-self that you have experienced so far through these body prayers. Allow each aspect of the self to express what it feels most in need of at the moment. Some may or may not be cooperative; if not, give them time. For those who do make a request, ask the help of all the healing and recovery powers of the cosmos to provide what is needed. Open to the possibility that these forces are present everywhere. Allow them to touch the presence, feelings, and sensations of each self.

If it feels appropriate in the moment, follow the healing powers back to the Source; catch hold of their wings . . . and fly, perhaps even to the sacred temple of Diversity. To conclude this body prayer, thank each aspect of the self, and thank the Source.

About Work and Rest Aramaic

An expanded translation of Matthew 11:28–29 from the Peshitta version of the Gospels

Isho'a said:

Tâw l'wâthî ḳ'lḳhôn layâ (28A)
wa shqîlay mâwblê (B)
wa inâ anyachḳhôn. (C)

KJV: Come unto me, all ye that labour (A) and are heavy laden (B), and
I will give you rest. (C)

> *Come to me,*
> *all of you, all of yourself,*
> *in your frenzied weariness,*
> *your movement without end,*
> *your action without purpose,*
> *not caring in your fatigue*
> *whether you live or die.* (A)

> *Come enmeshed by what you carry,*
> *the cargo taken on by your soul,*
> *the burdens you thought you desired,*
> *which have constantly swollen*
> *and now exhaust you.* (B)

> *Come like lovers to your first tryst:*
> *I will give you peace and*
> *renewal after constant stress:*
> *Your pendulum can pause*
> *between here and there,*
> *between being and not-being.* (C)

Sh'qôlw nîry wh'layḳhôn wa îlapw mêny (29A)
d'nyach inâ w'maḳhîḳh inâ blêby (B)
w'mishḳhîn antôn nyacha l'naphshâthḳhôn. (C)

KJV: Take my yoke upon you, and learn of me; (A) for I am meek and
lowly in heart: (B) and ye shall find rest unto your souls. (C)

Why not absorb yourself in my work—
here's newly plowed earth ready
for a crop of guidance and illumination.
Jump into the whirlpool of wisdom,
the impassioned spiral of understanding your self. (A)

Here's the peace you're looking for:
the softening of the heart's rigid
feelings and thoughts. (B)
In my way, you will find a
refuge of renewable energy
within the struggle and grasping
of your subconscious soul.
In my way, when you
wrestle for the knowledge of your Self,
the self you find finds rest. (C)

BODY PRAYER:
A REFUGE OF RENEWABLE ENERGY

Simple Presence with Depths of the Self

Return to the place of simple presence, breathing with each feeling
and sensation and following each to its Source. Allow the breath to
make a connection with the aspects of the subconscious self you have
experienced so far. Breathe in and out as much peace and simple presence as you are capable of breathing this moment, and allow this peace
to flood your *naphsha*. Sense the natural pause when the breath is either
all in or all out. In this instant of stillness, enter a deeper communion
with both your soul-self and the peace of existence from which it—and
all beings—arose.

Feel the breath as an ark of refuge on the sometimes troubled sea
of mind. The name *Noah* is derived from the same roots as *nyach,* the
peace of existence. Conclude this body prayer with thanks.

SPEAK UNITY'S NAME   Arabic

A meditation on the Holy Quran, Sura 112

Bismillâhir-rahmânir-rahîm.
Qul Hu-wallâhu 'ahad. (1)
'Allâhus-samad. (2)
Lam yalid wa lam yûlad. (3)
Wa lam yakul-la-Hû kufu-wan 'ahad. (4)

Mohammed Marmaduke Pickthall translation: Say: He is Allah, the One! (1) Allah, the eternally Besought of all! (2) He begotteth not nor was begotten. (3) And there is none comparable unto him. (4)

> *We begin in the name of Unity, from whose womb is born*
> *the Sun and Moon of Love.*
>
> *Speak Unity's Name.*
> *Support the Oneness of Existence.*
> *This sound, heard everywhere on the wind,*
> *combines the "yes" and "no" of being:*
> *all extending force toward a purpose*
> *and the entire abyss of nothingness.*
> *Say that every single and distinct object*
> *arose only from the passion of the One.* (1)
>
> *Ultimate Unity throughout the cosmos*
> *envelops and surrounds all dimensions,*
> *measurements, laws, and tendencies.*
> *It fulfills and completes all potentials that*
> *unfold in joy throughout the Universe.* (2)
>
> *Unity is the eternal Now—*
> *nothing is born from it and nothing produces it.*
> *It is the seed of both cause and effect.* (3)
>
> *There is no comparable existence.*
> *No metaphor, word, or sacred name*
> *can match or explain Universal Unity,*
> *the mysterious source of all of our*
> *personal and mutual dreams of being.* (4)

Body Prayer: The Mystery of Communion

The word *qul,* usually translated "say," also means to profess, teach, advocate, or support. Its roots point to the sound and voice of nature, especially that of the wind. The word *hu,* usually translated "he," relates to an older Semitic root pointing to the breath of existence that takes us from being to nothingness. This ending becomes defined as the masculine singular pronoun by the time Arabic is formalized as a language; it was not so earlier.

The word *Allah,* which we have seen in its various forms elsewhere, is directly related to its predecessors *Alaha* (Aramaic), *Elohîm* (Hebrew), and *Elat* (Old Canaanite). All are centered on the root EL or AL, which points to the oneness of existence. This word becomes used as the definite article (equivalent to our word *the*) to indicate that every individual and diverse being finds its distinct character in cosmic unity. In the seed root AL, one finds power with extensive movement that tends toward a purpose. The Aramaic and Arabic expressions also add the root LA, which refers to absolute nonexistence. It is movement without a goal, a line stretched out to infinity, to no-thingness. Even in the "no" of being, Unity exists.

The word *ahad,* usually translated "one," refers to every single, distinct object that is drawn or extracted from many. Its older compound roots refer to the passionate life and will in the universe (AH) which lead to the power of differentiation and diversity (AD). In other words, the Being and the Unity about which the sura is speaking is both the One and the one. The distinction between immanence and transcendence collapses at this point.

In the second verse, the word *samad,* translated by Pickthall as "eternally Besought," also means to defy, withstand, save, extend, supply whatever is needed or to fulfill the whole extent of any rules, customs, or measures. In verse 3, the words *yalid* and *yûlad,* Pickthall's "begotteth" and "begotten," are both based on the older Semitic root for bearing a child that we saw earlier in the Song of Songs. The roots point to an expansion of abundance born of division. The Unity we are talking about is not subject to such divisions: Everything is always connected and in communion.

In verse 4, the word pronounced *yakul* is spelled *yakun* and is based on the Semitic root for fixing, constituting, or grounding something in a body. According to the Quran, this is the word Unity spoke to create the cosmos. The phrase *lahu kufu,* usually translated "none comparable" or "none like," also means that nothing is equal, on a par, or equivalent. We may talk about Unity, the Universe Being, the One, or even God/God-dess, but these are only metaphors, place markers, signs pointing to a reality that is beyond philosophy, theology, mysticism, spirituality, and spiritual practice. No one owns it, no one can claim to understand it. But Oneness knows Oneness whenever and wherever its eyes and ears are open.

Sound and Embodiment

Both *ahad* and *samad* are included in the ninety-nine names of the One in the Sufi tradition. As with the other body prayers that use sound, begin by breathing the sound of each word with awareness centered in the heart. Then intone each name of the One a number of times with feeling still centered in the heart. Choose a note or tone that resonates best with your entire body. Traditionally the word *ya* (meaning "O"— used to address a person) would be added to the beginning of each phrase.

As you slowly intone "Ya Ah-hâd," connect in feeling and sound with each individual voice or self you may have experienced in these body prayers. Allow this sound to take you directly to the address of each aspect of the self and affirm its individuality as an expression of the desire of the entire cosmos. As much as possible, feel a connection of one to the One. After a few repetitions (perhaps eleven), intone "Ya Sâm-âd" and allow this sound to deliver from the One Being whatever is needed to fulfill the purpose of each aspect of being.

Then slowly alternate the sounds, "Ya Ah-hâd, Ya Sâm-âd," as you address the entire subconscious soul-self, the *nafs*. Finally, address your entire being, and feel its communion of one with the One. After some minutes, return to breathing both phrases, then release the sounds and breathe only with the feeling of each that remains. Follow the feeling and conclude with thanks for what was received.

Everyone Bows When the Friend Passes By   Persian

From the odes of the thirteenth-century Sufi poet Sa'adi of Shiraz

The world is greening—that suits me!
For everything has greened because of the Friend.
I love all worlds now since the Friend owns them.
Companions! Breathe in Christ's breath.
Wake up your dead hearts!
You will live again if the Friend breathes you.
Neither heaven nor the angels
own a truth that doesn't change.
But what you find in the core of
every human heart is from the Friend.
If my sweet one brings poison,

I am happy to consume it.
Pain and devotion come together.
Anyway, the Friend is also my medicine.
If the wound does not heal, all the better.
The Friend's glance relieves the rawness.
Is it wise to separate joy and sadness?
Bring wine! At least I know
my wound came from the Friend.

Rich, poor—it doesn't matter:
everyone bows when the Friend passes by.
Sa'adi, if the flood of longing washes out your house,
make your heart stronger.
The Friend will lay a new foundation,
which will last for eternity.

THE VISIT AND THE GIFT   Persian

Rendered from The Secret Rose Garden *by Sufi poet Mahmud Shabistari, thirteenth century*

At dawn, the moon,
like a creature of fantasy,
stole into my room
and woke me from some
lazy and unproductive sleep.
Her face quickly illuminated
the underside of my soul
and my own being stood
revealed in the naked light.
Sighing in wonder,
I faced my Self, which said:
"Your life so far has chased
the illusion of control:
You will not meet me on that path.
One flash of my glance
is worth a thousand years of piety."

Overcome by waste and loss,
my soul endarkened itself with shame.
But my moon-faced Self,
whose radiance equaled the sun,
filled a cup of Direct Experience
and urged me to drown my despair:
"No bouquet . . . no flavor . . .
but this wine can wash away
your being's whole historical library."

I finished the cup in one gulp,
and, intoxicated by its purity,
fell to the earth.
Since then I am not sure
whether I am here or not.
Neither sober nor drunk,
sometimes I feel the joy of
my soul's eyes looking through mine.

Other times I feel the curl of its hair
and my life bobs and weaves.
Sometimes, from sheer habit,
I'm back on the compost heap.
And sometimes,
when that glance finds me again,
I am back in the Rose Garden.

Textual Notes

1. *Facing Future, Embracing Past, Genesis 2:1–3.* In verse 3, the word *îbarekh,* usually translated "blessed," also means, as we have seen previously, to breathe with compassion, to invigorate with spirit. The word *îqaddesh,* usually translated "sanctified," points to setting apart or separating something for a specific purpose, to focusing or preparing the ground for something, and to establishing a central point, pivot, or motive upon which everything turns.

2. *The New Order: Everyone Breathes Like Everyone Else.* Version extracted from several Egyptian coffin texts (Cairo Museum 28083, 28085, and 28094) from literal translations by John A. Wilson in the collection of James B. Pritchard (1955, pp. 7–8) and J. H. Breasted (1933, p. 221).

3. *Wings of Healing in Diversity's Temple, Isaiah 6:1–2.* In verse 1, the word *'ereh,* usually translated "saw," can also refer to being impressed by a ray of power, particularly to a visionary state. The word *Adônâi,* usually translated "Lord," points through its roots to the elementary power of unity (A) that divides itself (DN) in order to give life and energy (I). The word *îsheb,* usually translated "sitting," is directly related to the same word we saw in Genesis: to return to its original state. The word *kisê,* usually translated "throne," can also mean the top, pinnacle, summation, or accumulation of everything or anything. *Râm,* usually translated "high," points to any straight movement that rises from a center and fills space in a very direct way. *Nîshâ,* usually translated "lifted up," points to any unstable, transient, whirling movement or to something that, because it is weak and unstable, needs to be carried and lifted.

The word *shîulâyw,* usually translated "train," refers to a being that is in equilibrium, with all parts in proportion and following harmonious laws, like the edge of a robe that follows the center from which movement arises. The word *m'lê'îym,* usually translated "filled," also means to overflow, satisfy, or complete. Images related to the roots of this word include setting a gemstone in its bezel so that it fits perfectly and consecrating a person in a holy office. The word *hêykhâl,* usually translated "temple," refers also to any place or way of doing things that assimilates power, that compresses life and causes it to come to fruition.

In verse 2, the word *'omdîym,* usually translated "above," can also mean gathered near, around, or in union with something. The word *mî'ma'al,* not translated in the King James Version, means to grow, extend, or be filled out with something, as through a natural development. The word *phânây,* usually translated as "face," also means the presence, countenance, atmosphere, or outer aspect of a being. By filling in what is necessary in their own beings, the recovery powers show how healing works.

The word *raglây,* usually translated "feet," also means all organs of motion and emotion, anything that moves a being (RG) and that connects with the orbiting, revolving movements in the whole cosmos. The word *whôphêph,* usually translated "fly," also refers to any rising, expanding, soaring movements, either inner or outer, that result from the instincts being enlightened, purified as if by fire, and cleansed of excess weight.

4. *About Work and Rest, Matthew 11:28–29.* In verse 28, the word *tâw,* usually translated "come," also carries the sense of lovers coming together for the first time. The word *layâ,* usually translated "labor," also means to be tired, weary, or exhausted. The phrase *shqîlay mâwblê,* usually translated "heavy laden," means more exactly to be enmeshed and enveloped by a desire (same root we encountered in the Song of Songs) that has turned out to be a burden, one that keeps swelling and expanding. *Anyachkhôn,* usually translated "give you rest," is another form of the same word we encountered in Jesus' "I am" saying in the last chapter: It is the repose of existence, a point of equilibrium, a rest and tranquillity after constant agitation. It is also a peace that moves toward a goal, one of guidance and health.

In verse 29, Jesus continues with a play on the words of the previous verse. Instead of being enmeshed in burdens created by a desire to possess something, he recommends absorbing oneself in *nîry,* a word usually translated "yoke" but that also means any labor and points to images of illumination and light (related to *îâor*) as well as of a newly plowed field ready for planting. The word *îlapw,* usually translated "learn," continues the image; the roots point to a wheel or vortex of mental energy that seeks to comprehend or understand existence.

The expression *makhîkh ina blêby,* usually translated "lowly in heart," is an Aramaic idiom that means to soften inner rigidities and blocks to feeling. A related phrase is used in the third Beatitude in Aramaic (Matthew 5:5). The word *naphshâthkhôn,* usually translated "your souls," is another form of the word *naphsha,* the subconscious soul-self, which we explored in part 2.

5. *Everyone Bows When the Friend Passes By.* This version is based on selections from the odes of Sa'adi from a literal translation of the Persian by R. M. Rehder in James Kritzeck's collection (1964, pp. 237).

6. *The Visit and the Gift.* This version is based on the previous literal translations from the Persian by Florence Lederer (1920) and E. H. Whinfield (1880).

Chapter Thirteen

ENDINGS —
PRAISE, THANKS,
AND BLESSING

All journeys of diversity, interiority, and communion end by looking backward and forward at the same time. Much has happened, much will happen. To realize ourselves as part of a living, sacred universe may be the most important gift of this or any spiritual tradition. To cultivate the quality of devotion may be the greatest antidote to the modern abuse of the natural world and of humans by one another. The Native Middle Eastern tradition points toward a way to pray, praise, thank, and bless that arises from our own wordless experience and does not depend on repeating any formula. In fact nothing is ever really repeated. If we are awake, we may catch the scent of the rose, we may hear the caravan's bell of departure.

A New Name for the Universe Being —
Day Seven, Part 2   Hebrew

An expanded translation of Genesis 2:4

*Elleh thô-ledôth ha-shamaîm w'ha-âretz b'hib-barâ'm b-îôm hashôth IHφH
Elohîm aretz w'shamaîm.*

KJV: These are the generations of the heavens and of the earth when
they were created, in the day that the Lord God made the earth and the
heaven.

The whole story narrated so far is a sign or symbol, a family
register for the way in which everything in wave and particle
has come about to satisfy a particular purpose. The Universe
has unfolded this story line in what may be seen as only one
luminous, intelligent activity, one Cosmic Day from *then*
until *now*.

During this Day, the Universe has been irresistibly
inclined to realize itself in its depths as a Being that simultaneously was, is, and will be. It is not a matter only of the past
affecting the future but, as we have seen, of the future affecting the past and both affecting the present moment. As a sign
of this new and ongoing awareness, the Universe Being (Elohîm) realized and named a new quality of its own essence:

*Life Squared (HH)
interpenetrated with both
its own Power to Manifest (I)
as well as the awareness of its own
original Being and Nothingness (φ):
IHφH.*

*And this Being of Beings,
another name for Unity,
continues to interpenetrate
the foundations of our existence—
all waves, all particles—
as the Seventh Day continues.*

Body Prayer: One Day at a Time

The Hebrew word *thô-ledôth,* usually translated "generations," can also mean origin, descent, lineage, family register, or genealogy. From its double set of roots, it points to a sign, symbol, hieroglyph, or story (THO) that has been born and unfolds for the purpose of satisfying some desire or purpose (LDTH). The word *b'hibbarâ'm* is another form of the word *bara,* with which this story began: to draw from the unknown into the known. The word *hashôth,* usually translated "made," refers to establishing the depths, foundations, or founding principles of something that moves toward an irresistible goal.

As discussed earlier, the mysterious word *IHϕH,* usually translated "Lord," is considered in the Jewish tradition to be the name too sacred to be pronounced. It is certainly nothing like the transcriptions Jehovah, Yahweh, or Yahuvah that Christians often use. As mentioned previously, it has many root derivations and mystical meanings because the roots interlace one another. The double root HH indicates universal life, breath, soul, and abstract being doubled in strength; as a verb it would be translated "to be being." This root is preceded by the sound I (*î*) pointing to a power that has manifested intelligible life as well as to a past that has been eternal. The letter is related to the human hand, to the forefinger pointing. In the middle of the HH root is placed ϕ (*ô* and *û*), which is the sign of a universal link between being and nothingness, the eye and ear, the door that converts one mode of existence to another.

D'Olivet comments that the being verb HH is "found placed between a past without origin and a future without limit. This wonderful noun therefore signifies exactly, the-Being-who-is-who-was-and-who-will-be" (1815, vol. 2, p. 68). He also points out that, if what were meant to be pure vowel sounds were hardened into consonants (as in YHWH), the name would point to a calamity or unfortunate existence, not a blessing. He speculates that this may have been the origin of the prohibition on pronouncing the name.

Heart Awareness

Return to breathing with awareness in the heart, and feel the heart as a mirror, as clear as possible for the moment. With a gentle breath, breathe in life from the universe, feeling the inner sound of the breath. Add to this the power of life to manifest, and remember all the life that has come into your body in the past. Finally, add your own sense of the goal toward which the whole universe is moving. Breathe in all the blessing you are capable of breathing in. Breathe out all the blessing you are capable of breathing out. Allow the mirror of your heart to contain the entire planet. Allow your heart to be contained within the heart of the Universal One. And let the mirror disappear. When this body prayer is ready to end, conclude with thankfulness.

The practice of feeling the heart as a mirror is used in many Sufi schools and is called *mujahida,* the struggle to keep one's inner impressions clear. When the mirror can hold the whole world, the practice, or grace-filled moment, is called *mushahida,* a greater witnessing and experience of Reality.

ISAIAH'S VISION, PART 2 —
THE POWER AND GLORY
OF DARK MATTER   Hebrew

An expanded translation of Isaiah 6:3

W'qârâ zeh 'el-zeh w'âmar (A)
Qâdôsh Qâdôsh Qâdôsh (B)
I-H-ɸ-H tzbâôth (C)
m'lô' ḳâl-hââretz ḳ'vôdô. (D)

KJV: And one cried unto another, and said, (A) Holy, holy, holy, (B) is the
Lord of Hosts: (C) the whole earth is full of his glory. (D)

> *Then each Power of Recovery*
> *named an essential medicine to the others*
> *and engraved it upon their mutual reality, saying:* (A)

> *Clear Intelligent Spaciousness:*
> *Matrix and Turning Point of the Cosmos:*
> *Focused Illuminating Emptiness:*
> *Holy Holy Holy is* (B)

> *IHɸH:*
> *The Life Force squared,*
> *past without beginning,*
> *future without limit,*
> *the Universe Breath behind all grasping and perceiving,*
> *the Soul of all hands, claws, tendrils, pseudopodia, orbits,*
> *the Self of all eyes, ears, antennae, protoplasm, atmospheres,*
> *the Being of Beings behind Being,*
> *Energizer of the Cosmic Story.*

> *This Ultimate Energy to Be is accompanied by*
> *a host of unfolding harmonic movement,*
> *the law-generating-and-revising principles of the universe.*
> *This crowd of illuminating order travels with Life*
> *just as the stars swirl through the stillness of the void.* (C)

This Universe Energy fills
the entire form of all elements,
the whole of earthiness in all its
imagined and unimagined shapes.
It burnishes all substance from inside
with the force of the Intelligent Abyss,
the abundant Depth of Depths,
the power and glory of Dark Matter. (D)

BODY PRAYER: THE TURNING POINT

Sound and Embodiment—Celebration of the Ability to Praise

It is uniquely human to be in awe of and praise the cosmos around us. To the extent that our culture has isolated us from both fear and awe, making praise unfashionable, it has prevented us from achieving the clarity about our place in the cosmos that older native traditions attained. Yet both mysticism and the new findings of science promote an experience of both fear and awe. In both arenas, what we do matters a great deal: No act is insignificant. Reawakening the ability to praise, even when not in words, is essential to real communion with the Universe. Recognizing that we are part of something sacred is the matrix and turning point of the cosmos.

Begin by breathing the sound "qâdôsh" in the heart. Then intone it slowly on one note, focusing on the intention of opening a space for praise and devotion in your life. In many native traditions, one gives praise and thanks for things one has not yet received, thereby creating a focused spaciousness that the Universe can fill. As with all of the sound practices, a melody of your own may make its appearance. All traditional music came from the hearts of devotees, just like this. Only in the last three hundred years have humans in modern culture "professionalized" music to the extent that we have been isolated from our own urge to sing and to create. Unself-conscious praise has been in the human repertoire much longer than that. This body prayer begins, proceeds, and ends in thanksgiving.

THE DEPTHS OF SHAMASH   Babylonian

A version of a hymn to the sun, approximately seventh century B.C.E.

First lines of Ferris J. Stephens translation: Those who traverse the wide
earth, Those who tread upon the high mountains, The monsters of the
sea which are full of terror . . .

> *We humans travel the breadth of the earth.*
> *We place our footsteps on the highest peaks.*
> *The sea contains terrible monsters*
> *as well as unknowable creatures in its depths.*
> *The rivers spawn their own life cycles.*
>
> *All these, O Shamash,*
> *live in your unfolding circle.*
> *They occupy a sphere of name,*
> *a glorious place of vibration*
> *that has no "outside"—*
> *your border continues to expand.*
>
> *You dress the mountains with your brilliance.*
> *Every region warms itself by you.*
> *You even illuminate light's absence and*
> *cause darkness itself to shine.*
> *You open the depths and unfurl space.*
>
> *From the bright days, torrid with midday heat,*
> *to the long nights of cold and frost,*
> *you open the ears of the whole world.*
>
> *On the twentieth day of the month, you rejoice.*
> *You eat and drink in ecstasy.*
> *Taverns open their pure wine and aged beer.*
> *Everything is poured out in your remembrance.*
> *The flood goes over some of our heads,*
> *but you drink with all pure toasts*
> *of desire, love, and gratitude.*
> *Everything asked in this spirit*
> *will surely come to pass.*

O Breathing Life   Aramaic

An expanded, then condensed translation of Matthew 6:9–13 and Luke 11:2–4 from the Peshitta version of the Gospels

Isho'a said:

Abwûn d'bwashmayâ (A)
Nithqadash shmâkh (B)
Têtê malkûthâkh (C)
Nihwê' tzêbwyânâkh aykanâ' d'bwashmayâ âph b'ar'âh (D)
Habwlan lachmâ d'sûnqânan yâwmânâ (E)
Washbwôqlan châwbayn (wa chtâhayn)
aykanâ dâph ch'nan shbwâqn l'chayâbayn (F)
Welâ ta'hlan l'nêsyônâ
Elâ patzân min bîshâ (G)
Mêtol dîlâkh-hî malkûthâ wachaylâ watêshbûchtâ
l'âhlam 'âlmîn. (H)
Amêyn. (I)

KJV: Our Father which art in heaven. (A) Hallowed be thy name. (B) Thy kingdom come. (C) Thy will be done in earth, as it is in heaven. (D) Give us this day our daily bread. (E) And forgive us our debts, as we forgive our debtors. (F) And lead us not into temptation, but deliver us from evil. (G) For thine is the kingdom, and the power, and the glory, forever. (H) Amen. (I)

> *O Breathing Life, your Name shines everywhere!* (A)
> *Release a space to plant your Presence here.* (B)
> *Envision your "I can" now.* (C)
> *Embody your desire in every light and form.* (D)
> *Grow through us this moment's bread and wisdom.* (E)
> *Untie the knots of failure binding us,*
>   *as we release the strands we hold of others' faults.* (F)
> *Help us not forget our Source,*
>   *yet free us from not being in the Present.* (G)
> *From you arises every Vision, Power, and Song*
>   *from gathering to gathering.* (H)
> *Amen—*
>   *May our future actions grow from here!* (I)

BODY PRAYER: A PRAYER FOR THE COSMOS

Simple Presence

Return again to a place of simple presence. Sitting comfortably, eyes closed, feel the rise and fall of the breath. With each breath, reach out to whatever feelings or sensations arise, and feel the breath illuminating each with awareness. Without needing to add anything, feel each sensation that rises to awareness as already illuminated, already radiating with brilliance and remembering its own home in the wave and particle reality of the cosmos. Feel each sensation giving thanks and returning, in its own language of feeling, a prayer of vision, power, and song to the cosmos.

A Blessing of Lucid Fire
and Secret Grace   Hebrew

A translation of a blessing from the Qumran [Dead Sea] Community, about 100 B.C.E.–100 C.E.

l'bârekhâh b'khôl tôb, (A)
w'îshmôr hhâh mî'kôl râ'h, (B)
w'yâaîr lîbkhâh bsêkhel chayyîm, (C)
w'yâchônkhâh b'da'ath 'hôlâmîm, (D)
w'îshâ phnêy chasâdâyw l'khâh,
lîshlôm 'hôlâmîm. (E)

A. M. Habermann translation: May He bless thee with all good (A) / And
keep thee from all evil. (B) / May He enlighten thy heart with immortal
wisdom (C) / And grace thee with eternal knowledge. (D) / May He Lift
up His merciful countenance upon thee for eternal peace. (E)

> *May the Being of the Universe*
> *breathe into you the light of blessing and ripeness,*
> *the fulfillment of health and balance;* (A)
>
> *May it protect you from*
> *distractions brittle and bent*
> *with a sphere of lucid fire;* (B)
>
> *May it enlighten*
> *the heart of your passion*
> *with the contemplation of living energy;* (C)
>
> *May it uncover the*
> *hidden strength within you,*
> *insight gathered from the eternal* now; (D)
>
> *and May it show you its face*
> *of secret grace and silent refuge*
> *in a communion of deep peace.* (E)

THE GIFT OF THE ROSE   Persian

From the fourteenth-century Sufi poet Hafiz

The breeze at dawn shines with a gentle breath of musk;
  the old world has become young again!
The tulip opens its cup to the jasmine;
  the narcissus flirts with the anemone.
Mourning spreads to the palace of the rose
  as the nightingale says its painful farewells.

Yes, I left the mosque for the tavern yesterday,
  but don't blame me too much.
The weekly sermon went on and on—
  valuable time was slipping away!

My heart, if you delay collecting today's pleasure
  until tomorrow, who will guarantee that
  your life's account will still show a balance?
The month of daylight fasting gets closer—
  don't let the wine cup leave your hand:
  This sun disappears until Ramadan is ended.

Smell the rose's gift as it passes! Its presence is priceless.
  It enters the garden one way and leaves by another.
Musician! We're all friends here—get on with your song!
  Enough of the chorus "As it was, so shall it ever be."

Hafiz entered the garden of life for you—enjoy him and
  say good-bye, for he will soon be leaving!

A Song About a Journey   Persian

From The Diwan of Shams-i-Tabriz *by Sufi poet Mevlana Jelaluddin Rumi, thirteenth-century Anatolia*

Calling all lovers! It is time to break camp in this material
        world!
From the Universe, I hear the drum of departure calling me.
The driver was up long ago and prepared the camels.
He says it's not his fault we are still asleep—wake up!
The hubbub of departure surrounds us—camel bells behind
        and ahead.
Every moment a soul leaves on a journey to the unknown.

Look! From these upside-down candles in the night
        sky bowl
            magnificent beings arose so that the mystery could
                unfold.
This whirling of planets and stars brought you a sound
        sleep.
For a life so light, be careful of a sleep so heavy!

My inner self—seek the Self of love!
My inner friend, seek the Friend!
Inner witness, stay alert! It's not your job to fall asleep.
The streets are full of torches—chaos and din are
        everywhere!
Tonight this grasping-getting world gives birth to an eternal
        one.

It's simple: You thought you were dust and now find you are
        breath.
Before you were ignorant, and now you know more.
The One who led you this far
will guide you further on as well.

BODY PRAYER: GUIDANCE

In the Native Middle Eastern tradition there is a prayer that asks the Universe to choose the right prayer, which affirms that we don't always know what to ask or how but want to open ourselves to guidance anyway.

In the Hebrew language, the prophets often used the phrase *hînênî,* meaning "here I am, use me." In Aramaic, the fourth line of the Lord's Prayer asks that the desire of the universe come through us, equally in form and vibration, wave and particle, heaven and earth. In Arabic the Beautiful Name used is *Ya Hâdî,* the One who Guides (a form of this word is used in Sura Fateha). Related is *Ya Wakil,* the Solution to All Challenges and Problems.

Chanting or breathing any of these prayers, open yourself to the next step in guidance. If you are willing to allow the heart of the Universe to change your life, let it speak to and through you for the benefit of all beings. Allow it to lead you "further on."

GAZE GENTLY ON THESE BLOSSOMS

Rendered from The Secret Rose Garden *by Sufi poet Mahmud Shabistari, thirteenth century*

I have plucked this bouquet of scent
from a place I have called
"The Secret Rose Garden."
There roses bloom that reveal
the mysteries of the human heart.
There the lilies' tongues really sing,
and the narcissus sees everything perfectly.

With your heart's eyes,
gaze gently on these blossoms
until all your doubts fade away.
Hopefully, you will find some wisdom,
both practical and mystical,
all detailed and arranged clearly.

Don't use cold eyes to find my mistakes:
The roses may turn to thorns.
Ingratitude usually reveals ignorance,
and the friends of truth are thankful.

If you remember me, please
send a little breath of mercy my way.
As the tradition goes, I sign off with my own name,
   Mahmud:
"May all I do and am return to praise the One."

TEXTUAL NOTES

1. *The Power and Glory of Dark Matter, Isaiah 6:3.* The word *Qâdôsh* is another form of the word *qadesh,* which was used to name the Sabbath day in Genesis. It is usually translated "holy"; it also relates to a central point, pivot, focus, or motive upon which everything turns as well as to setting apart something for a specific purpose or preparing the ground for something to happen. The word *tzbâôth,* usually translated "hosts," is often associated with the movement of stars or angels. The roots point to something that leaves material limits behind, breaks the bounds of the past, and is clear and radiant (TZA) as it progresses and moves (BA) toward an unnameable future (TH).

In the last line, the word *m'lô',* usually translated "full," is related to the word we saw in the previous two verses: It is what satisfies all needs, is abundant, strong, and pregnant. The word *k'vôdô,* usually translated "glory," can also mean weight, wealth, esteem, or, in a more figurative sense, the soul. Its roots point to a centralized force that acts from the abyss of existence or from the inside of all beings with power, light, and abundance. This "heavy glory" shines from the soul of all particular existence, according to this passage.

2. *The Depths of Shamash.* This version is based on a fragmentary text translated by Ferris J. Stephens from the Akkadian manuscripts in the library of Ashurbanipal, 668–633 B.C.E., in James B. Pritchard's collection (1955, p. 389).

The name *Shamash* is clearly related to the Semitic root SHM, the vibratory wave reality of the cosmos. Although most scholars consider the Babylonian Shamash to be male, there is equally good evidence that she was part of a long Middle Eastern tradition that embodied the sun and sky as female. For a thorough discussion of sun/sky goddesses in many traditions, see Janet McCrickland's study *The Eclipse of the Sun* (1990).

3. *O Breathing Life, Matthew 6:9–13 and Luke 11:2–4.* The word *abwoon,* usually translated "father," can also mean birther, parent, father-mother, or, from its roots, the breathing life (U) that comes from (B) the All (A). The word *tzêbwyânâkh* in line 4, usually translated "will," can also mean heart's desire or confidence. In line 5, the words *shbwôq . . . shbwâqn,* usually translated "forgive," may also mean to untie, embrace with emptiness, or return to its original state. Matthew's version uses the word *shbwâqn* as the object of this releasing, usually translated "debts." The word also means hidden past or stolen property. Luke's

version in this line, on which this particular translation is based, uses the word *chtâhayn,* usually translated "sins." The word can also mean failures, mistakes, frustrated hopes, or tangled threads.

Line 8 uses the phrase *welâ ta'hlan l'nêsyônâ,* usually translated "lead us not into temptation." The Aramaic says literally, "and let us not enter forgetfulness." The word *nêsyônâ* can also mean being lost in superficial appearances or materialism, the image of forgetting the Source. In the next line, the King James Version renders *elâ patzân min bîshâ* as "but deliver us from evil." As we have previously seen, the Semitic sense of *bîshâ* means unripe action, that which is out of its proper time or continued beyond the appropriate time. The word *patzân* also means to loosen the hold of, to free, or to break the seal that binds.

In the last line the word *têshbûchtâ,* usually translated as "glory," can also mean song, especially the harmony of the stars as it was envisioned by the Native Middle Eastern tradition. The phrase *l'âhlam 'âlmîn,* usually translated "forever," means literally "from gathering to gathering." All other words have been considered in some form elsewhere in these notes. For a more complete discussion, please see my earlier work (1990).

4. *A Blessing of Lucid Fire and Secret Grace.* This blessing is a variation of the one in Numbers 6:24–26 (KJV: May the Lord bless thee, and keep thee: may the Lord make his face shine upon thee, and be gracious unto thee: The Lord lift up his countenance upon thee, and give thee peace). I have retranslated it from the transcription in Nahum Glatzer's collection (1967, p. 319) using A. M. Habermann's translation as a reference.

In the second line, the word *îshmôr* means to protect or keep, as though with a sphere of light or fire. The word *râ'h,* another word for "evil" in Hebrew, means that which is abnormally bent or brittle compared with its natural state.

In the third line, the word *lîbkhâh* is another form of the word we have previously encountered for "heart," the center of one's passion and energy. The word *sêkhel* means consciousness, contemplation, meditation, intelligence, or wisdom.

In line 4, the word *yâchônkhâh* means to grace with or to uncover what was hidden, especially a strength or virtue. The word *da'ath* means knowledge, insight, or any understanding of diversity and presence that satisfies a particular purpose. The word *'hôlâmîm* is the Hebrew form of the Aramaic word *'âhlam,* which we encountered in the previous text:

the eternal light of intelligence in all gatherings, all mutual bonds of sympathy.

In the last line, the word *chasâdâyw* (based on the word *chesed*) can mean love, kindness, benevolence, favor, mercy, grace, or beauty. Here is yet another word for love in the Semitic language; in this case it is again a silent, secret action that sympathizes with another, that offers a place of shelter and refuge. The word *shlôm* is another form of the word for peace and happiness, the note that unites and harmonizes sounds previously heard as dissonant.

5. *The Gift of the Rose.* This version is based on number 98 from "Ghazals from the Divan of Hafiz," translated by Justin Huntly McCarthy (unpublished manuscript) and by H. Wilberforce Clarke (1891).

6. *A Song About a Journey.* This version is based on the first part of the literal translation of number 36 in the collection by R. A. Nicholson (1898, pp. 140–43).

7. *Gaze Gently on These Blossoms.* This version is based on the previous literal translations from the Persian by Florence Lederer (1920) and E. H. Whinfield (1880).

A Tradition of Translation

Translation is never objective. It is a purposeful act, and I have tried to present my intention and biases about what I think I am doing and why it is important. I would give an inaccurate impression if I did not acknowledge those who connected me to this method of Middle Eastern mystical translation. My work arises from a tradition of translation that is older than, albeit quite different from, the methods that have been used in orthodox academia and religion for the last two hundred to three hundred years.

First and foremost I was inspired by my late friend Shemseddin Ahmed. When I met Shemseddin fourteen years ago in Lahore, he seemed a perfectly ordinary, elderly Pakistani Muslim. Except that he was also a saint. I met Shemseddin during a trip to Pakistan and India that involved visits with a number of other Sufi, Hindu, and Buddhist teachers. Shemseddin had no particular following and ran a very unprepossessing cooperative bookstore focusing on religion and Islamic culture. When my traveling companions and I met him, we immediately felt a deep, unconditional love, a love that did not call attention to itself or fascinate one with its power or magnetism. Shemseddin was eager to teach us the Quran, but there was no time during that trip.

About a year later, my friends and I raised money to bring Shemseddin to the United States. He said that he felt we were his real family, and that his own family treated him merely like an eccentric old man.

As we began classes in the Quran, everyone was a bit skeptical. Most English translations of the Quran seem at best confusing and prosaic, at worst peremptory, demanding, and quarrelsome. Yet the Quran is a work that requires more than a superficial reading. Many Muslims believe it was written in several "dialects" of meaning, layer upon layer, and that one must explore these layers deeply until one comes to the ineffable Being behind the words.

When I returned from Pakistan, I began to take Arabic classes at a local university. Since I had an undergraduate background in languages, I was not put off by the difficulty, even though the teaching methods I encountered left something to be desired.

The root and pattern system was immediately intriguing: Words were organized by families of meaning, and variations radiated out from a central core, much like the families of scales or ragas in Indian music. However, the teachers at my university had no interest in the Quran, and their methods seemed destined to keep us for several years in the purgatory of "How do I get to the airport?" I was also aware that, since all classical Arabic grammar was based on the Quran, young children learned the language directly from the holy book itself. So there had to be another way.

As Shemseddin began to teach, he simply started at the first sura (chapter) and proceeded from there, word by word. Every word opened a variety of meanings, and our repeated question was, "Which does it mean here?" He then began to show us how all the meanings can be seen individually and simultaneously as holding wisdom depending on which aspect of life one viewed. One verse often took us an hour to consider, which included much discussion and questioning related to our own life experience and what we believed. In fact it seemed impossible to contain the discussion to get at "one translation." Compared with these discussions and with the richness of sound and music of the Arabic phrase, the usual English translation in the text we used lay on the page like a stone. I began to see how the Quran could be a lifelong study and why it held such power for those who honored it as their primary holy book.

I want to emphasize that Shemseddin was not a famous academic or a published author. He said that he learned this method of Quranic translation from his teacher, who had learned it from his. We attempted to record Shemseddin in order to put his wisdom into a book, but the immediacy and magic of what he offered could not be held by these forms. To the extent that I have been successful in this book, I owe much to his inspiration.

During this time I also decided to finish an editing project I had begun six years earlier, which involved compiling for publication the diaries of an American Sufi and Buddhist teacher, Samuel L. Lewis (1896–1971). Lewis is best known as the founder of the Dances of Universal Peace, a modern form of sacred folk dance and movement-meditation-for-peace. I had been learning these dances and studying in the Sufi path with Lewis's students since 1976. His diaries and letters ranged over a vast field of comparative religion, organic horticulture and agriculture, meetings with various government and spiritual leaders, travels in the Middle and Far East, and his own mystical experiences.

His habit was to rise before breakfast and write five or six long letters on various topics to correspondents around the world, keeping a carbon as his diary. There was so much material that, as far as I know, no one had ever been through it all. In one letter he wrote that he wanted to start a revolution by "chanting the Lord's Prayer in Aramaic" but elaborated no further. Nor could anyone who knew him remember him doing a chant like this. Because Lewis was so interested in the power of sound and the mystical interpretations behind conventional scriptures, this statement remained with me. It took me, in fact, on a search that led to both chanting and translating the Aramaic Lord's Prayer and the Beatitudes.

Included in Lewis's papers also were transcripts of lectures he had given at a local Christian brotherhood. Some of these concerned alternative translations of the Book of Genesis according to Kabbalistic (Jewish mystical) methods. Lewis was born into a Jewish family, but his father prohibited him from pursuing spiritual studies and disowned him. Most of the Kabbalistic methods were passed down orally, and Lewis had learned what he knew directly from a Jewish teacher in San Francisco. He also mentioned in his diaries the existence of writings on these methods by a nineteenth-century French mystic and Hebrew scholar, Fabre D'Olivet. A translation of D'Olivet's book was in Lewis's private library and reaffirmed the existence of a long tradition of "expanded," multileveled translation, or midrash, in the Semitic languages.

In his *Hebraic Language Restored,* D'Olivet undertook a mystical retranslation of the first ten chapters of Genesis (the "Sepher of Moses"). Unfortunately, in both French and English, he limited himself to the use of nineteenth-century metaphysical language, relying on long, often excessively hyphenated phrases to help him squeeze in all the multiple meanings. D'Olivet translates Genesis 1:1, for instance, as: "At-first-in-principle, he-created, Elohim (he caused to be, he brought forth in principle, HE-the-Gods, the Being-of-beings) the selfsameness-of-heavens, and the-selfsameness-of-earth." More valuable for my work was D'Olivet's extensive scientific, grammatical, and historical commentary on the Hebrew language, exposing the literal, sound-by-sound basis for Kabbalistic interpretations involving at least three levels of meaning: literal, metaphoric, and mystical.

The correlation between D'Olivet's work and the methods used by Shemseddin Ahmed, backed up by the same tradition of expanded translation mentioned in Islamic literature, was uncanny. Using these methods, even normal dictionaries and lexicons of Hebrew, Aramaic, and Arabic reveal another way to derive meaning from these sacred texts. However, this way depends on both a knowledge of the sound meanings of each word root as well as a willingness to open oneself anew to the mystery of the cosmos.

The way also demands an ability to concentrate on sound, feeling, breath, and atmosphere, which is taught by the classic spiritual practices of the mystics in these traditions. Poetic skill, intuitive awareness, the ability to recognize and work with spiritual experiences, linguistic facility, phenomenological understanding, and grammatical knowledge must come together in one moment for the translation to convey wisdom rather than mere concepts. This way of translation opens us to questions about our life and its purpose. It does not mean to answer them with definitive statements from an outside authority.

To the extent that I have been successful, I thank my teachers, as well as those before them who kept this ancient tradition of translation alive when it was unpopular or dangerous to do so. May all we do and are return to praise the One!

A MYSTIC'S PEACE PLAN

While lecturing and teaching on Middle Eastern spirituality, I am often asked whether I have any special insights on political peace in the region. I mentioned some of my thoughts about this in the Preface; namely, that the West's interventions in the Middle East in this century have been at best ignorant of the Middle Eastern mind and at worst manipulative for its own benefit. The West needs to do less until it understands more. In addition, the recent history of violence and human tragedy on all sides has produced an extreme climate of fear and mistrust. Any peace efforts must deal with this climate of fear before any effective agreements can be made.

A plan that addresses these points was offered by Samuel L. Lewis (1896–1971), the American Sufi mystic who studied the spirituality of the region extensively and lived there for a number of years. Lewis was born a Jew and studied Jewish mysticism and Kaballah in depth along with his Sufi work. His ideas arose from discussions with Muslim and Jewish spiritual leaders in the 1960s and reflect an attempt to change the atmosphere (or "wave-reality") of the region as a preparation for any specific political changes in the "particle-reality." Lewis felt that only careful confidence-building efforts on spiritual, semantic, economic, ecological, and cultural fronts would effectively prepare for long-term political solutions. The basis of the plan has been endorsed by several former U.N. officials, including Gunnar Jarring and Robert Mueller. The main points of Lewis's skeleton plan follow.

1. *Spiritual:* Place all religious holy places in the entire region under international protection, including the entire Old City of Jerusalem. All people should be protected in their worship and spiritual practice. The spring 1994 massacre at the mosque in Hebron shows how important such a measure could have been. This part of the plan also involves setting up "safe corridors" so that devotees of all traditions and religions feel safe to travel between all shrines and places of worship. Lewis felt that this would establish a spiritual network of prayer and peace, much like the "cities of refuge" in medieval Europe. Because the spiritual life is so important in the Middle East, one must denationalize holy places to both stop arguments about them and secure them for worshipers, he felt.

2. *Semantic:* Obtain agreement from all parties in all peace processes to use terms consistently or not at all. For instance, one side's "security" cannot be another side's "terrorism." One side's "dispossessed persons" must be judged equally with another side's. The use of words like "home" and "historic home-

land" must be judged by objective criteria and applied equally to all sides or eliminated from the discussion. Lewis felt that using words as emotionally laden weapons to escalate wars of public relations prevented all sides from dealing seriously with one another at the bargaining table. As a student of Korzybski's "general semantics," Lewis also felt strongly that these unhealthy linguistic habits, usually associated with politicians, obscured the real problems at hand under a cloud of fuzzy meaning and thinking. "The reason we often don't solve problems," said Lewis, "is that their answers get in the way of our concepts."

3. *Ecological and Economic:* Regional conferences must be held to resolve the fair use and trade of natural resources in the entire Middle Eastern bioregion. This would include honest discussions about the use and conservation of water, minerals, and oil. The current political borders and boundaries in the Middle East have largely been imposed by the strategic interests of Europe and the United States. They do not necessarily serve the people of the region, who have been divided artificially into haves and have nots by outside forces wanting to exploit the resources for their own use. When the people of the Middle East can meet to decide the best use of the earth's resources in their area, then the ground will be prepared for just determinations about land and borders. "I shall continue in desert reclamation research," said Lewis in 1967, "knowing that sooner or later Israelis and Arabs will both have to drink from the same well."

4. *Cultural:* The West should officially sponsor cultural exchange on all levels with the Middle East, including sponsorship of Middle Eastern tours of music, dance, and art. It should seek to educate its people as much as possible about Middle Eastern culture in order to diminish racism and anti-Semitism. With the same goal, it should sponsor exchanges of citizen diplomats between the West and the Middle East (much as was done in the former Soviet Union). At the same time, the West should support tours of the best of its own folk arts, music, and dance to the Middle East. It should ban the export of the worst aspects of Western pseudoculture to the Middle East, including pornography and movies that exploit violence and fear. Lewis supported all means whereby ordinary people could come together simply to recognize their mutual humanity. Only this recognition would prove stronger than the modern economic and political forces that drive the many apart for the benefit of the few. "My main peace theme is: eat, pray and dance together," he said.

Texts Cited and Resources for Further Study

A cassette tape with pronunciations of selected sacred phrases, chanting, and music for use with the body prayers in this book, prepared by Neil Douglas-Klotz, is available from the Abwoon Study Circle, 10441 Phar Lap, Cupertino, CA 95014 or the office of the International Center for the Dances of Universal Peace, 444 N.E. Ravenna Blvd., Suite 306, Seattle, WA 98115. In Europe it is available from the Dances of Universal Peace, European Network, Crescent Moon Cottage, Holwell, Dorset DT9 5LW England.

Ali, A. Yusuf, trans. *The Holy Quran: Text, Translation, Commentary.* Lahore, Pakistan: Sh. Muhammad Ashraf, 1938.

Arberry, A. J. *The Koran Interpreted.* New York: Macmillan, 1955.

Black, Matthew. *An Aramaic Approach to the Gospels and Acts.* Oxford: Clarendon Press, 1967.

Boyce, Mary. *Zoroastrians: Their Religious Beliefs and Practices.* London: Routledge & Kegan Paul, 1979.

Breasted, J. H. *The Dawn of Conscience.* New York: Charles Scribner's Sons, 1933.

Brock, Sebastian. "Early Syrian Asceticism." In *Numen XX, Fasc. I.* Leiden: E. J. Brill, 1973.

————. "St. Isaac of Ninevah and Syriac Spirituality." *Sobornost* 7, 2 (1975).

————. "The Priesthood of the Baptised: Some Syriac Perspectives." *Sobornost/Eastern Churches Review* 9, 2 (1987).

Budge, E. A. W. *The Book of the Dead: The Papyrus of Ani.* London: British Museum, 1895.

————. *A Hieroglyphic Vocabulary to the Book of the Dead.* London: Kegan Paul, Trench, Trübner & Co., 1911a.

————. *Osiris and the Egyptian Resurrection.* London: Medici Society, 1911b.

————, ed. *Facsimiles of Egyptian Hieratic Papyri in the British Museum, Second Series.* London: British Museum, 1923.

Clarke, H. Wilberforce. *The Divan of Khwaja Shamsu-d-Din Muhammad-i-Hafiz-i-Shirazi.* 1891. Reprint, London: Octagon Press, 1974.

Cragg, Kenneth. *Readings in the Qur'an.* London: Harper Collins, 1988.

Dawood, N. J., trans. *The Koran.* Harmondsworth: Penguin Books, 1956.

Dhalla, Dastur M. N. *Homage unto Ahura Mazda.* Bombay: H. T. Anklesaria, 1942.

D'Olivet, Fabre. *The Hebraic Tongue Restored.* Translated by Nayan Louise Redfield. 1815. Reprint of 1921 edition, York Beach, ME: Samuel Weiser, 1991.

Douglas-Klotz, Neil. *Prayers of the Cosmos.* San Francisco: HarperSanFrancisco, 1990.

Drower, E. S. *The Mandaeans of Iraq and Iran.* Leiden: E. J. Brill, 1962.

————, trans. *The Canonical Prayerbook of the Mandaeans.* Leiden: E. J. Brill, 1959.

————, trans. *The Thousand and Twelve Questions (Alf Trisar Suialia).* Berlin: Akademie-Verlag, 1960.

Eisenman, Robert H., and Michael Wise. *The Dead Sea Scrolls Uncovered.* Shaftesbury: Element Books, 1992.

Elliger, K., and W. Rudolph, eds. *Biblia Hebraica Stuttgartensia*. Stuttgart: Deutsche Bibelgesellschaft, 1966–1967.

Erman, Adolf. *The Literature of the Ancient Egyptians*. Translated by Aylward M. Blackman. London: Methuen & Co., 1927.

Errico, Rocco A. *The Message of Matthew: An Annotated Parallel Aramaic-English Gospel of Matthew*. Irvine, CA: Noohra Foundation, 1991.

Errico, Rocco A., and Michael J. Bazzi. *Classical Aramaic, Assyrian-Chaldean Dialect, Elementary Book I*. Irvine, CA: Noohra Foundation, 1989.

Fitzmyer, Joseph A. "Did Jesus Speak Greek?" *Biblical Archaeology Review* 18, 5 (1992): 58–63.

Fox, Matthew. *Original Blessing*. Santa Fe: Bear & Co., 1986.

———. Foreword to *Prayers of the Cosmos*. San Francisco: HarperSanFrancisco, 1990.

———. *Creation Spirituality*. San Francisco: HarperSanFrancisco, 1992.

Friedlander, Rabbi Albert H. *Five Scrolls*. New York: Central Conference of American Rabbis, 1984.

Gadd, Cyril John. *Sumerian Reading Book*. Oxford: Clarendon Press, 1924.

Gaster, Theodor H. *The Dead Sea Scriptures*. Garden City, NY: Doubleday & Co., 1956.

Glatzer, Nahum N. *Language of the Faith*. New York: Schocken Books, 1967.

Hixon, Lex. *Heart of the Koran*. Wheaton, IL: Theosophical Publishing House, 1988.

Horne, Charles F., ed. *The Sacred Books and Early Literature of the East*, vol. 6, *Ancient Persia*, and vol. 7, *Medieval Persia*. New York: Parke, Austin, & Lipscomb, 1917.

Hornung, Erik. *Conceptions of God in Ancient Egypt: The One and the Many*. Translated by John Baines. Ithaca, NY: Cornell Univ. Press, 1982.

Jafarey, Ali A. *Fravarane: I Choose for Myself the Zoroastrian Religion*. Westminster: California Zoroastrian Center, 1988.

Kritzeck, James. *Anthology of Islamic Literature*. New York: New American Library, 1964.

Lamsa, George M. *The Holy Bible from Ancient Eastern Manuscripts*. Philadelphia: A. J. Holman, 1933.

———. *Gospel Light: Comments on the Teachings of Jesus from Aramaic and Unchanged Eastern Customs*. Philadelphia: A. J. Holman, 1939.

———. *New Testament Origin*. San Antonio: Aramaic Bible Center, 1979.

Langdon, Stephen. *Babylonian Liturgies*. Paris: Librairie Paul Geuthner, 1913.

———. *Sumerian Liturgical Texts*. Philadelphia: Univ. of Pennsylvania Museum, 1917.

Layton, Bentley. *The Gnostic Scriptures*. Garden City, NY: Doubleday & Co., 1987.

Lederer, Florence. *The Secret Rose Garden of Sa'dduddin Mahmud Shabistari*. Lahore, Pakistan: Sh. Muhammad Ashraf, 1920.

Lewis, C. S. *The Best of C. S. Lewis*. New York: Iversen-Norman Associates, 1969.

MacRae, George W. "The Thunder, Perfect Mind." In *Nag Hammadi Studies*, vol. 11: *The Coptic Gnostic Library: Nag Hammadi Codices V, 2–5 and VI with Papyrus Berolinensis 8502, 1 and 4*. Edited by Douglas M. Parrot and James Robinson. Leiden: E. J. Brill, 1979.

McCrickland, Janet. *The Eclipse of the Sun.* Glastonbury: Gothic Image, 1990.

Nicholson, R. A. *Selected Poems from the Divani Shamsi Tabriz.* Cambridge: Cambridge Univ. Press, 1898.

————. *Translations of Eastern Poetry and Prose.* Cambridge: Cambridge Univ. Press, 1921.

Pagels, Elaine. *The Gnostic Gospels.* New York: Random House, 1979.

————. *Adam, Eve, and the Serpent.* New York: Random House, 1988.

Pasha, Johnson. *The Secret Garden.* 1903. Reprint, London: Octagon Press, 1969.

Pickthall, Mohammed Marmaduke. *The Meaning of the Glorious Koran.* New York: New American Library, 1953.

Pritchard, James B. *Ancient Near Eastern Texts Relating to the Old Testament.* 2d ed. Princeton, NJ: Princeton Univ. Press, 1955.

————. *The Ancient Near East.* Princeton, NJ: Princeton Univ. Press, 1958.

————, ed. *The Ancient Near East: Supplementary Texts and Pictures Relating to the Old Testament.* Princeton, NJ: Princeton Univ. Press, 1969.

Robinson, James, ed. *The Nag Hammadi Library in English.* San Francisco: HarperSanFrancisco, 1978.

Robinson, Theodore H. *Paradigms and Exercises in Syriac Grammar.* Oxford: Clarendon Press, 1962.

Rogers, Robert William. *Cuneiform Parallels to the Old Testament.* London: Henry Frowde, Oxford Univ. Press, 1912.

Scholem, Gershom G. *Zohar, The Book of Splendor.* New York: Schocken Books, 1949.

————. *Major Trends in Jewish Mysticism.* 3d ed. New York: Schocken Books, 1954.

Schonfield, Hugh J. *Secrets of the Dead Sea Scrolls: Studies Toward Their Solution.* New York: Thomas Yoseloff, 1957.

Spretnak, Charlene. *States of Grace.* San Francisco: HarperSanFrancisco, 1991.

Suhrawardi, Shahab-ud-din. *The 'Awarif-u'l-Ma'arif.* Translated by H. Wilberforce Clarke. 1891. Reprint, Lahore, Pakistan: Sh. Muhammad Ashraf, 1979.

Swimme, Brian, and Thomas Berry. *The Universe Story.* San Francisco: HarperSanFrancisco, 1992.

Syriac New Testament and Psalms. Based on the 1901 Clarendon Press edition prepared by G. H. Gwilliam. Istanbul: Bible Society in Turkey, n.d.

Syrian Patriarchate of Antioch and All the East. *Peshitta Syriac Bible.* London: United Bible Societies, 1979.

Vanderburgh, Frederick Augustus. *Sumerian Hymns.* New York: Columbia Univ. Press, 1908.

Vermes, Geza. *The Dead Sea Scrolls in English.* London: Penguin Books, 1987.

Wacholder, Ben Zion, and Martin G. Abegg. *A Preliminary Edition of the Unpublished Dead Sea Scrolls: The Hebrew and Aramaic Texts from Cave Four, Fascicle Two.* Washington, DC: Dead Sea Scroll Research Council, Biblical Archaeology Society, 1992.

Whinfield, E. H. *The Gulistan of Shabistari.* London: Trubner, 1880.

Whish, Henry F. *Clavis Syriaca: A Key to the Ancient Syriac Version Called "Peshitta" of the Four Holy Gospels.* London: George Bell & Sons, 1883.

Wilson, Epiphanius, ed. *Sacred Books of the East.* London: Colonial Press, 1900.

Zaehner, R. C. *The Teachings of the Magi.* New York. Oxford Univ. Press, 1956.